Rejecting

D1352595

Many nations recognize the moral and legal obligation to accept people fleeing from persecution, but political asylum applicants in the 21st century face restrictive policies and cumbersome procedures. What counts as persecution? How do applicants translate their stories of suffering and trauma into a narrative acceptable to the immigration officials? How can asylum officials weed out the fake from the genuine without resorting to inappropriate cultural definitions of behaviour?

Through in-depth accounts by asylum applicants and interviews with lawyers and others involved, the book takes the reader on a journey through the process of applying for asylum in both the United States and Great Britain. The book describes the conflicting needs of states to protect their citizens from terrorists and the influx of hordes of unwelcome economic migrants, and to adhere to their legal, moral, and treaty obligations to provide safe haven for those fleeing persecution.

Rejecting Refugees is an insightful, and fresh evaluation of the obstacles asylum applicants face and the cultural, procedural, and political discrepancies in the political asylum process. This makes it ideal reading for students and scholars of political science, international relations, sociology, law, and anthropology.

Carol Bohmer is a lawyer and a sociologist. She teaches at Dartmouth College, USA and works pro bono for asylum applicants.

Amy Shuman, a folklorist, is Professor of English, Women's Studies, and Anthropology at the Ohio State University, USA.

Rejecting Refugees

Political asylum in the
21st century

**Carol Bohmer and
Amy Shuman**

 Routledge
Taylor & Francis Group

LONDON AND NEW YORK

First published 2008
by Routledge
2 Park Square, Milton Park, Abingdon, Oxon, OX14 4RN

Simultaneously published in the USA and Canada
by Routledge
270 Madison Avenue, New York, NY 10016

Routledge is an imprint of the Taylor & Francis Group, an informa business

Typeset in Times New Roman by
Keystroke, 28 High Street, Tettenhall, Wolverhampton
Printed and bound in Great Britain by
Antony Rowe Ltd, Chippenham, Wiltshire

British Library Cataloguing in Publication Data
A catalogue record for this book is available from the
British Library

Library of Congress Cataloging in Publication Data
Bohmer, Carol.
Rejecting refugees : political asylum in the 21st century / Carol
Bohmer and Amy Shuman.
p. cm.
Includes bibliographical references and index.
1. Political refugees. 2. Political refugees–Government policy.
3. Asylum, Right of. I. Shuman, Amy, 1951– II. Title.
JV6346.B64 2007
325′.21–dc22   2007016952

ISBN 10: 0–415–77375–X (hbk)
ISBN 10: 0–415–77376–8 (pbk)
ISBN 10: 0–203–93722–8 (ebk)

ISBN 13: 978–0–415–77375–1 (hbk)
ISBN 13: 978–0–415–77376–8 (pbk)
ISBN 13: 978–0–203–93722–8 (ebk)

To Ned, whose idea it was . . . and to Amy

Contents

Acknowledgments

Acknowledgments usually mark the completion of a project and gratitude for all of those who have made it possible, and we are indeed grateful for the support and generosity of many people. However, as we complete this book, the political asylum crisis is only intensifying. Perhaps someday this book will become an historical record of a difficult time, but for now it represents the stories of desperate people seeking safety from persecution in countries unprepared to address their needs. We know that many of the individuals and institutions who helped make this project possible did so out of recognition of those needs and the urgency of serious discussion of the problems. We have endeavored to write a book that might reach a wide audience of all of the people involved in the political asylum process as well as people interested in learning about it.

Our thanks begin with the many people whose stories are represented here. In the book we changed not only their names but also any circumstances that might make them traceable. Finding asylum is not necessarily an end to fear. To all those who talked to us, we cannot name you here in our acknowledgments, but we thank you for so generously sharing painful stories, and we hope we have done them justice. We have done everything possible to prevent you from any harm, and we also hope that this book will help, rather than harm, others in your situation. That much said, we fully acknowledge the risks taken in a public statement such as this. Political asylum is all about risks.

Carol Bohmer was working as a volunteer lawyer at Community Refugee Immigration Services (C.R.I.S.) in Columbus, Ohio when she teamed up with Amy Shuman, a folklorist and scholar of personal experience narrative. People who become the witness to so many tragic stories have an obligation, and we decided that our obligation was to use our skills to untangle some of the inconsistencies and injustices in the system. We could not have carried out the project without the full support of C.R.I.S. and all the dedicated people who work there.

The many lawyers and others who work with asylum seekers do this as a job, but many work for substantially less money than they would make in other areas of the law. These are people for whom time is money, but they never asked us for compensation. No one ever refused our request for an interview. We thank them all: Navtej Ahluwalia, Cheri Attix, Miranda Avery, Megan Berthold, Michele Butz, Susan Coutin, Ana Deutsch, David Dunford, Ezinda Franklin-Houtzager, Serena Forlati, Simonetta Furlan, Maurice Gee, Loraine Gelsthorpe, Lea Greenberger, Sheila Grewell, Mark Hetfield, Martin Heisler, Joe Hohenstein, Leah Hurwitz, Catroina Jarvis, Robert Joyce, Walter Lamb, Judy London, Jane McGrew, David McHaffey, Lisa Nolan, Angie Plummer, John Quinn, Melanie Ryan, Andrew Schoenhold, Prakash Shah, Farzad Simon, Fran Tobin, Joy Van Berg, Bill Westerman, Gita Williams, Jenny Willoughby, Erika Woodhurst, and Colin Yeo.

Several people need a special mention: Dan Berger who has been there for every question, large or small; Judge Ian Borrin, who has been a one person clipping service since the project began; and Dave Burgoon who started it all by rashly handing over asylum cases for Carol to handle

Our work was supported by the Mershon Center for International Security Studies, the Department of English, and the College of Humanities at The Ohio State University, Dartmouth College, and the Institute for Criminology at Cambridge University.

We have presented our research at various fora including The International Society for Political Psychology, the American Anthropological Association, the American Folklore Society, The International Studies Association,The Ohio State University Moritz College of Law, Ethnography and Literature: Theory, History and Interdisciplinary Practice Conference at the Hebrew University Institute of Advanced Studies, Jerusalem, the Western States Folklore Conference, the Peter

Wall Institute for Advanced Studies, University of British Columbia, Vancouver, The University of Pennsylvania Center for Folklore "Take/Cover" Conference, Common Ground: New Directions in the Humanities Conference, Prato, Italy, the Department of Political Science, University of California, Irvine, the Legal Studies Group, Dartmouth College, the Cambridge Socio-legal Group, Cambridge University, United Kingdom, the Political Science Departments at the Universities of Queensland, Australian National University, and the Sociology department of the University of Tasmania, in Australia. We are very grateful for all the feedback we received from these audiences.

Amy thanks her family, Amy, Evan, Lino, and Ariel, for allowing this project to become part of daily life, and her support system: Tim Hewitt, Pilar Hewitt, Derek Rutter, and Mike Wiatrowski. She also thanks her mother, Noni Shuman, for family stories and editorial help.

Carol thanks her family for all their support and feedback on drafts.

We are grateful to Craig Fowlie and Natalja Mortensen at Routledge, U.K. and Sophie Richmond and Colin Morgan for their careful attention to this publication.

We are grateful to Ken Pyne, cartoonist, and *The Spectator*, for permission to reprint the cartoon on page xii.

We hope to follow this project to its next steps.

'How does the prisoner plead? Innocent
or asylum-seeker?

(*The Spectator*, 6 May 2006)

Introduction

In 1939, the *St Louis* sailed from Nazi Germany with 937 Jewish refugees on board and headed for Cuba where the passengers had landing permits. The passengers were nevertheless not allowed to disembark. The ship's captain, the passengers, and an American Jewish refugee organization pleaded for asylum in the US, to no avail. The *St Louis* ultimately returned to Europe, where almost three-quarters of the refugees were later killed in death camps. In retrospect, the plight of the *St Louis* has come to represent a moment of national shame.[1] Nevertheless, we continue to do similar things every day. Immigration officials deny entry to people fleeing persecution and deport many of those who make it to the West seeking a safe haven from persecution. Some of those people are tortured or killed on their return. Mostly this happens without public knowledge or public outcry.

The US proclaims itself to the world as the permanently unfinished nation. Immigration is a national rite of passage. We pride ourselves that taking in the world's tired and poor, with its image of huddled masses, is not just our origin myth, but also our actual history. But in fact we have restricted access to immigrants, especially asylum seekers, arguably the most desperate of immigrants. Our narrow criteria for granting asylum have become even more limited since the end of the Cold War and September 11. Other liberal democracies also pay lip service to the obligations of providing shelter to those fleeing persecution, but have been, if anything, more restrictive in accepting those seeking political asylum.

This book is about the disconnect (even hypocrisy) between the ideas of a nation welcoming asylum seekers and our actual practices. We in the West talk a good game about providing a safe haven for those fleeing persecution, but we also talk a lot about securing our borders. We tell those responsible for immigration to control our borders and process asylum seekers rapidly, but then not only do we not provide adequate resources for them to do so, we also create obstacles that prevent legitimate applicants from succeeding in the process. We say we treat people from all nations equally, but the path is much smoother for those with white skin or, ironically, those who come from countries which are our enemies. We use political criteria for deciding who gets in and who doesn't, so some applicants are sent back, perhaps to die just like those on the *St Louis* did.

We have undertaken research both in the United States and the United Kingdom to give our analysis a wider frame. We also refer to reports about other asylum receiving countries, including Canada, Australia, and Europe. Observing both the differences and the similarities of the US and the UK, we see how they affect the ways the process plays itself out in each state. Do the different immigration histories of the two countries have an impact on the asylum process? Do the two countries have a different sense of their obligation to asylum seekers? To what extent is the problem we describe an inevitable result of the conflict between the ideals of a liberal democracy and the sense of threat both countries feel as a result of the rise of terrorism and the huge numbers of potential asylum seekers washed up on the shores of civil war and political unrest?

The process of applying for asylum both in the US and the UK involves a complex legal, administrative terrain. In this book, we will describe this complexity through stories about particular asylum applicants and the legal and community workers who help them. We start with the stories asylum applicants tell when they first seek help from a community legal aid center or a lawyer, and we describe the process of translating those trauma stories into a document that will be recognizable by the authorities. Using these stories, we explore the criteria for asylum, especially the concept of a "well-founded fear of persecution." How does asylum policy work in practice? Does practice accurately reflect the laws governing asylum? Where does the system fail and why? What should our policy be? How can applicants prove that they have been persecuted as members of a group (political, racial, religious, or social) when the persecution is personal? How can the system walk the line between accepting those genuinely in need of protection while avoiding the misuse of the asylum system as a back door to entry for those who have not been persecuted but who seek a better life? How has asylum policy changed as a result of September 11? What is the effect of changed attitudes toward women on the recognition of gender-based persecution?

We differentiate among three kinds of asylum claims, all of which we will examine in the chapters that follow. The first are those applicants who clearly deserve asylum but have problems because of the way the system functions. These cases tell us where the system is flawed in practice. The second type of application is the one which is, in fact, not genuine. The fear of granting asylum to a "bogus asylum seeker" to use the term which has gained currency in the UK, occupies much of the attention of the asylum authorities. These cases are important as they tell us much about how successful the system is in weeding out the genuine from the false, as well as illustrating the arbitrary nature of asylum, which includes only those cases defined as deserving within the wording of the law. The third kind of application is from those who push the envelope of asylum law, whose cases fall into gray areas. Those cases are important because they force us to think about what asylum is and should be about. We argue that our practices don't match our goals in the asylum process. We criminalize people for illegally crossing borders, and this includes people who cross for safe haven. As we will discuss, the conditions that drive people from their homes do not necessarily create a distinction between economics and the need for asylum. Our central thesis is that the questions we ask, as well as the way we ask them, about the identity of the applicants, the credibility of their stories, and the possibility that they will face persecution should they return to their countries, may not be the most necessary or useful means for determining who is a genuine asylum seeker.

This book is about an important legal and public policy issue, and it has implications for both policy and law. It discusses these issues in the framework of the narratives of those who have direct experience of asylum, rather than in legal or policy terms generally. On the general issues of asylum law and policy, there is a large scholarly literature, to which the interested reader is referred (see e.g. Goodwin-Gil, 1996; Guild, 2001; Joly, 1996; Joppke, 1999; Shah, 2000; Whittaker, 2006).

Asylum is a very personal issue for the authors. As the stories in the next chapter illustrate, both of us have connections to asylum seekers. But it is not necessary to have such close connections to see it in personal terms. We can easily understand and even identify with the plight of those who seek what we already have, a place to live in peace, free from the persecution which forces people to flee their homelands. Asylum resonates with our sense of who we are as individuals and as members of a nation. It tells us a lot about what kind of nations we are now and what we aspire to be.

The first chapter of the book, "No More Huddled Masses," introduces the reader to the historical, political and cultural dimensions of asylum. We include a short history of asylum policy in the US and the UK since its inception after World War II. We also explain what asylum means, and its connection to politics, using stories as illustrations. We trace the rise and the fall of asylum as a public policy issue through the numbers of those seeking asylum and the places from which they flee.

Chapter 2, "The System," examines how the process has evolved in practice in the period since World War II, when asylum first became a separate legal category. We follow the process though its typical stages in the US and the UK and compare the two systems. We look closely at actual hearings in the US and in the UK to better understand the cultural obstacles that applicants face. Because the political asylum process is a legal proceeding, applicants who do not meet legal requirements are often labeled as criminals and detained in special detention centers or prisons. We review the specific consequences of the laws for people seeking asylum in the US and in the UK, especially recent legal and policy changes designed to severely limit the numbers both of those seeking asylum and of those who succeed in their quest.

Chapter 3, "Are You Who You Say You Are?," examines the central issue of identity in the asylum process. The applicants have to prove that they are who they say they are. The need for identity proof is based on an assumption that everyone has access to written documentation.

In this chapter, we describe the cases of people who pitch their documents en route to conceal identity from pursuers, people who never had any documents, and people who use illegal documents. Official policy acknowledges that people seeking asylum may have false documents, or no documents, but authorities nevertheless make the whole process much harder in practice for those in this position. Even applicants with documents can face obstacles. Individuals with legitimate passports acquired by bribing an official often face additional scrutiny and suspicion.

Chapter 4, "Did This Really Happen to You? The Problem of Credibility," describes how asylum hearings are dominated by a search for the "truth" as determined by the asylum officials and based on their evaluation of whether the applicant's story contains sufficient organization, coherence and detail. Officials spend a lot of time checking and rechecking the details of the story, often as a way of "catching out" applicants, and thus as evidence that they are lying and that their stories are therefore fabrications. The problem is that stories of the horrors of persecution often don't lend themselves to the kind of presentation demanded by the authorities. Asylum applicants have to demonstrate that they will face harm if they return to their native country, and they have to convince the officials that they have reason to be fearful. How do asylum applicants prove that what they say happened really happened? Of course, written documents carry the most weight, but in their absence, asylum applicants have only their own stories, and if they are fortunate, the testimony of witnesses. Everyone, at every stage of the process, faces limited knowledge, from the people who experience violence but don't necessarily understand the motives, to the secrecy of escape, to the asylum official's knowledge about political circumstances in particular countries.

Chapter 5, "Politics Get Personal: What Counts as Persecution?," returns to the issues raised in the first chapter to describe in detail the various categories of persecution. What is the difference between having been persecuted and fearing future persecution if you go back to your country? How bad does it have to be? Does the story fit into one of the defined categories of persecution (race, religion, national origin, political opinion, or membership in a particular social group). Asylum is considered on a case-by-case basis, but claimants must prove that their persecution is on account of one of these legal categories, as well as political (by the government or due to the government's failure to provide protection) rather than personal. The asylum process involves rewriting a personal narrative of trauma to contextualize the persecution within the legal categories recognized by the asylum officials.

Chapter 6, "The Personal is Political: Taking Gender into Account," describes how, until recently, all gender persecution was regarded as private and domestic, falling outside the purview of the definition of political persecution. Now gender persecution counts as long as it is not just personal violence, but has a political element, somehow involving the government. In this chapter, we trace the changing policies regarding gender; this is one of the few areas offering new possibilities for claiming asylum. We describe the cases of women who have experienced rape, who are fleeing female genital mutilation (FGM, also known as female genital cutting, FGC), honor killings, and other cultural practices, and whose political activities, often in the domestic, rather than public sphere, have not been considered political by the asylum officials. Some gender discrimination, especially persecution based on sexual orientation, affects men as well as women. Persecution based on gender raises complex issues requiring rethinking how the personal and the political intersect and overlap. Asylum officials seem more ready to grant asylum when discrimination against women is part of non-Western cultural practices regarded as "barbaric" in the West. Persecution that more closely resembles Western discrimination against women, such as rape or domestic violence, is less readily regarded as political.

Chapter 7, "Safe Haven for Whom?," the concluding chapter, discusses asylum as a fundamental part of the value system of the United States, crucial to what it means to be an American. We compare this to the British historical experience, which leads to a different perception of asylum within the culture of the country. As first world nations, both countries have an obligation to provide safe haven for people needing protection from persecution. We know, for example, that we want to protect people who are trying to defend democratic practices in their own nations; we know that we want to protect people against genocide or ethnic "cleansing." However, we wonder whether political asylum can continue with present practices, which seem designed to constrain it so it no longer serves the purposes for which it was intended. How can we have a fair and just policy, especially at this period in our history in which there is a record number of refugees around the world, as well as an unprecedented concern about controlling our borders? We conclude by reviewing what we have found to be the primary inequities in the system, parts of the process that criminalize and dehumanize the applicants and that fail to serve the stated goals of determining who are the legitimate asylum seekers.

Note

1. As Lisa H. Malkki points out, locating the genealogy of the refugee in World War II Europe carries the danger of eurocentrism, but at the same time, "There are also justifications for this specific localization," including the creation of the legal category of the refugee (1995: 498). Our book begins with both European and African stories. The European categories remain important, but today's asylum seekers come primarily from Africa, Asia, and Latin America.

1 No more huddled masses

Max Zisman (his real name) arrived in the US in 1901 from Lithuania, at the age of 31. He brought with him his entire family, including his wife and two children, his parents, and his eight siblings and their spouses and children. At his point of entry, in Boston, he faced a battery of health tests, but no one asked him to prove his identity, account for his political affiliations, or even explain why he had left. No one wanted to know why he was afraid of being forced into the Russian army, why didn't he want to serve, was he a deserter, what would happen to him if he were to return? In fact, he did not face certain death or torture in Lithuania, although few young men in his village ever returned from service in the Czar's army. The truth is that Max Zisman (who was Amy's great-grandfather), was searching for a better life, and his story, like that of so many immigrants of his time, is about both escaping from a dangerous political situation and searching for greater economic opportunities.

Berti Bohmer (his real name) was a Viennese Jew. On August 1, 1938 (the Germans were already in Vienna) he sent his wife and sister, Anny and Mitzi, out of Vienna on a train, with no money. They had been given permits to go to Britain as domestics – Anny as a cook and Mitzi as a servant – by a rich English woman (with no humanitarian motives). They tried without success to get a permit to go to the US. Hitler entered Prague in March 1939. Berti needed a permit to leave Prague, which he managed to get after three futile attempts. He was finally successful because he met a German soldier, a high-ranking Nazi, who threw Berti into a small room, but then said that he recognized Berti as he knew his father and his father had been good to him. So he arranged for the permit for Berti to leave. He left two days before war was declared, crossing the Dutch border on a train full of German soldiers who thought he was English as he didn't talk to them. Mitzi had applied for permits for Berti (who had been a businessman in Vienna) to be a farmer and for Anny to be a cook in Sussex. Berti was then interned as an alien, first in Scotland and then on the Isle of Man for six months where he learnt to cook. Mitzi joined the army. Berti and Anny worked in Britain until 1947. After the war, Berti made a number of trips back to Vienna trying to reclaim his property, which he ultimately succeeded in doing. They moved back to Vienna permanently in 1949. Berti and Anny (who are Carol's uncle and aunt) were given refuge in the UK from the persecution and almost certain death they would have suffered at the hands of the Nazis had they stayed in Vienna during the war. The rest of the family were not so lucky. With the exception of Carol's parents, Gusti and Hugh, who fled to New Zealand from Czechoslovakia in May 1939, they all perished in Auschwitz.

Henri (not his real name, unlike Max and Berti whom we do not need to protect), is an asylum seeker of the twenty-first century. He is a refugee from the Central African Republic, who has no possibility of returning to his homeland. He is an educated man with an advanced university degree, and in his homeland he was active in opposition politics. In fact he was slated to hold high office had the coup he was involved in succeeded. When it failed, he went into hiding, in fear of his life. Unable to find him, his political enemies killed his father, his wife and two small children. Henri had no idea what had happened until later. Today he bears the guilt of these deaths, as well as of the shooting of his brother and the beating of his mother, not to mention the exile of other family members. They and he attribute all this horror to his having been active in a failed coup attempt. Henri is applying for political asylum. He is not so much looking for a better life as trying to avoid the fate that would await him should he return to the Central African Republic. Life holds little promise for him now that he has lost much of his family and is estranged from the rest of it. His claim is based on his "well-founded fear of persecution" because of his political activity. When Carol first met him, he had been in the US for several months as a student at a local university. He was shabbily dressed and barely able to communicate because he was so traumatized by what had happened to him. His student visa was part of an effort by the leader of his political group to get him and some other activists out of the country to save their lives. When the university had to deny him admission for the second semester because he couldn't pay the fees, they referred him to the agency with which Carol was working.

Carol worked with Henri over a period of several months, preparing his asylum application, through many difficult and sometimes tearful sessions in which he was forced to relive the horrors of his terrible experience. Tragically, the more ghastly his experience, the "better" his case appears to the immigration authorities. So Carol had to keep asking, "What exactly happened to your wife? How do you know she was raped? Was your father killed first and then dismembered, or the other way around?" By forcing him into going over this experience, we built his case. While he wept at his loss, Carol made notes on each horrific episode. If the details are unclear, his case is weaker. At the interview, the asylum officer interviewing him would be likely to view this vagueness as a sign that he had made the whole thing up, which is the most common reason applications such as Henri's are denied. So we went over and over his story, hoping to prevent his being caught out in an incorrect detail by the interviewing officer.

Since Max Zisman arrived in the US about a hundred years ago, the US has moved from being a nation that welcomed the huddled masses with open arms to one frantically trying to keep its borders secure by allowing only a select few to enter. Every applicant for immigration or asylum is a potential terrorist. When Barney Shuman fled the Czar's army last century, neither the US nor the UK had an official category of political asylum. Berti and his family, who would have qualified, instead had to rely mostly on good luck and perseverance to escape persecution. They were lucky to get a visa as part of the UK's half-hearted program to accept a few refugees fleeing Hitler (Schuster, 2003: 89). In the nineteenth and early twentieth centuries, political asylum wasn't a necessary category because people didn't have to justify their claim to admission. In the US, until the 1920s, anyone in reasonable health was allowed to immigrate (with the notable exception of the Chinese, the subject of a special racist exclusion statute in 1882, and the Japanese, by treaty). Today we have a category for the likes of Henri, but we are frightened to use it except in the most obvious and sympathetic cases. We fear that if we use it too enthusiastically, we will open the floodgates to all the miserable, needy, people fleeing war or crisis, so common in our current world. So we quiz asylum applicants endlessly, to convince ourselves that they are really fleeing persecution and not lying to us so they can slip into a safer country in search of a better life. The whole process is riddled with the fallout from this fear. We are not arguing that the asylum system is never misused by people who are not really fleeing persecution, but rather that the fear of the "bogus" asylum seeker permeates the system to the detriment of genuine asylum seekers. Asylum seekers are guilty until proven innocent.

We make rules to ensure a legal, fair process for asylum applications, and then we enforce them in ways that minimize the number of people eligible for asylum. We say we are concerned about processing cases in a timely manner, but we provide the immigration agencies with insufficient money to achieve this goal. We also have an elaborate system of hearings and court appearances but they are weighted against the asylum seekers, and we are careful to appoint judges to the courts and appeals board who are cynical and reluctant to grant asylum

(Bernstein, 2006; Liptak, 2005). We keep tightening the law to make it harder and harder for asylum seekers to be successful in their claims.

Why do we treat asylum seekers this way? It is because we are deeply ambivalent about our responsibility for providing safe haven to anyone who needs it. On the one hand, the US has a history of taking in the world's "tired, huddled masses, yearning to breathe free." The UK has had a "right to asylum" since the early twentieth century and has taken in some refugees over the years. Both have accepted the 1951 UN Convention and the 1967 Protocol on refugees. On the other hand, we have limited concern for those suffering as a result of wars which are far away and in parts of the world about which many of us know nothing and care less. It is difficult for many Americans or Britons to empathize with the victims. How many readers know that there has been a war festering in Sudan for well over 20 years, of which the current crisis in Darfur is only one part, and that people have been fleeing persecution in significant numbers? Or that religious minorities are routinely persecuted in countries ranging from Uganda to Pakistan? Or that, in many countries, frequently women who are married to political activists are raped just because they are there when government forces round up their husbands?

It is not only the policies but the cultural dimensions of border crossing that have changed. Along with requirements for passports, procedures for obtaining visas, and various forms of border checks, there are institutions producing fake passports, media reports of remarkable border crossings, and informal networks assisting people in various ways. Not all borders are the same, and some countries have internal check points, refugee camps, and less visible borders, as well as forms of transport that present opportunities for greater anonymity. Not only the informal networks and practices but also the state strategies for controlling borders have cultural dimensions. A cultural approach to the political asylum process can help us to understand the conditions in which some individuals and groups of people seek political asylum. Our interviews with asylum seekers point to the need to take apart our assumptions about migration, both the idea that people move from one stable place to another and the idea that the association among people, language, culture, and land is stable and uninterrupted.

As we shall see in later chapters, an individual faces a number of obstacles when seeking asylum. These obstacles are practical, legal, and cultural. So, in addition to having to run the gauntlet of a daunting bureaucracy with complex laws and regulations, asylum seekers often find their applications stymied because their claims are misinterpreted as a result of cultural and political barriers. We will show the many ways in which the cultural predispositions of asylum officers and judges influence (and distort) their understanding of the details of a particular claim. Couple this with the general ambivalence toward asylum we mentioned, and many applicants with good claims fall through the cracks. Some of them are forced to return to the horrors of their homeland from which they have fled; others wait in detention, often in the company of ordinary criminals, for months or even years until their claims are dealt with by the system. Some commit suicide while waiting; one UK asylum seeker who tried to hack himself to death left a note which said "You have to kill yourself in this country to prove that you would be killed in your own country" (Moorehead, 2005: 163).

In those rare situations where an individual case is picked up by the media, we learn enough to identify and feel sympathy. Take, for example, Fauziya Kassindja, whose story we will tell in Chapter 4. She escaped from her small village in Togo on what would have been her wedding day, to avoid FGM (female genital mutilation, a process which is customary in many parts of Africa) (Kassindja, 1998). As we will discuss later at greater length, FGM falls into a nebulous category that includes issues of cultural practices, the rights to state sovereignty, and political persecution based on gender. Fauziya first fled to Germany, but then came to the United States, where she had relatives and where she spoke the language. She used a borrowed passport, which she told the authorities about when she arrived at Newark airport. She was handcuffed and sent to jail to await a hearing. In jail, she was treated like a criminal, and was moved from detention center to prison after a riot, ending up in a maximum security cell with an American criminal. Eventually, she acquired a lawyer (a luxury for those in her position, though he handed the case over to a law student) and had a hearing before a judge. The judge treated both the law student and

Fauziya with impatience and insensitivity, and immediately denied the asylum application because he found Fauziya's disjointed and superficial story unconvincing (he had not allowed her to go into the details of FGM). She was again jailed pending an appeal.

So far this case is pretty typical. What is really unusual is what happened next. The law student persuaded her teacher, Karen Musalo, a leading authority on asylum law, to take on the case. Musalo made it her business to make sure that this case received widespread publicity. Articles about Fauziya, including one by Gloria Steinem, appeared in newspapers such as the *Boston Globe* and on the front page of the *New York Times*. On the day the *Times* story appeared, Musalo was contacted by a representative of the film star Sally Field, who was so outraged by what had happened to Fauziya that she wanted to help. When a case gets picked up like this, with media coverage and the support of public figures, the result is a successful asylum claim. So, Fauziya was granted asylum and also received the traditional perks of one who hits the front page, appearances on talk shows and a lucrative book contract.

Fauziya has a British counterpart whose story also hit the headlines, and as a result her asylum denial was overturned. Mende Nazer, as we will learn in more detail in Chapter 6, was enslaved for eight years in Sudan, her home country. She was sent to Britain to work in the household of a member of the Sudanese Embassy in London, where her treatment was not much better. She escaped and claimed asylum, which was initially denied. She was befriended by a journalist who publicized her case in the British media and worked with her on writing a book, which became a bestseller on its publication in 2003 (Nazer and Lewis). The British Home Office specifically recognized the power of publicity in its decision:

> In view of the widespread publication of her book and the high profile given to her claims both in Sudan and elsewhere, I am satisfied that Ms. Nazer would face difficulties which would bring her within the scope of the 1951 convention were she to be returned to Sudan. For these reasons it has been decided to recognize her as a refugee and grant her Indefinite Leave to Remain in the United Kingdom.

Interestingly, in both Fauziya Kassindja and Mende Nazer's cases, media attention was itself taken into account in determining asylum status. As we will observe, visibility and profile are crucial elements of asylum cases; visibility can make an applicant's situation more dangerous, as the officials recognized in Ms. Nazer's case. Also, visibility can give the officials heightened and more precise awareness of an applicant's situation and can serve as a corrective for the officials' cultural assumptions or lack of understanding.

Those whose cases don't hit the headlines may vegetate in detention until they are deported back to the country from which they fled or, if they are a bit luckier, like Henri, spend the time awaiting the result of the application living hand to mouth, ineligible for any government support or even permission to work legally until six months after the application is filed. In the UK, while applicants are usually provided with benefits, they are not permitted to work while awaiting the outcome of their applications.

Asylum policies are often carried out arbitrarily. So much depends on where the person comes from. If an applicant is unfortunate enough to be persecuted by a government that is a friend of the US or the UK, the chances of getting asylum are minimal. If, on the other hand, they come from an "enemy" country, they stand a much better chance. In the bad old days of communism, those fleeing persecution from communist countries had no trouble getting asylum either in the US or the UK, which shared the US enthusiasm for anticommunists. Those fleeing countries which the US was involved in supporting, like Guatemala, or countries with which we have fragile but important trade relationships, such as China, may find it more difficult to claim persecution. A recent study showed that between 2000 and 2004, applicants from Cuba were granted asylum 82 percent of the time, while the figures of those from China (25 percent), Haiti (11 percent) and El Salvador (3 percent) were much lower (Bernstein and Santora, 2005). For example, in 1993 the ship *Golden Venture* ran aground in New York Harbor with 296 Chinese aboard; they were incarcerated for years until political activists and folklorists brought them to the attention of President Clinton, in part through an exhibition of their folded paper sculptures, made in prison (Westerman, 1996). Some were fleeing China's sterilization policies (they had more than one child and faced or had already experienced forced sterilization). The US has been reluctant to offend the Chinese government by categorizing those policies as political persecution, even though it has now decided that those fleeing the one-child policy are officially defined as fleeing persecution. It is typical of the fragmented nature of the system that this policy doesn't help the women from the *Golden Venture*. In the UK, Kurds from Turkey have a very hard time convincing the authorities that they are persecuted. In the past, Kurdish members of the PKK (Turkish Workers Party) were able to claim persecution by the Turkish government, but since the passage of the Terrorism Act of 2000, belonging to the PKK has been deemed a crime in the UK.

Of course, asylum policy isn't the only area of law that is arbitrary. The death penalty has recently received publicity in the US because of new information about its arbitrary nature. There is now a widespread movement to change the way it is administered, which may eventually result in its being abandoned entirely. The arbitrary quality of the death penalty has in fact been known for a long time, but was something that policy makers did not want to admit. The recent availability of DNA evidence has shown that change is necessary. The public does not yet know that asylum is arbitrary, but here, too, attitudes may change if this fact comes to public attention at a time when people are receptive. The time is clearly not right now, when people are so exercised about the whole subject of immigration that they are unlikely to care that the system is inconsistent if not arbitrary. Similarly, people generally don't realize that sending someone back to a country that persecuted them can itself be a death penalty.

Asylum law: the background

The US

US asylum law is based on the Immigration and Nationality Act of 1952, which made it possible for individuals fleeing persecution to find a haven. That Act followed Article 33 of the 1951 UN Convention (though the United States never signed the Convention). The need for protection came from recognition of the failure of countries to offer safe haven from the Holocaust. The prime example of this is the infamous case of the *St Louis*, which we described in the introduction to the book.

In retrospect, the plight of the *St Louis* has come to represent a moment of national shame. At the time, however, polls show that 88 percent of the American public were opposed to allowing more refugees to enter. After we discovered the horrors of the Holocaust, the US changed its views as did the West in general (hence the passage of the UN Convention). So the US incorporated the words of the 1951 UN Convention into legislation. Under s. 208(a) of Immigration and Nationality Act, asylum can be granted to a "refugee," a definition which includes those who can show that they are unwilling or unable to return to their home country because of past persecution or a "well-founded" fear of persecution on account of race, religion, nationality, membership in a particular social group, or political opinion. Like so many legal definitions, this sounds quite straightforward. In practice, however, it is complex. What exactly is a "social group"? What does "on account of" mean? When is the persecution personal and when is it on account of one of the listed categories? Does the government have to do the actual persecution or is it enough that they look the other way? What does an applicant have to fear? Death? Torture? How likely does it have to be that this will happen? These questions have special meaning for women who fear rape. Does it matter whether the rapist acts on behalf of the government or is just a member of the military who sees rape as a benefit of his position? Does it matter if one is a high-profile political activist or a relatively innocent member of a persecuted group? In the rest of the book, we will show, through the cases of specific individuals, how these rules work in practice, including the ways in which they are arbitrary or unfair.

In 1953, Congress passed the Refugee Relief Act, which granted permanent residence to 214,000 European refugees, and in 1957 the Refugee-Escapee Act, which granted special status to refugees fleeing communist regimes. This special provision for those fleeing communism (which was repealed in 1980) can be explained as part of an effort to redress the wrongs done to people like the passengers on the *St Louis*, but it can also be seen as part of the Cold War efforts to rescue people from the vise of communism. Despite these pieces of legislation, the US commitment to refugees after World War II was fairly limited.

For example, Congress did not pass a Displaced Persons Act until 1948, and even though the law allowed for the admission of up to 200,000 refugees, it was circumscribed so most of the displaced Jews in Europe could not get visas (Tichenor, 2002: 187). In 1965, Congress passed a significant immigration law, which dismantled national origin quotas that had been in force since the 1920s. For the first time, refugees were given a percentage (6 percent) of the total number permitted entry each year. The quota, however, continued to limit refugees to those fleeing from the Middle East and Communist countries.

In 1980, Congress passed the Refugee Act, which expanded the number of refugee admissions and required the development of a system to adjudicate asylum claims. Before (and also after), the President responded to major political crises on an *ad hoc* basis, using his "parole powers," which then came into conflict with the quotas in the law. For example, President Eisenhower offered asylum to 10 percent of the 200,000 refugees created by the Hungarian revolution in 1956. Only about a third of those could actually be given visas under the Refugee Relief Act, so Eisenhower then used his parole authority to admit the rest. President Lyndon Johnson had to use his parole power rather than the 1965 law to admit the Cubans he invited to seek refuge in the US, because they did not come from Europe. Those Czechs in the country following the Soviet invasion of Czechoslovakia in 1968 were given asylum, as were Indochinese refugees after the Vietnam War (Tichenor, 2002).

The 1980 statute was a response to a recognition that the previous haphazard system wasn't working too well. For the first time, it created a new legal status, that of asylum, and it incorporated the definitions of the 1951 UN Convention and the 1967 Protocol (Gibney, 2004: 152). Like the previous legislation, most of the Act was focused on refugees overseas, but for the first time it made it possible for people already in the country, legally or otherwise, to seek asylum if they met the definition of refugee. This new law was a huge administrative burden because of the arrival of floods of people from Cuba in the Mariel boatlift, and later from Haiti, Nicaragua, Guatemala, and El Salvador.

After the passage of the 1980 Act, the Reagan administration continued to use the asylum process to serve its own Cold War foreign policy agenda, rather than for the intended humanitarian goals of the new law. The new regulations required that the Immigration and Naturalization Service (INS) consult with the State Department before granting anyone asylum, and they almost always followed the opinion of the State Department. So those fleeing the Soviet Union were far more likely to be granted asylum than those fleeing those regimes supported by the US, such as Haiti, and El Salvador Only 3 percent of those seeking asylum from countries supported by the US received it, despite a well-documented record of human rights abuses in some of those countries (Einolf, 2001: 14). As a result of this unfair administration of the asylum law, a grassroots movement sprang up among church groups, who provided sanctuary for Salvadorans and Guatemalans. They also filed class-action lawsuits claiming that applicants' due process rights were being violated through the administration of the law. Many of the cases were successful, and the biggest of these (known as ABC for the plaintiff American Baptist Church), which was settled in 1990, resulted in more than 250,000 Salvadorans and Guatemalans becoming eligible to apply for asylum.

Cuba has always been a special case. After Castro came to power, the US admitted virtually all Cubans who were able to reach its shores. Following the Mariel boatlift, people began to reconsider the blanket assumption that every Cuban who arrived in the US was fleeing persecution. Efforts were then concentrated on keeping Cubans from reaching US shores. This "wet foot, dry foot" policy (i.e. those who are picked up at sea are sent back; those who make it onto US soil are taken in) is still in effect (Goodnough, 2005). The aim was to prevent as many Cubans as possible from actually reaching the US, so that the issue of their status need not become the political hot potato it would otherwise have been, because of the outspoken Cuban exile community. Publicity about efforts to prevent Cubans from landing on US soil raised awareness of the disparity between the treatment of Cubans on the one hand, and Haitians and others fleeing the region on the other. This disparity provides further illustration of the conflict between humanitarian concerns and concerns about the country being flooded with expensive and troublesome refugees, as well as the role of foreign policy versus domestic concerns in the implementation of asylum.

In 1990, as the class action cases were being settled, the administration of the process was streamlined to make it more efficient and
fairer. A distinct asylum unit was set up to operate separately from the
INS district offices, and special officers were to be trained as asylum
hearing officers. These reforms worked well, except they didn't
eliminate one huge problem, the backlog, which grew each year. The
new asylum officers couldn't keep up with the new arrivals from all
over the world, let alone deal with the 250,000 new cases generated
by the ABC settlement we mentioned above. This resulted in delays
and the related problem of fraud. People were able to apply for asylum
and immediately get a work permit, which gave an applicant many
years of work before their case (whether meritorious or not) came
before the authorities.

The 1990s saw a battle in Congress to drastically change asylum
law, as part of a movement to restrict immigration generally (Schrag,
2000). Like the general public, legislators are not generally informed
about asylum law and policy and saw asylum as a "foot in the door"
for unsuitable people to lie their way into the country. Their views
had some merit. In the 1980s tens of thousands arrived in the US without proper documentation and requested asylum. This exacerbated the
backlog (over 400,000 by 1994) because the INS was unable to deal
with the cases fast enough. So applicants were simply given work
permits and a date for a hearing later. Many of them just disappeared
into the woodwork and didn't show up for their hearings. Even if they
did appear for the hearing, and the asylum application was ultimately
denied, they had in the meantime had years of working legally before
their case was heard. How many of those 400,000 applicants were
"real" asylum cases is unknown, though at least some of them must
have been genuinely fleeing persecution and not just seeking economic
advancement.

As is so often the case, the result of the battle in Congress was a
compromise. Asylum law (part of the Immigration Control and Fiscal
Responsibility Act of 1996), was maintained, with a few important
restrictions which we will discuss later (Schrag, 2000). Special
categories are still part of the political landscape. The Lautenberg
Amendment, passed in 1989, was named after Senator Lautenberg,
who persuaded Congress to make it easier for Soviet Jews to immigrate

as refugees. Despite much debate prior to the passage of the 1996 statute, it is still in force. The 1996 law amended the definition of refugee and provides a special category for those fleeing China's one-child policy, in response to the previous INS policy of denying asylum to those who fled China's coercive population policies. This is another example of the way Congress sometimes intervenes in "special cases" in response to political pressures, in this case a strange coalition of Chinese asylum supporters and right-to-life activists (Hing, 2004: 256).

After September 11, 2001 Congress passed legislation merging a number of agencies within the government into the Department of Homeland Security, whose responsibility includes those previously held by the INS. In 2005, the REAL ID Act was passed as part of the general crack-down on immigrants. It mostly focuses on ways to make it harder for undocumented immigrants to obtain drivers' licenses, but it also tightens some of the rules for obtaining asylum in ways which make it harder for an application to succeed.

The UK

Before 1905, Britain was known as a place of refuge because of its laissez-faire attitude to entrance policies in general (Gibney, 2004: 113). Like the US, the UK began limiting the entrance of foreigners early in the twentieth century. In 1905 and 1914, as a result of public fear of foreigners, legislation was passed limiting entry to the UK. Also like the US, between1919 and 1938 there was no distinction between immigration and asylum, though the UK did not have the same allure for workers as the US. The UK was also part of the group of democracies that were mostly unwilling to accept those fleeing Hitler (Berti Bohmer was a lucky exception). Anti-Semitism, always pronounced among the British elite, made the government unresponsive to Jews seeking entry into the country. Despite this reluctance, Berti was one of about 50,000 refugees fleeing Germany and Austria between 1933 and 1939 who were allowed into the UK (Gibney, 2004: 114; Schuster, 2003: 88). After World War II, the UK asylum policy was based on "the combination of discretion and unpredictability" (Gibney, 2004: 114). Many thousands of refugees were settled in the years immediately after the war. The UK was one of the first signatories of the UN

Convention of 1951 (Lynch and Simon, 2003: 128). Since then, it has also signed the 1967 Protocol, though neither treaty was actually incorporated into the law, so in fact, signing them didn't really affect the way asylum seekers were treated, nor did it lead to much increase in the numbers of those admitted (Gibney, 2004:114). Like the US, the UK did, however, resettle refugees from post-1956 Hungary and post-1968 Czechoslovakia. Apart from these special cases, the UK didn't pay much attention to refugees until the 1980s. Attention was instead directed at problems caused by a big influx of immigrants from the former British colonies, especially from those parts of the Commonwealth that were non-white. The plight of British citizens who were expelled from Kenya and Uganda in the late 1960s and early 1970s created problems for the British government because of negative public sentiment toward letting in large numbers of refugees with dark skins (Shah, 2000). The concern about admitting "too many" foreigners, as well as a negative economic climate in the late 1970s and early 1980s led to greater attention to the issue in the 1980s, even though only 14,897 refugees were resettled between 1981 and 1990 (Loescher, 1993: 135), a figure which was much lower than those of other European countries for the same period (Gibney, 2004: 122). One of the policy reasons for this relatively low rate was that, early on, the UK required visas for asylum seekers from countries that were the source of many applicants. Also, in 1987, the Immigration (Carriers Liability) Act imposed heavy fines on carriers that brought passengers to the country without adequate entrance documents. This continues to be an effective tool for limiting asylum seekers; it has since been extended to trucks and the Eurostar train. The widespread use of executive discretion gave the government the power to change such policies as the benefits received by asylum seekers with very little judicial oversight until recently (Gibney, 2004: 125). The Home Office has the power to make the rules, change them, and enforce them at their discretion. This is a result of the particular system of government in Britain, where rules and laws, unlike in the US, are not subject to constitutional oversight (Maiman, 2005: 422).

Despite this combination of executive discretion and early prevention efforts, the UK's worst fears were fulfilled when the numbers of asylum seekers began to skyrocket in the late 1990s; applications rose from 27,685 in 1996–7 to 79,125 in 2000. The crises in Kosovo, Albania, Iraq and Afghanistan contributed to this increase. Britain responded by granting asylum in a very low percentage of cases, using administrative discretion, special "fast-track" procedures for those from "safe" countries (an ever expanding category), by dispersing asylum seekers throughout the UK, and by eliminating cash benefits to applicants. All these measures were intended to deter people from coming to the UK to seek asylum.

The increase in asylum seekers to the UK came about because many of the previous barriers diminished in importance. The geographical isolation of the UK was no longer an advantage, as a result of the opening of the tunnel under the English Channel and organized trafficking of asylum seekers into the country. Economic woes were no longer an issue, making the UK a more attractive destination for asylum seekers and economic migrants alike. Also, the executive discretion that had earlier been so useful was "whittled away by the courts since the mid-1990s" (Gibney, 2004: 127). In addition, the incorporation of the European Convention on Human Rights into British law in 1999 provided an important tool for lawyers contesting the bureaucratic decisions of the Home Office, as well as making available another route to contest cases to the European Court of Human Rights.

At the same time, other European countries began tightening their asylum laws, which also made the UK a relatively more attractive destination, especially for those with an emotional and linguistic tie to Britain because of its colonial past. In 2002, the UK had 51,400 asylum applicants, compared to 36,259 in Germany and 24,761 in France, the closest competitors. In the last few years, however, the British government has made an all out (and successful) effort to dramatically cut the numbers of those seeking asylum. These reductions have come as a result of several recent measures, such as moving UK immigration controls to France, before people make the journey across the channel. A law passed in 2004, the Asylum and Immigration (Treatment of Claimants, etc.) Act, assumes that those who arrive in the UK without documents are not credible, which makes it very unlikely they will obtain asylum. The statute also merged two levels of appeal in asylum cases and limited jurisdiction of immigration tribunals, which speeds up the process of appeal and removal (Maiman, 2005: 413). It also makes it possible to arrest people for immigration crimes, such as bigamy and forgery. Other actions also make it easier to remove those whose claims fail, such as an agreement with China to take back failed asylum seekers; and there have been efforts to remove Somalis, even though there is really no country to which they can return.

Until very recently the UK had no mechanism for taking in refugees from abroad as a special category of asylum applicants, as distinct from allowing those who made it there to stay, under the rules for granting asylum. As part of its push over the last few years to make it harder and harder to obtain asylum in the UK, the government in 2002 finally included a small (500 each year) refugee resettlement program (Gibney, 2004: 130–1). The Gateway Resettlement Programme has been hampered by problems with local authorities, so at the end of the first year only 150 refugees had gained entrance through this scheme, a tiny contribution compared to other refugee-accepting states, such as the US, Canada, and Australia (Gee, 2005).

Asylum seekers, refugees and economic migrants – what is the difference?

We need to clarify the distinction between asylum seekers and refugees. Much of the public information on this subject refers to "refugees," rather than asylum seekers, who are the subject of this book. There is a vast literature on the subject of refugees (e.g. Castles, 2000; Gibney and Hansen, 2004; Loescher, 1993; Zolberg and Benda, 2001). The word "refugee" is commonly used to describe anyone who has been forced to flee his or her country, but in the law and international policy it has a more technical meaning. It refers to the legal status that someone receives which allows them to be brought into a country at government expense and to receive certain public benefits. Many refugees from wars end up in refugee camps in a third country. There, some of them are processed and given refugee status. They get refugee status because of a general recognition of their group's vulnerability. In some ways, getting refugee status outside a refugee-accepting country is easier than claiming asylum after arrival in the country, because it is already recognized that they, as a group, would be persecuted if they had to return to their country (Tichenor, 2002). However, displaced people in refugee camps often wait many years for a country to accept them for resettlement (Moorehead, 2005).

Asylum applicants, by contrast, who are the subject of this book, are those who travel to the US or the UK under their own steam and then apply for asylum. Some asylum seekers come legally on other visas, as Henri did, on a student visa or on a visitor's visa. They may intend to seek asylum when they arrive, or may determine after their arrival that they can't go home. Mohamed, for example, came to the US from the United Arab Emirates where he had been living with his Filipino wife. He converted to Catholicism, which made him feel very unsafe in the UAE or any other Muslim country where Christians are persecuted. He is afraid that radical Muslims will hunt him down. "For a Muslim to kill us, they would go to heaven," he said. Mohamed and his wife came to the US on a visitor's visa in 2002 to visit his brother, who had earlier been granted asylum.

Applicants like Mohamed intend to apply for asylum when they come; for others, circumstances may change in their country while they are here, which makes it impossible for them safely to return home. A civil war may break out or someone may find out that the authorities are looking for him when he contacts his family at home, thereby forcing him to stay here. Tun, a Burmese activist, whose story we will tell in Chapter 5, decided to seek asylum while he was in the US studying because the Thai government publicly announced that it no longer supported pro-democracy activists like him, making it too dangerous for him to go back to Thailand where he had been living after his escape from Burma.

Other asylum seekers come with false papers or no papers, as we saw in the case of Fauziya, whose story we discussed above. They are fleeing persecution and are looking for a safe haven, though they may not know the word "asylum" or understand the process of applying for it. In Diallo's case, which is typical, someone provided him with a passport to get through immigration and then later he applied for asylum in his own name. Diallo, a Mauritanian, is an educated Fulani, an ethnic group targeted by the government as part of its goal of ethnic cleansing to get rid of black Mauritanians. He worked in the tax office, which made him an identifiable target. He was arrested several times and beaten in jail. After searching for a safe haven in Senegal and Morocco, he finally paid a smuggler to bring him to the US on someone else's passport. As is typical in such situations, the smuggler disappeared with the passport as soon as they had passed through immigration. Diallo applied for asylum several months later through CRIS (Community Refugee and Immigration Services in Columbus, Ohio), the agency with which Carol worked.

When Mustapha was 17, he stowed away on a ship departing from Freetown, the capital of Sierra Leone, to escape being drafted into the rebel forces. He had been shot in the leg when he leapt out of a car driven by rebels just before it blew up. After spending some time in hiding, he believed that he was not safe from either the rebels or those on the other side, whom he feared would believe that he was a rebel himself. The ship on which he stowed away went first to Brazil, but after spending some time there he decided he would be better off in an English-speaking country. So he got back on the ship and arrived in a small town called Louisiana, Texas, where he was apprehended by officials. They jailed him for a couple of days, but he was a lot luckier than Fauziya, because they then let him go. Under the law, a person claiming asylum can be let go if the authorities believe he has a credible fear of persecution should he return to his homeland. A local agency helped Mustapha buy a bus ticket to a Midwestern city where they believed he would be better off because there was a Sierra Leonean community there. Mustapha clearly left Sierra Leone with the purpose of finding a safe haven, though he had no idea then where it would be. He had no passport and, of course, no visa to enter the country legally.

To someone trying to stay in the US or the UK, asylum looks like a tantalizing possibility. Like the general public, lots of immigrants don't really understand what is required by the law to file a successful asylum application. For example, Carol saw Sheila, a Tamil woman, who arrived in the US on a visitor's visa. Sheila was brought in to CRIS by someone in the social services department of a local hospital. They thought that if she got asylum, she would be eligible for Social Security and Medicaid, which would help her deal with her medical problems. When Carol asked Sheila about what she was afraid of in Sri Lanka, she described a general fear of being in a disrupted area where there was fighting. She had no direct personal experience of that violence, nor did any member of her family. Carol had to tell Sheila that, however afraid she might be of a volatile situation, she had no basis for a claim of asylum.

Ignorance about asylum can sometimes mean a failed claim. One of the best examples of this ignorance and its effects was Halima, a young Somali woman who had been smuggled in on a false passport. When Carol asked her why she wanted asylum she said that she wanted a work permit, and for the child she was then carrying to be born in the US. In the end, she settled for some help in finding furniture. Halima is a classic case of someone seeking a better life in the US. She came from Somalia, a country ravaged by violence, where members of many ethnic groups were (and are still) persecuted, and many of those ended up in refugee camps in Kenya and Ethiopia. Many of them were given refugee status in the camps and then resettled abroad. The problem for Halima was that she had not been personally persecuted, nor had she been in a refugee camp, where she could have been given refugee status, but instead had come to the US illegally, and too late. The number of Somalis being resettled had by then diminished to a trickle. She had missed the bus. Many other Somalis were granted refugee status abroad as a group and did not have to prove that they were personally targeted for persecution. By taking matters into her own hands and coming to the US illegally, Halima became an individual claimant who had to prove that she personally had been persecuted. She also had to overcome the barrier that the INS had decided by then that, except in very rare cases, Somalis were no longer considered suitable candidates for asylum. This was not, of course, an overt policy, but rather something that those in the business of helping asylum seekers knew on the basis of past cases. It is one of the ways in which the system for obtaining asylum is arbitrary. Just as the media and media audiences suffer what has been called "compassion fatigue," growing weary of a particular bad news story, the asylum bureaucracy suffers from a parallel syndrome in which a "hot spot" of political persecution goes "cold." Of course there is a relationship between media attention and the perception of a spot as "hot." In any case, sympathy for others' political plight seems to be driven by the seemingly arbitrary matter of media interest and attention span. When Halima made her application, Somalia was old news and therefore Somalians were no longer people to whom asylum was to be granted. For a while, CRIS advised Somalis seeking asylum to go elsewhere in the country, where they seemed to get a more sympathetic hearing, but later, that, too, no longer helped them.

Of course, "hot spots" can go cold for perfectly legitimate reasons, which make them no longer suitable places from which to claim asylum, as the authorities are the first to argue. When a crisis has passed, there is much less need for someone to flee the persecution generated by that crisis. Political changes may also change the likelihood that asylum will be granted. This has happened in the UK, with the addition of new countries to the European Union in 2004 and 2007. Before that time, a number of Roma (Gypsies) from Romania, the Czech Republic and elsewhere claimed that they were being persecuted because of their ethnicity. Now that they come from European Accession states, they are no longer considered candidates for asylum whether they are still persecuted or not. Their home countries are among those countries classified as "safe."

Seeking a better life is not enough for an asylum claim. After all, millions of people would like a better life in the United States or the United Kingdom. These are economic migrants who may be able to enter or stay in the country under other immigration rules. Asylum, by contrast, is carefully reserved only for those who are fleeing persecution. Asylum seekers have to be able to prove that they have been persecuted in the past and/or that they fear future persecution if they return to their country. Persecution has been defined in different ways by various courts, but the general meaning is similar in asylum-accepting countries, as we shall see in later chapters. We will also learn, however, that what counts as persecution is not interpreted consistently and that the category must be assessed culturally, as well as legally. In addition, we shall see that while asylum seekers and refugees are clear and distinct legal categories, the distinction between asylum seeker and economic migrant is very murky. Many people flee difficult conditions to improve their lives, both economically and otherwise. The asylum court in London where we observed asylum appeals was full of Kurds fleeing the difficulties they faced as members of a minority in Turkey and Iranians fleeing the hardships of life in Iran.

Some of them had indeed been persecuted, while for others the conditions they left were not considered to constitute persecution.

Who are the asylum seekers?

What do we know about people seeking a safe haven? Unfortunately, not as much as we would like in the US, though more in the UK, which seems to keep more informative statistics. We do know that people from many countries seek asylum in the US, though as we have seen, the figures are also a measure of changing regions in crisis. There is a steady stream from Africa, though the countries change; the Americas account for the most applicants, but Asia is well represented also, with some from Europe making up the total. The top ten source countries from which people were granted asylum in 2005 were, in order, the People's Republic of China (accounting for 20.7 percent), Colombia (13.4 percent), Haiti (11.7 percent), Venezuela (4.4 percent), Ethiopia (2.9 percent), Albania (2.8 percent), Cameroon (2.6 percent), Russia (1.9 percent), Indonesia (1.9 percent), and Armenia (1.7 percent) (United States Department of Homeland Security, 2006). The latest figures from the UK show that the leading countries from which asylum seekers came were Eritrea, Afghanistan, Iran, China and Somalia (Home Office, 2006). Both countries receive those whose need to flee persecution is greatest, though more people make it to the US from the Americas than the UK, and more from the Middle East go to Britain, for reasons of geography.

So how many applicants were successful in their claims? The short answer should come as no surprise by now: many fewer than there used to be. The US Citizenship and Immigration Service's (USCIS) approval rate of affirmative cases (those heard by a hearing officer) was on average 19 percent over the five-year period from 2000 to 2004, but only 9 percent in 2004, the last year for which these figures seem to be available, though that figure fluctuates significantly depending on the country of origin. For defensive asylum claims (those referred to the court or those begun as defensive claims) the rate has remained steady over the period, with only 1 out of 5 (19.8 percent) being granted asylum. It should be noted that many of the defensive claims are not heard at all for one reason or another (withdrawn, abandoned, or received an alternative resolution – 48 percent) (TRAC Immigration Report, 2006). The UK figures are lower than both those for the US and in comparison to earlier figures; in 2004, a total of 24 percent were granted asylum; very few of those were granted asylum at the initial hearing (4 percent). In the UK, there is less fluctuation among countries of origin, though the success rate does still vary by country. For example, only 4.5 percent of Turks were successful, while 14 percent of those from Cameroon were; 1.5 percent of Ghanaians, and 18 percent of Eritreans received asylum or leave to remain (Home Office, 2006).

In the last few years, as we have seen, both the UK and the US have made great efforts to limit the numbers of people seeking asylum. In the UK this was a response to a sudden increase of asylum applicants in the early 1990s, which caused great public concern. Ever since, this has been a front-burner political and media issue. As a result, attitudes toward asylum seekers have shifted. People are now more inclined to believe that people seek asylum for economic reasons and less because they are fleeing persecution (MORI, 2002). In response to this concern, several laws have been passed and implementation policies changed, which have had the effect of making asylum much more difficult both to apply for and to obtain in the UK. The number of applicants in the UK fell by 25 percent in 2005 compared to 2004, and 70 percent compared to 2002 (UNHCR, 2005a: 5). In the US, a similar legal and administrative process has occurred, though asylum has never had the political importance there that it has had in the UK. September 11 has had the effect of pushing the changes further and the result in the US has been similar to that in the UK: fewer asylum seekers getting in and fewer grants of asylum. In Chapter 2 we will look at the nature of those changes and their effects.

Conclusion

Asylum statistics are a mirror of politics. As civil wars heat up and cool down, so do the numbers of those fleeing the results of the seemingly inevitable persecution. In the 1990s, it was Bosnians, Kosovans, Albanians, Iraqis, and Afghanis who sought asylum. Africa always has one country or more where there is civil war creating many refugees, some of whom make it to the US in refugee resettlement programs, like the Somalis in the late 1990s. Others come as asylum seekers on their own, from Sierra Leone, Liberia, and, more recently, Cameroon and Eritrea. China is a perennial source country for those seeking asylum in both the UK and the US. People flee religious persecution (most recently the Falun Gong), coercive population policies, and, of course, the political persecution characteristic of that repressive regime. For the Tibetans it is both religious and political persecution that has resulted in a small, but steady, stream of people seeking asylum. Cuba, the US's neighbor and permanent enemy, is a regular source of asylum seekers, as are places in constant turmoil, like Haiti and Colombia. While there are many similarities, the differences in country of origin of those who go to the UK and the US are a result of geography, history, and chance.

The overall reduction in asylum applicants to both countries is part of a worldwide trend. The office of the UN High Commissioner for Refugees (UNHCR) reported that:

> . . . [the] number of asylum-seekers in Europe and in the non-European industrialized countries analysed in this report continued to decline sharply in 2005. In the 50 countries included in Table 1, 336,100 applications for refugee status were submitted in 2005, 15 percent fewer than in 2004 (394,600) . . . Since the latest peak in 2001, when 655,100 asylum-seekers were registered by these 50 countries, applications have halved (–49%).
>
> (UNHCR, 2005a)

The UNHCR also reports that the number of refugees has dropped as many people are able to return home after crises have passed. Some countries that were previously the sources of many asylum seekers are no longer, like Afghanistan and Turkey. The UNHCR reports: "Since 2001, the number of Afghan asylum applications has fallen by 85 percent. Similarly, the number of Turkish asylum-seekers has decreased by 61 percent over the same period" (2005a).

However, like the US and the UK, many other industrialized countries have responded to the view of their people that asylum is out of control by passing restrictive legislation. So it is hard to tell how much of the drop in applications comes from a lower demand for asylum and how much from more stringent procedures to deal with asylum seekers.

Many questions about asylum seekers remain. Why do some people from ghastly war-torn places in the world fail to get asylum, while others from what seem perfectly calm places, like Hungary, succeed? What is it about the claims of those originating from some countries that makes them more likely to succeed? Is it that there is simply more persecution in those places? Or is it that some nationals are better at putting together a claim, more likely to have resources to hire a lawyer, or more articulate at the hearing? Do individuals with high political profiles have an advantage over applicants who have suffered as a result of their membership in an ethnic or religious group? And does the system favor people fighting for democracy, the right to protest, or religious freedom over those whose political views may not be in accord with our values and politics? Does it matter whether you are Christian or Muslim? What about women who suffer gender persecution? What kinds of applicants are being accepted? Who is being rejected? Can we identify patterns in the policies and in the stories of individual cases? What role does culture play in officials' evaluations? Are these questions answered differently in the US compared to the UK? How does the interplay between the legal changes and administrative actions work in this case? We can't find the answers to these questions in the dry pages of immigration statistics. But we can provide some answers through the detailed accounts of particular cases of asylum applicants. Only in this way can we address the complexity of these questions. The next chapters will look at the whole asylum system in the US and the UK to find some answers and explanations.

The asylum system may be on the way out. The British Home Office sends out frequent press releases about the new tough measures they have taken to reduce the number of asylum seekers. They focus on "deterrence" and cutting the numbers as if applying for asylum is a crime to be prevented. They trumpet their "successes" proudly, only occasionally paying lip service to the needs of genuine asylum seekers. The belief that liberal democracies have a moral and international obligation to those fleeing persecution seems no longer to be part of the discourse either in the US or the UK. Any concerns for the plight of those who suffer as a result of persecution are overridden by domestic fears within the country. For the UK, the fear is of being overrun by economic migrants masquerading as asylum seekers for their personal gain at the expense of the country; in the US, in addition to the fear of economic migrants, the fear is of being overrun by terrorists posing as asylum seekers to get into the country and then cause havoc. These fears are becoming interchangeable; after the bombings on the London underground in July 2005, Britons also fear asylum seekers as potential terrorists, while in the US asylum seekers are lumped in with "illegals" generally, as those stealing jobs and benefits from Americans. Whether the fears have any basis in reality is not considered by the policy makers. In fact, none of the nineteen hijackers on September 11 were asylum seekers, though some of those arrested in Britain for terrorist activities have been.

How will all this end? Will victory be declared by a Home Office press release when they have cut the numbers of asylum seekers to zero? It goes without saying that the wars and the crises that make asylum seekers leave their countries have not and will not stop, however tough the measures of the governments toward potential asylum seekers. Can governments abdicate their responsibilities toward those in need of protection? Or are these responsibilities no longer relevant in the security minded twenty-first century, despite the continuing validity of the UN Convention? The rest of the book will discuss these questions in detail. We will show the effects of a combination of new laws and policies and the reframing of the problem in such a way as to guarantee that only those few applicants defined within certain cultural and political frameworks are classified as "genuine" asylum seekers deserving of protection.

2 The system

Nikolai, in the US on a visitor's visa, sees an ad in a Russian-language newspaper, which offers help to people seeking asylum. He is very excited that this may be a way for him to stay in the US, so he makes an appointment with the "expert" who promises him easy sailing with his asylum application. He manages to pull together the money the "expert" requires to begin to process it. Months go by, and Nikolai hears nothing. He is stopped by the police for failing to have a current inspection sticker on the car he is driving and all hell breaks loose. He finds out that the "expert" has done nothing on his asylum claim, so he is detained for overstaying his visitor's visa.

On the other side of town, a dozen asylum lawyers are gathered in a modest room at the Windjammer Inn on the outskirts of Burlington, Vermont, on a chilly November morning to learn the tricks and finer points of assisting asylum applicants who will arrive in the lawyers' offices knowing nothing of the process. Sara Ignatius, a woman from an asylum referral organization in Boston called PAIR (Political Asylum/Immigration Representation Project), is running a workshop like many she offers in cities across the country. In these sessions, lawyers learn the nuts and bolts of the application process; they leave with a training manual and notebook full of notes and the feeling that they are in control of what is a very complicated and byzantine process.

Elijah, who recently escaped with his life after being arrested for writing an article critical of the Liberian government, arrived in the US on a visitor's visa. From educated friends in the US he learns about what is required for an asylum application. He goes to the local public library, locates the forms, downloads them, and fills them out. When he left Liberia, he knew he would need to support his claim, so he brought as much evidence with him as he could. He has the newspaper articles he wrote, news reports about his arrest and sham trial, as well as letters from friends in Liberia and the US corroborating his story.

It is perfectly possible for someone to apply for asylum themselves in the US, without the help of lawyers or "experts." It does occasionally happen. However, it's certainly not typical, and in all but the rarest cases (like Elijah's) the worst advice that could be given to any asylum seeker without significant resources and education, would be to do this themselves.

Hassan arrives in London after escaping from Turkey and goes immediately to his cousin's house. He is taken by the cousin to the public call-in unit at Lunar House, the main office of the immigration service, where he has an initial screening interview with a Home Office case worker in which he is asked who he is and how he got there. His photo and fingerprints are taken and he is given an ARC (Application Registration Card) so he can get benefits, and what is known as an SEF (Statement of Evidence Form), which he is told he has to complete and return in ten working days. On the form is the name of a couple of nongovernmental organizations (NGOs) which might help him. Luckily for Hassan, his cousin knows how to get him to one of them, the Refugee Legal Centre, where he sees a case worker who helps him fill in the form.

Because legal aid is available for asylum in the UK, applicants' stories are less varied than they are in the US. Asylum seekers are more likely to find a lawyer than their US counterparts, for whom no government paid legal aid is available, though lawyers in the UK complain that cutbacks in fees paid to them make it increasingly difficult for them to represent clients adequately. Most applicants in the UK are no longer legally represented at their initial interview, although the Legal Services Commission, which oversees the legal funding for lawyers, does provide up to five hours compensation to prepare for this interview, though not to attend it. In the US, the process of finding a lawyer is much more haphazard.

For the average person, the process of applying for asylum is a bureaucratic maze requiring a native guide and the help of others who have been through it before. This is not only a perception; the asylum application process is indeed very complicated, and there are all sorts of "tricks" known by those familiar with the system, knowledge that increases the chances of success. Of course, the average person from another country is unlikely to have a clue about how to go about jumping through the bureaucratic hoops. We know from interviews with applicants that many of them don't even know there is such a thing as asylum when they arrive, let alone what it involves. Peter, an applicant from Cameroon, was helped to escape and told how to get in and what to do with his borrowed passport, but was never told that he had to apply for asylum once he got here. Fortunately, the person with whom he stayed when he reached California knew and sent him to a lawyer.

There is also the "word on the street" about the whole asylum process, which is sometimes accurate but often sadly misleading. Perhaps the most widespread "story" is that asylum is the way to get legal residence. Many people who have not been persecuted apply for asylum, which has the result of making their presence and whereabouts known to the authorities and triggering the deportation process. In California, for example, huge numbers of Mexicans were deported after they applied for asylum because they had been told it was the only way to get legal residence. Lawyers of course know this, and warn their clients of the risk of getting onto the radar screen, but, as we've already seen, many people in the US don't ever see lawyers. The statistics make it abundantly clear that the chances of success at every stage of an asylum claim are significantly increased with the help of a lawyer. Schoenholtz and Jacobs' research indicates that asylum cases where the applicant is represented are four to six times more likely to succeed than claims without legal representation (2002: 740). A lawyer can evaluate the various options available for an asylum seeker, which may involve other processes than an application for asylum. But in the US, as we have mentioned, the government provides no legal help to applicants, nor can many nonprofit agencies find the funding to do so. The odds of finding a lawyer to take the case *pro bono* (without fee) varies from virtually impossible in some parts of the country, to pretty good in others. In Columbus, the Department of Homeland Security (DHS) had a list of lawyers and agencies which ostensibly provided free or low-cost help; in fact the list was completely inaccurate. In Los Angeles, by contrast, a nonprofit agency both represents asylum seekers and coordinates lawyers from corporate law firms who take cases as part of their *pro bono* activities. Those lawyers spend vast amounts of time preparing the cases and generally have a lot of success. But, in other parts of the country, asylum seekers have much more difficulty finding someone to represent them. Most asylum seekers have no money to live on, let alone pay for a lawyer.

It was the story of the Mexicans using asylum as a potential route to legal residence, as well as others like it, that provided some of the ammunition for the tightening of the asylum process in the US in 1996. Because asylum is so much a front-burner issue in the UK, there is more of a sense that people know what to do. We don't hear the same stories of ignorance about the process that we hear in the US. Most people, like Hassan, seem to find a relative or countryman who helps them get to the Home Office for an initial interview and then they can find themselves an agency. Here is an exchange in an asylum appeal we witnessed in 2006, which is pretty typical and which illustrates the relative sophistication of asylum seekers in the UK (*R* is the lawyer for the applicant, *AP* is the applicant):

R: Would you please recount what happened when you arrived in the UK, things such as who did you stay with?

AP: A friend of my cousin's. I stayed with her for eight days. Then she left me at the Home Office because she said she couldn't keep me any more.

R: Did you know you could claim asylum as soon as you got to the UK?

AP: My cousin told me I couldn't stay without getting asylum.

There is more help available from agencies, because of government funding to help asylum seekers in the UK, despite the recent cutbacks. Nevertheless, there are still those in the UK who get into serious difficulties because they don't apply soon enough, or because they don't get any help filling out the SEF form.

In the US, some smugglers apparently advise their "customers" to tell a policeman that they want to claim asylum. Some of the smugglers even include a completed application form in the services they provide, to be used if the asylum seeker is picked up. Not surprisingly, these are usually boilerplate applications based on previously successful cases and are unlikely to be suitable for that particular asylum seeker (Schoenholtz and Jacobs, 2002: 748).

In every city in the US, there are "fixers" or "experts" (often called *notarios*) who operate outside the law to "help" people file asylum applications. They are particularly prevalent in communities with big Latino populations and trade on the fact that in other countries, *notarios* are much like lawyers. They charge for their services, but much less than a private attorney, whose representation goes far beyond the filling out of Form 589, the application form. In Columbus, the going rate was $150 (cheap by comparison with rates in other cities where the costs can rise to several thousand dollars) to fill out the application. CRIS had a policy of refusing to hand out blank copies of the form, in an attempt (probably not very successful) to deter the "fixers" from operating. Their attraction is that they profess to know the way through the bureaucratic maze that is so daunting to the average applicant. It is a rare applicant (Elijah is the exception) who is educated enough and has sufficient command of English to be able to fill out the complicated form themselves. Half the time the fixers take the money and say they will file a 589 and do nothing, which is what happened to Nikolai. In fairness, some of the people involved, often in the communities from which the applicant comes, do a pretty good job of helping applicants through the maze that is form 589. They have the advantage of speaking the language of the applicant and knowing the conditions in the country from which they have fled.

In some parts of the US the most damage to applicants is done not by unqualified *notarios*, but by people who are qualified lawyers, who make their money doing a volume business for asylum applicants. They charge less than a good lawyer would, but provide very little by way of preparation in what is labor-intensive legal representation. In California, these inadequate lawyers charge between $3,000–4000, compared to about $10,000 for a private attorney who undertakes the extensive preparation necessary to file a good application. Because of the economics, and because it is very difficult to find a *pro bono* attorney or non-profit agency who will take the case without fee, many applicants end up with bad representation by an unprepared lawyer. A report by the Vera Institute found that immigration professionals perceived the vast majority of lawyers either nominally qualified or totally unqualified, and many of them maintained huge caseloads and spent very little time preparing each case (unpublished report, cited by Schoenholtz and Jacobs, 2002: 757). Bad legal advice exists even when the government pays for it. In the UK, lawyers have also been providing advice that is "variable," and sometimes downright bad (Greater London Authority, 2005).

US lawyers tell stories of having to repair the damage done by others, both bad lawyers and *notarios*. At the very least it can be a problem figuring out what has actually been filed. In some cases, the applicant has been told that they can't get asylum unless they claim to have been tortured by electroshock, or raped. So the application will contain this information, even though it is not true and even though in many cases the applicant has a perfectly good claim based on the true facts of the persecution. What usually happens is that the case is denied at the hearing level and then is referred to the court. The lawyer who ends up with the case then has to try to turn an inadequate application into one what will result in asylum being granted by the court, which is much harder than writing a good application in the first place. If the applicant has been told to lie, as is often the case, the lawyer then has to explain convincingly why that happened.

The system is different in the UK. Because of the public legal aid available for asylum claims, applicants do better, even with the recent effort by the government to limit the availability of this aid at various stages of the process. Nevertheless, some asylum seekers suffer from inadequate legal representation exactly as their US counterparts do. For example, in one case:

> . . . private solicitors failed to notify a 35-year-old Eritrean woman of her right to appeal by the deadline, then failed to take any further action. The woman was referred by a community organization to another private solicitor who charged £300 to lodge a completely inadequate application, which did not explain why the appeal was late. Failure to lodge an appeal in time resulted in the woman losing her local authority accommodation, where she had lived for

> five years. The new representatives had to make an application for
> judicial review in the High Court . . .
>
> (Greater London Authority, 2005: 68)

In the UK, there is now a new system of policing bad asylum
advisors, and a push to make sure they are properly certified. Because
they can benefit from available funds, there is an incentive for agencies
to employ only certified advisors. We are told that this push toward
professionalism seems to have reduced the number of bad advisors.
Because of the power of the organized Bar, lawyers are not covered
by these new procedures, so complaints about them are treated (as is
the case in the US) by the authorities who control the behavior of the
Bar in general. The reduction in legal aid has also reduced the numbers
of lawyers available to do this work; many really good practitioners,
we are told, have found it no longer financially viable or too cumbersome to deal with the new bureaucratic rules for reimbursement and
have stopped representing asylum seekers.

The application process is supposed to discriminate between legitimate and false claims. The 589, the US form, is a multi-page document which used to be even more complicated than it is now. It was
recently updated and the language simplified somewhat. It is now
possible to download it directly from the web. The SEF, the UK
counterpart of the 589 is also multi-paged and pretty complicated. On
the basis of these forms, the asylum seeker has an interview with an
asylum officer. Asylum may be granted after this hearing; otherwise,
in the US, the case is referred to the Immigration Court, in the UK to
the AIT (Asylum and Immigration Tribunal) for another hearing of the
asylum claim.

The 589

The 589 form itself is a combination of lots of detailed information
about the applicant's history and some open-ended questions about the
basis for the claim. Many of the questions seem simple enough. Given
the nature of asylum law and policy, however, almost every question
can be a minefield for the unwary applicant. It starts with the usual
questions about name, address, and phone number, which in itself may

be a problem, as many applicants don't have a fixed address or phone number. Often, like Henri, they move every time their hosts run out of patience with a nonpaying guest. If they have a lawyer or someone in an agency is helping them apply, they can use the address of the lawyer or agency. If not, they *must* use some address, but run the risk of not receiving communications from the authorities if they are no longer at that address and the current occupant doesn't forward their mail. We have heard many stories of mail being left unforwarded, or in some cases even thrown out. If applicants don't receive the mail telling them to appear on a certain date, they will be shown as having missed the appointment and the case will be dropped. One ex-employee of the USCIS told us that this is the single most difficult problem – the expectation that they will show up as requested, on time, etc. About one-quarter of those given a date on any particular day do not show up. If they miss an appointment, they have to start all over again, but by then they are likely to have missed the one-year deadline (more on that later). If a lawyer finds out fast, it may be possible to repair the damage by contacting the asylum office to reschedule, but if the date is past, it is on to court for that person. This is true even if the applicant doesn't receive the letter giving the date, as happened to a Burmese applicant who then had to have his case heard in court. When a case is referred to court it becomes, as we shall see, a much more difficult process, where a lawyer is almost essential if the applicant is to have any chance of success. So this "small" problem has big ramifications.

After the basic information, the applicant is asked about nationality (past and present) and things such as tribal affiliation, native language, other languages spoken. All this seems quite simple, but it, too, can be the source of problems later on. The form then asks a host of questions about the applicant's spouse and children. They look easy to a Western educated person, but to someone from a very different culture, even these questions may be problematic, and the way they are answered may have ramifications down the road. For example, many people, especially Africans, who marry under customary law, and have no marriage certificate, do not remember exactly when they married. Children are also more complicated than we might think. For example, some cultures have a custom under which a person marries his widowed sister-in-law and takes on the responsibility for the children of the marriage (his nieces and nephews). Also, in times of war, from which many applicants are fleeing, when a parent dies, the children are taken in by an available relative. Because these children usually have not been legally adopted, they are not considered the applicant's children under American law. If the applicant puts them on the form as his children, he can later be accused of lying. If he does not, he can't bring them in as dependents, assuming the authorities will buy a legal argument that this is a valid, if informal adoption. Sometimes, applicants get lucky; they say the children are theirs (as they believe they are) and the authorities never find out that under US law they are not.

Some of the questions may be clear to those who are used to filling out forms, but they may be very difficult for those who are not. Some may even be a challenge to ordinary Americans. For example, the applicant is asked: "What is your child's current status? What is the date of expiration of his/her status? Status when last admitted?"

Then there are the questions that require the memory of an elephant. Asylum seekers are asked about educational history and last five years of employment. This includes details about the name of the school or employer and exactly when one attended it or worked there (the month and the year of the beginning and the end). Imagine the effort of remembering exactly when one entered the equivalent of kindergarten. Or trying to figure out what to call the type of school in a system which is very different. Or to remember the name and address of an employer from several years ago. Dev, about whom we shall learn more later, had a hearing which was dominated by a mistake he had made in filling out the form, despite having had legal help. He said:

> There was a little mistake in the application form about which I was thoroughly questioned. I lived in my maternal uncle's place in Birtamod for about three months between third week of September 2002 and last week of January 2003. I had this information in my declaration but I forgot to mention about it in the form where I had to provide information about the places I lived in last five years. It was an accidental mistake.

But the *really* tricky questions are those which form the meat of the application. "Why are you applying for asylum?" one of them asks. Or

"Have you, your family, or close friends or colleagues ever experienced harm or mistreatment or threats in the past by anyone?" "Do you fear harm or mistreatment if you return to your home country?" The way these questions are answered can mean success or failure of the application. When an applicant has the help of a lawyer, many hours of interviewing are focused on developing good answers to these questions. Most people who do not have help answer the questions briefly, assuming that the two-inch space available on the form is all the space they should use, even though there is, in small print, a statement which reads "attach additional sheets of paper as necessary." In fact, an application completed by a lawyer will answer these questions with a multi-paragraph affidavit of several pages or more, and maybe also a personal statement by the applicant. The lawyers are very careful not to say anything that might be negatively perceived or misunderstood by the asylum officer. Without legal advice, of course, the average applicant has no idea what might be a problem. They don't understand the importance of a clear chronology, the inclusion of things that are considered by the asylum officer to be relevant and the exclusion of "irrelevancies."

Lawyers sometimes also unintentionally include things that attract the officer's attention. In Henri's application, for example, we included a sentence that said "Kolingba put me in charge to ensure that there were enough weapons, and to provide the people with food to meet their needs." That short sentence raised a red flag with the officer who questioned him in minute detail about whether he himself had been involved in the fighting and responsible for human rights violations, which would be a bar to granting him asylum.

Often the questions that might seem simplest to the asylum officials – who the asylum seeker is related to and what groups they belong to, how they got to the US – can be complicated to answer. Mustapha's case shows how difficult the simple question "How did you get here?" can be.

Mustapha, the young man from Sierra Leone, whom we met in Chapter 1, came to CRIS one day seeking asylum. At the time he was about 18 years old. He was disoriented and had difficulty talking. He was wearing sweat pants and a rather grimy sweatshirt. It was not until our second interview that it became clear that these were his only clothes, which he had been given by a charitable agency in Texas on his arrival in this country. He was very grateful when Carol gave him some hand-me-downs from her teenage son. We also found out later that he was living on rice and sardines in the basement of the home of another Sierra Leonean who was not happy about having him to stay. He told a garbled story of leaving his homeland and arriving in the US. To illustrate how difficult it is to put together a cohesive story for the application, here is a transcript of Carol's first interview with Mustapha.

C: Why did you leave Sierra Leone?
M: I left there on the 7th July.
C: This year?
M: 2000.
C: Why?
M: The rebels were killing them, cut hands, that's why I left the country. They cut hands when you catch the person. These people were just doing things.
C: How did you get out?
M: I was working at the port, I took a Greek ship. I got a ship.
C: How did you do that?
M: I was working on the inside of the ship . . . When they catch me the other time, they shot me.
C: So you've been shot by the rebels?
M: Yes. This was even for 9 months. This happened when they came to the city. They ruled for 9 months. There was one man, his name was Johnny Koroma. He was in prison, when they came they took him out of the prison.
C: When did you get shot?
M: . . . was the President, he had to leave. Then ECOMOG came, when they were pushing people into the city, they were mad . . . to kill people, both hands. They caught me with other guys. They pushed me inside a car.
C: And then what?
M: They put fire to the car. I got shot inside the car, that was just the shot back.
C: What about your family?

M: I lost them, I don't know their whereabouts since the problems that took place . . . I was living at the . . . I was in school, they came there, they burned down the school, all of us just ran away.

C: When was that?

M: 1999. The time I leave, I was seeing a lot of troops, it was United Nations, something, so they bring a lot of ammunition then I heard they were heading against the city. I already came there. They caused a lot of problems. I heard they were coming so that made me to risk taking the ship. I just got in and hide there . . . It was later, about four or five days, they found me inside the ship.

C: Where did the ship go?

M: The ship was heading for Brazil . . . they dropped me . . .

C: So how did you get from Brazil?

M: The same ship dropped me there. I don't know the place, language, I was just sleeping in the streets . . . So I just took a ship that was headed to . . .

C: Where did that ship go?

M: That ship was first going to Louisiana.

C: What happened then?

M: The immigration, they found me inside the boat, and they take me in prison for two days. We arrive a Friday. They found me these trousers . . . then they told me to move to Houston, Texas. The same ship took me to the same place the night that was Sunday they bring me at the ship and they said these guys have to keep going, don't behave bad, something, you have to go with us. So in Houston Texas, they will contact . . . the Sierra Leonean Embassy in Washington. Anything they say you will accept or some details. They contacted the Sierra Leonean Embassy. In reaching Houston, Texas, they contacted them, the Sierra Leonean, why we come to America, we don't stay, because we speak the language, even I tell him I speak the tribal language. All he knew that I'm a Sierra Leonean, but I don't know what he's trying to talk about. He said it's the problem why I'm coming to America . . . he has a brother there, the problems going on there, you asking me questions, and . . . he determined this is not our brother. We don't know what he is talking about. So keep cool, be still, we're going to contact you, what we will see about you guys. Then later we don't see one of them come back again. Then the place they put us, there are 17 or 16 in the room, we don't come out, we're just being there.

C: And how many people were you with?

M: There was two of us. Other guy went to Atlanta, Georgia, one of his brother . . .

C: What happened then? How did you get from Texas to here?

M: Other people even inside the room. They don't seem to be, they say you guys, I don't know what they're saying because they just came and talked to me . . . we are trying to help you, we don't know what the program so, we are inside. Later on they take me out of the room we are in. People give us . . . they take us out of town and from town . . .

C: These are the people from the ship?

M: I don't know if it was the people because it was late, immigration, the people who did that. The people who came to take you outside, they don't bring, they don't say nothing, so we don't know nothing, like who did this. When we go out we talk to people, they say in Washington a lot of Sierra Leoneans, because in Houston I think there is no Sierra Leoneans, so they just say we are putting you on.

C: So you went to Washington?

M: No, I just come to Columbus and then after later I see some Sierra Leoneans. I was talking to them to help me find a place to sleep, even to say they don't just want to keep me like that, this around I found this Sierra Leonean.

C: Who was the man who brought you here?

M: A Ghanaian, we go to the mosque and pray together and then he said well, I'm going to help you and found these people for you because I was trying, really trying to found me something you see.

C: Do you have any political background? Why did they put you in the car and shoot you?

M: They found out that young . . . the young ones to train us, they will decide to do any kind with us . . .

C: So it was because you refused to join the rebels?

M: Yes, they put us inside, about five or six of us. Suddenly they saw the ECOMOG came there so they ran away and tried to save us.

From this narrative, the lawyer has to assist the applicant in creating suitable answers to the questions on the form.

The UK forms

The UK form, known as the SEF (Statement of Evidence Form) is designed to serve the same purpose as the 589. Unlike the US form, it is not readily available to anyone who decides to seek asylum, but instead is handed directly to an applicant to fill in later, usually at the first interview designed to determine eligibility for benefits. It is not the first form they are required to complete. At this first interview claiming asylum, a 14-page questionnaire is completed called 'Screening Form Level 1'; questions are asked about the person's name, date of birth, nationality, marital status and full details of the spouse, dependants, passport details if available, health, last employer, journey details. These are very detailed, including for example questions about the number of meals provided on the plane, identifying features on the lorry etc., parents' details, educational history, immigration history, information on other family members who have applied for asylum or leave to enter or remain in the UK and any other country. The applicant has to write in their own language and script their name, date, and place of birth and last address in the country of origin and the telephone number. At this stage, a temporary Home Office reference number is given. No questions are asked about the substantive claim for asylum here; that is left for the SEF, a 19-page form, which has to be completed in English within ten working days of the claim of asylum. This is a very short period of time for something so important, especially given that most asylum seekers don't speak English. If it isn't returned in time, the application is refused on "noncompliance grounds" (about 15 percent of the time) and the applicant then has to appeal that refusal. The form asks the "basis" on which asylum is claimed, meaning whether it is based on religion, political opinion, etc., the grounds in the 1951 UN Convention. That is already a decision that has important implications for whether the applicant will be granted asylum and, in some cases, requires a strategic decision which the applicant isn't in a position to make. The SEF only suggests that an applicant provide more information on supplemental sheets of paper in the case of a claim based on membership in a social group, rather than the other bases, an omission which is unexplained. Like the 589, it asks questions that the applicant would find hard, if not impossible, to answer. For example, the applicant is asked to provide the claim number of relatives who have also claimed asylum.

Because the time is so short, many people fill the SEF out themselves, or with the help of a "friend," which has similar negative consequences in the UK as it does in the US. In the appeal cases we watched in London, a remarkable amount of time was devoted to asking an applicant why they said one thing in the SEF and another in the follow-up interview. If an applicant finds her way to a lawyer (or an agency where a case worker can help them), the form is then filled in briefly, with a statement of the basis of the claim attached to it, similar to the way US lawyers operate. A lawyer is reimbursed by the government for up to five hours' work in interviewing the client and completing the form. Even though lawyers tell us that this payment doesn't cover the time usually spent preparing the application, it is still better than the situation in the US, and a higher percentage of applications do get some kind of help at this stage in the UK than in the US.

US asylum hearings

Since the initial asylum hearing in front of an asylum officer is behind closed doors, it is difficult for us to get in to observe. We are told that even a person's therapist sometimes has trouble going in to the hearing, including when they have an important role in keeping the applicant focused and preventing them from having a breakdown. In one case, the therapist had to choose between being the "representative" and therefore not being able to talk themselves, or being a witness so they could give evidence, but then having to stay outside the room except when they were testifying.

Carol attended Mustapha's asylum hearing, as his advisor. At the hearing, he was asked a number of questions, and it became clear that the asylum officer had trouble making sense of his story. The officer began by asking him how he got to the US, and he went into his long rambling account about that. He revealed a few new details, but basically the story was the same as the one we heard at our first interview described above. The officer seemed to have particular difficulty with the sequence of events in Sierra Leone, as he was very vague about what he was doing between 1996 when the rebels came in and 1999 when he had the encounter in the car. It was unclear also how much time he had spent doing their bidding. He did not answer directly the several questions she asked about it, which is a fairly frequent problem. At a couple of points, the officer was so confused that she asked Carol to elucidate. At the hearing he described what happened to him in the car when he was escaping the rebels much more graphically, though he did not mention that he was shot. He broke down and wept when he was describing the rebels coming into the village and burning the school and having to escape without his parents. He mentioned that he did not know where his parents were several times. At the end, the hearing officer said she said that she had enough, though she admitted that she did not have full information about the chronological details. Carol explained that Mustapha wouldn't have thought in that way, to which the officer replied "They don't think like that," so she appeared to understand that it was not deviousness that made it impossible for him to answer the questions about dates. He seemed to have been told he would need to be specific about dates at the hearing, so he had someone to write out the sequence of political events, though not what he was doing at the time, which was what the officer wanted to know.

Mustapha's application was ultimately denied at the hearing stage, and his case referred to the Immigration Court. He was referred to the court in Cincinnati and several months later we went down to a court appointment to get a date for a substantive hearing. That date was then well over a year away, and when that date came around, it was put off again; at the time of writing it has not yet taken place. Mustapha spent time frantically trying to find an affordable lawyer (Carol is no longer in the area where Mustapha lives) for yet another hearing date. When we last spoke to him, he still had no date for the hearing of his claim, now more than six years on from his initial application. In the meantime, he has a work permit and is working at Walmart. He seems to have a more stable place to live and, with money, his situation has improved. He is no longer living from hand to mouth, relying on handouts from other Sierra Leoneans, and other charity.

Carol went to Henri's hearing as his translator so he could also have a lawyer present. After we waited several hours for our turn, the officer told us that it would take about an hour and a half, but it took well over two hours. Several issues came up which the officer was concerned about. The first was about when and how Henri got his passport. The officer kept asking for chronology about when Henri got his passport, who filled out the forms when he got the visa, who was involved in that, where he was when he got the passport. He was asked how he got a passport in 2001 when he had been involved in three coups in 1996, and had been imprisoned and tortured then.

Henri was also questioned about his escape into Cameroon. The officer wanted to know exactly how he got to Cameroon, what method of transportation he used, how many people he was with, what time things happened. There was a long story about what happened at the border. While they were waiting at the border, a friend of Henri's who was the Commissioner, came by, patrolling, saw Henri and told him there was a warrant out for his arrest, but snuck him across the border anyway. Clearly the officer had some difficulty believing Henri's luck in this situation, and kept asking things like:

> Where were you at the time? What time did the Commissioner come by? How come he could sneak up on you from behind if you were hiding in the bush, and he was on a scooter? Which border was closed? Were you physically together with the others?

Henri answered pretty well, though it was very hard to get him to give a direct response to some of the questions. One thing came out in the middle, which clearly the officer had not considered, which was that Henri and the Commissioner were communicating by cell phone.

The officer also quizzed Henri about his role in the coups. He described himself as a sort of organizer of supplies, but the affidavit said that he supplied weapons, food, etc. to those involved in the coup. This raised the issue mentioned earlier, whether Henri himself had been involved in the fighting and responsible for human rights violations. The officer went over and over exactly what Henri did, what happened when someone needed weapons and ammunition. Henri said that his guys didn't shoot anyone, just fired over their heads. He kept saying that it was Patassse's troops who were solely responsible for the killing, and denied that any RDC (Rassemblement Démocratique Centrafricain) people had been responsible for killing. The officer asked if civilians were killed and by whom. He also wanted to know how it was that the RDC had control of half the city of Bangui if they didn't actually fight. We finally answered that by explaining that that part of the city was Yakoma territory and the Yakoma was basically synonymous with the RDC.

The officer also asked about Henri's's time at the university in the US, trying to pick up inconsistencies in his story; at one point he said he didn't study, while at another he said he was a student for several months. Carol pointed out that he did study English, but did not have the money to enroll in the accounting program he was planning to do.

The last thing he was quizzed about had to do with what happened to his family, who had all been killed by Patasse's troops. The officer was quite kind, saying he knew this was difficult but he had to know what happened to Henri's family and how he knew about it. It was a truly dramatic moment as he told the story, though he had trouble beginning, and then a tear rolled down his cheek. There was a silence while he tried to compose himself. The first thing he said was that he was responsible for what had happened to his family and that he had suffered greatly from this. The officer also wanted to know what was Henri's reason for leaving and why he didn't want to go back. He talked about what had happened to his colleagues, and then said simply: "I would be killed."

What the officer was doing was questioning him about the things that did not seem to hang together. At the end of the interview, the officer said that we would hear in two weeks. Three years later, Henri's case was finally referred to the Immigration Court. The referral notice from the USCIS said:

> . . . you directly and indirectly supplied RDC soldiers with everything from money and food to weapons and ammunition

which resulted in multiple civilian deaths and the execution of political opponents by RDC soldiers. As such, you have been found ineligible for asylum based on the persecutor bar . . .

Henri of course denies this. This is one of the most difficult aspects of asylum policy. It is not uncommon for high-profile individuals involved in civil wars to be somehow involved in, or even responsible for, receiving or procuring arms. When is such a person eligible for asylum? How involved can one be in violent situations? How likely is it that asylum seekers will be only victims of violence without having defended themselves, or more, participated in violence? We will address these questions in Chapter 5.

The UK interview

The first interview applicants in the UK have is to find out how they got to the UK and to decide whether they are eligible for benefits. If they are, they are given a card and fingerprinted. Even though this initial interview is not supposed to be substantive, it can be used later against the applicant to pick up on inconsistencies with subsequent statements. The substantive interview comes within a short period after the SEF is submitted. Lawyers are no longer paid to be present at this interview, though, unlike Italy where they are forbidden to be present, they are permitted to be there. According to one lawyer we interviewed, the officer often hasn't read the witness statement (the document the lawyer prepares to go with the SEF), even though the interview is based on the SEF and the witness statement (Yeo, 2005). But a recent Appeals Court case says that the Home Office can't refuse requests to have the interview taped, which is likely to improve the quality of the interview.

Now they prepare, as they are tape recorded, only on request. There is some information that people are bullied into not having interviews taped. The lawyer has sent in a letter saying they want it taped, the person is told that, then the HO [Home Office] says you don't really need this, your lawyer said not to . . . they are isolated examples.

(Yeo, 2005)

The person who conducts the interview isn't the person who makes the decision, though the Home Office is trying to change that, as part of their new streamlined asylum model. This might also improve the quality of the interview.

The UK appeal hearing

If an application is turned down (as most of them are), a person is entitled to have her case heard before an Administrator of the Asylum and Immigration Tribunal. For this, she is entitled to a lawyer paid for by the government, if the lawyer can show to the Legal Services Commission that there is some merit in the claim. If not, the person can fill out the forms (which can be downloaded) for the appeal herself. Again, however, the questions asked are complicated enough that it is very difficult for someone to do this alone.

Below are excerpts from an extensive court hearing of Marthe, a Cameroonian woman whose application was turned down at the initial substantive interview. The excerpts highlight the assumptions made by the authorities and the difficulties applicants have responding to those assumptions. It also shows the emphasis on telling the same story each time. We will examine both these issues in more detail in Chapter 4.

The Home Office (*HO*) is represented by a hearing officer; *R* is the lawyer representing the applicant; *AP* is the applicant; and *AD* is the administrator (the judge).

R: You explained in detail about the timing of your asylum case, but just to confirm, your sister who lives here, what is her status?
AP: She has leave to remain.
R: Permanent?
AP: Yes, indefinite.
R: How long has she been here?
AP: More than fourteen years.
AD: How come she came here?
R: She's my half sister, she used to live in Togo.
AD: You say she's your half sister? Which part do you share?
AP: Same mother.

R: You say you contacted your uncle in Cameroon to get your sister's phone number. You said he also told you, Para 16 of the first statement, he told you you shouldn't go back to Cameroon because you were still wanted.

AP: He said I'd be killed.

R: How did he find that out?

AP: He said he listened to notices on the radio.

R: Just to confirm have you ever had a passport [Cameroonian]?

AP: No, not yet.

    . . .

R: Just two other questions about your political activities. Did you have a particular role in organizing and carrying out meetings?

AP: In fact we worked together, the young people and organized everything together. I was not the only decider.

R: How many of them were there?

AP: Twenty.

R: Did the organization have a name?

AP: It was just a group; it had no name.

R: In detention, were you questioned about your role in the group?

AP: No.

R: Were you charged formally? Did they accuse you of something?

AP: I would say I was charged because we protested against the government.

R: But you were not taken to court?

AP: No.

R: Did you understand why you were held in detention? Why was that?

AP: Because they believed we offended the government. We organized marches and they didn't agree with it.

R: You said you organized a march in 2001 and you didn't do it continually but you did another one in 2004.

AP: It was the Anniversary march.

R: When was the march?

AP: October 1, 2004

R: And the one preceding that?

AP: It took place one or two months before that one.

R: How many people were at the march?

AP: A lot of people. I am not in a position to give a figure. I was not counting.

R: Was it more than 100 or less than 100?

AP: It was a good gathering, quite a large number of people because it coincided with the SNCC [Southern National Cameroon Council].

. . .

R: What did you do between 2001 and 2004 about marches?

AP: I said we organized marches but not regularly.

R: You said the first march in 2001 was regarding the nine people who died in Bependa.

AP: Yes.

R: Were the other marches for the same reason?

AP: Yes, certainly it was for the same reason.

R: Referring to paragraph 61.8, were you aware there was a trial of people who were alleged to have killed the people before you left Cameroon?

AP: Could you repeat the question?

R: Before you left Cameroon, there was a trial regarding the disappearance of the Bependa nine.

AP: Yes, I knew that.

R: What was the outcome of the trial?

AP: I knew that a trial took place but I didn't pay much attention to it.

R: You marched for four years but you didn't pay much attention to the trial on the same subject?

AP: If I said I didn't pay attention, it was because we knew the government had to run justice and we didn't fear anything.

R: You've said you were arrested and detained at the demonstration in 2004?

R: Were you the only person detained?

AP: No there were a lot of people.

R: The cell you were staying, was that guarded?

AP: Yes, it was guarded. Cells in prison are always guarded.

R: Were the guards armed?

AP: Certainly.

R: You've said you escaped while you were in hospital, while you went to the toilet.

AP: Yes I was having a drip but I had to visit the ladies. They removed the handcuffs, I was escorted to the door.

R: Did the guards check the toilet for open windows?

AP: I don't know if they checked before but when I expressed the need they removed my handcuffs and escorted me to the toilet.

AD: What about the drip?

AP: I could move around with it.

AD: You went to the toilet with the drip?

AP: Yes I removed it in the toilet myself

R: Ma'am, I'm referring to Q 86 in the HO interview. In the HO interview you said the doctor removed the drip.

HO: She said she removed it the doctor disconnected it. There is a difference.

AD: Start at the beginning. Ask about how she removed the drip. If what the appellant is saying is right the doctor doesn't seem to get involved. The point is we were using different words.

R: That's not my point.

AD: If you'd ask her to describe the drip.

R: I don't mind rephrasing the question at all.

AD: I'm not sure I understand the difference between disconnecting and removing the drip.

R: You can remove the needle.

AD: We need clarification.

R: Before you went to the toilet did the doctor disconnect the drip?

AP: I recall that the doctor came from time to time to check. When they put the needle in I was bleeding and he used to come and check it.

AD: Ask her Q 85 because there appears to be a discrepancy.

R: In your interview with the HO, I'll read the question, the question you were asked: "If you were connected to the transfusion, how could you leave the bed?"

HO: There are two different matters. Ask Q 84.

AD: Let me ask some questions to set the scene. Mr. Hollis wants to ask you some questions about the treatment you received in hospital. I want to go back to the beginning when you were admitted to hospital. Am I right in saying you were in hospital two weeks, no I'm not right. How long were you in hospital?

AP: I'm not sure of the answer.

AD: You went to hospital. How long were you there?

AP: I found myself in hospital with the drip. It was finished about 3–4pm. The drip finished about 3–4pm.

AD: You call it a drip. What was it doing for you?

AP: It had yellow liquid because I was ill. I knew I was receiving treatment.

AD: Did you receive any transfusion at all?

AP: No they were not giving blood. From time to time they were putting things into the drip, not blood.

AD: Do you think the drip was for glucose to give you sustenance?

AP: Yes I would say so, because I was tired and had a bit of a temperature.

AD: Mr. Hollis, would you pick up? Start at Q 94. Can I ask the interpreter when you translate transfusion and drip, is there a difference?

Interpreter: I personally wouldn't use the same word ever.

HO: In Q 84 of the interview you said you were having a transfusion. Did you mean drip?

AP: It was the drip, not the transfusion.

R: The word in French is perfusion, quite similar.

HO: In Q 85 of the interview, so if you were connected to the drip, how did you manage to leave the bed? You response was, because at that time the drip was already finished. It finished at 4pm and they disconnected it so I could go to the toilet. At Q 86 you were then asked who disconnected it and you said the doctor did. In your evidence before you said you removed it in the toilet. Can you explain the difference?

AP: I recall that the drip was finished around 3.30–4pm and I told the guard that I needed to visit the ladies. They removed the handcuff and they escorted me to the toilet.

AD: So you didn't have the drip?

AP: It was already removed.

AD: You told me earlier that you already removed it

AP: You know when you had a drip in your hand they will not remove the whole stuff they leave the needle in. I removed that because if I were outside and people noticed that I was a patient outside . . .

AD: Sorry, when the doctor at 3.30–4pm disconnected did he not take the tube, was the drip into your hand? So when he disconnected, did he not take it out of your hand?

AP: When the drip is finished, they remove it, they put cotton and bandages.

AD: Over the puncture hole?

AP: Yes, when I had the drip.

AD: I need to know this. You were handcuffed together. How were you handcuffed?

AP: When I found myself in bed one hand had a drip and the other was handcuffed to the bed.

AD: When they took the handcuff off where was the handcuff?

AP: It was taken off my hand.

AD: So when you went to the toilet you didn't have any handcuff?

AP: No, I didn't go to the toilet with a handcuff.

AD: What were you clothed in?

AP: I had a skirt, and a T shirt and the skirt I had to . . . a bit because I was bleeding.

AD: Did you have anything on your feet. So were your feet bare?

HO: You've said after you jumped out the window you went to the taxi cab.

AP: Yes, they were parked outside.

HO: How far away?

AP: Not even two minutes. I was running, but not very fast because I was in pain.

HO: Could you see the taxi rank from the hospital?

AP: Sure, there are taxis waiting for people going home.

HO: Could you see the taxi rank from the toilet?

AP: No.

AD: Did you know this hospital? Did you know the layout?

AP: Yes, very well.

AD: How did you know the layout?

AP: I was familiar with the hospital. My children were born there.

HO: You also said that you heard shots when you were running for a taxi.

AP: Yes, but I was already beaten up from the detention and the jump I made from the window, it increased my panic.

HO: Could you hear shots from the taxi?

AP: Yes, I heard a gunshot behind, but not at the taxi rank. They didn't reach me, they had to go around to catch me.

HO: You said the taxi driver took you to a relative's house.

AP: My friend.

HO: Was the taxi driver aware that you had escaped from hospital?

HO: He noticed it, because he asked when we were in the taxi and I told him I was in danger.

HO: How did you pay the taxi driver?

AP: When we got to my friend's house my friend paid.

HO: You say you were in hiding in a shop in Cameroon. How long was that for?

AP: It was the shop of the man who helped me to travel. About nine days.

HO: Did you have any problems from the authorities?

AP: I was wanted. That's why I didn't stay with my friend. She heard notices on the radio and she suggested to go to the person who helped me escape, in hiding.

AD: She heard notices on the radio so she said you couldn't stay?

AP: Yes, and even people from the neighborhood learned I had escaped. It was not a small problem.

AD: How far was the hospital from your friend's?

AP: It was far.

AD: How long?

AP: About four hours with the traffic . . . because of the traffic. If the traffic is heavy.

AD: Lucky we don't have four-hour traffic jams. How many kilometers?

AP: It's far, more than ten.

AD: In what suburb? What area?

AP: Nevelle.

AD: Is that the area you lived in?

AP: That's where I dropped my children before I attended the march. My friend lived in Nevelle. I lived in Bependa.

AD: How far was your friend's house from yours?

AP: It was one and a half hours without traffic.

AD: Did she look after your kids on a regular basis?

AP: When I had things to do.

AD: This one and a half hour journey . . . did you have your own car?

AP: No, I used taxis.

AD: By the time you arrived at your friend's house, there was an announcement on the radio that you had escaped?

AP: That's what she told me. I can't confirm these things.

AD: The way you can confirm these things to me is by telling me exactly what happened. This is why we ask questions about distances.

HO: The appellant says her friend had heard about her on the radio, but that is not in the statement, she gives different reasons (for leaving her friend's house). In your statement in paragraph 9 you said you had to explain the fact surrounding the arrest and you didn't say she had heard you had escaped on the radio. Can you explain why you now say that?

AP: She knew I was involved in the march because of the nine persons (who disappeared). She knew I was going to the march when I dropped my children.

AD: That isn't the question. In your reasons, you didn't say that she had heard it on the radio so you couldn't stay with her.

AP: Because I had escaped and I was wanted and they were looking for me, they'd be directed by the neighbors, so it wouldn't be safe.

AD: You said that before you arrived, she'd heard it on the radio.

AP: That's what I'm telling, that's what I heard.

AD: She told you that she had heard it on the radio.

AP: Yes, that's what she told me and it was not safe to stay. If the neighbors would see me they would tell the police.

HO: The question we're asking . . . you said your friend told you that she'd heard you escaped on the radio

AP: Yes.

HO: Why have you not mentioned that in your statement?

AP: When you are giving a statement through questions sometimes some details can go unnoticed and you don't dwell on them.

HO: You said you left Cameroon by an airport.

AP: Yes.

HO: Was it a major airport?

AP: Yes.

HO: If you were wanted by the authorities, can you explain how you left by an airport?

AP: I was at this gentleman's house for nine days. I never went out. This man made the arrangement to get me outside the country. I don't know.

HO: What was this gentleman's name?

AP: Moninga Pol.

HO: So no immigration authorities asked you any questions when you left the country?

AP: No.

HO: You arrived in the UK in October 2004?

AP: Yes.

HO: And you went to see your half sister?

AP: Yes.

HO: And your half sister said you should claim asylum?

AP: Yes because she didn't want me to stay in this country illegally and she told me she would take me to claim asylum.

   . . .

HO: Why did you not claim asylum on arrival in the UK?

AP: I didn't know the procedure in this country and I was following the instructions of a man.

The Home Office representative made the following remarks about the evidence in his summation:

> There is a difference in evidence given today and paragraph 9 regarding how the friend found out about her escape: today she claims the friend knew from the radio.
>
> The marches – she claims she organized marches. She said she didn't know the outcome of the trial. If someone had involvement over such a period of time, they'd know more about the subject

of the trial and what happened. The applicant's escape claim – she was beaten on a daily basis so much so that she had to be taken unconscious to the hospital, but she still could escape, jump from the first floor [in US the second floor], get to a taxi with shots being fired. She was guarded – I submit it was unlikely that the guards would just have let her go to the toilet without checking whether the window was open. Her four-hour ride, with no money, it is implausible. She didn't claim asylum until 8 months later. She met a man in the airport, he offered to help her claim asylum. There is an issue, credibility-wise of the sister's phone number. She claims she memorized it, but couldn't remember . . . The medical reports, paragraph 13, the psychiatric report, says she has a moderate mental health problem, but the paragraph below says she can function on a day-to-day basis. Paragraph 16 says she would not be suicidal if she returned to Cameroon.

Regarding Ms G's return, I submit she would not be at risk. There was no risk from her father in 2001, no problems due to her father's activities. She has attended marches between 2001 and 2004. There is no evidence to support her claim that she is wanted. She had no problems staying in Cameroon for nine days, had no problems leaving from the airport.

The Home Office representative makes several assumptions here. The first is that a taxi driver would not take someone who had no money to pay, even though he was paid at the other end, a common practice in other countries as well, though perhaps not in the UK. He also questions how she remembered the phone number, even though it is certainly possible she could remember something so important to her. He further assumes that she isn't in trauma because she functions on a day-to-day basis, in contradiction with the medical literature on PTSD (Post-Traumatic Stress Disorder). He also questions how she was able to leave without being monitored. This assumes both a level of organization which might not exist in Cameroon, as well as the absence of bribery on the part of the "gentleman" who helped the applicant flee. Her responses also rely on assumptions, for example in her explanation of why she didn't pay attention to the outcome of the trial. She says: "If I said I didn't pay attention, it was because we knew the government had to run justice and we didn't fear anything." For her, "paying attention" to the outcome of the trial would mean changing her protest in response to government actions, which she regards as perfunctory ("the government had to run justice"). For the asylum officials, it makes sense to pay attention to the outcome of a trial when one is protesting the incarceration of those involved in the trial. The protester, in contrast, regards the trial as the government's effort to incite fear. What we see here is not one correct way of thinking but rather the vast differences in assumptions that prevent easy assessment of what makes sense.

Recent changes in asylum law and practice

As we discussed in Chapter 1, both the UK and the US have made it more difficult for applicants to get asylum. There are basically two ways in which this has happened: laws passed to tighten up the rules for getting asylum, and changed practices by bureaucrats which do not have a legal basis but are a response to a general feeling in both countries that asylum law should be more restrictive. These two forces intertwine, but it is possible to look at them separately. The next section of the chapter will look at the recent laws in the US and the UK which have had the effect of making it more difficult to get asylum.

Applying in time

Both the US and the UK have changed their rules about when a person can validly apply for asylum. In the US, the law was changed in 1996, as part of the Immigration Control and Fiscal Responsibility Act, to what is now known as the one-year rule. Under that law, a person has to apply for asylum within one year of coming to the United States. What this means in practice is that the person must be able to prove when they arrived, so they can show the government that they haven't been in the US over a year. The legal standard is that a person must show by "clear and convincing evidence" that they arrived no more than a year before applying, or that there are exceptional circumstances which affected their ability to apply in time. The people who are in trouble here are those who came without any documents at all, or with a false passport. As one lawyer we interviewed put it:

> . . . clear and convincing evidence is code for "we want to see documentation of your entry". The I-94 [the form visitors receive when they enter validly] is clear and convincing evidence; a person's statement isn't. The new section made it all but impossible for EWI [those who enter without inspection] to be granted political asylum. The point here is the amendment has the effect of denying political asylum to the vast majority of genuine refugees who come in . . . If a person comes in legally, they have gone to the US consulate, got some visa – if the US consulate says he thinks the person is an honest to God visitor, then he is not a refugee.

> (Quinn, 2002a)

So here is another of the many ways an applicant is caught between a rock and a hard place: either he is a refugee and so he needs to flee fast and arrives without the proper papers, or he is a "real" visitor with a visitor's visa, so how can he be a refugee? Asylum applicants often have good reasons for missing the one-year deadline. Many of them are traumatized, and since the US doesn't provide any financial support, they need to devote primary attention to survival when they first arrive. As we already know, language and access to any kind of legal help can be a serious problem. The one-year rule was intended to reduce abusive claims; Schoenholtz asserts that there is no evidence that it does so. One can assume, however, that many genuine claimants have not sought asylum because of it (Schoenholtz, 2005: 346).

The new rule has had a significant effect on the total number of asylum claims heard. Schoenholtz shows that between 2000 and 2003, more than 25,000 asylum seekers were referred to the Immigration Court because they did not meet the one-year deadline requirement. We do not know how many of those were granted asylum by the court, though doubtless many of them weren't. We do know that many claimants withdraw their claims at the Immigration Court level, or simply don't show up for the court hearing. Schoenholtz and Jacobs show that 30 percent of all applicants without lawyers didn't show up at court, while only 3.5 percent of those who were represented didn't appear (2002: 744).

Sometimes the one-year deadline may be a convenient way of dealing with a case which has other problems (e.g. credibility). One lawyer told us that he talked to the Director of the Asylum Office who said that if there is a credibility issue and a one-year issue, they refer it to the Immigration Court on the one-year filing issue; "it is a kinder thing to do because there is less derogatory information going into the files" (Mc Haffey, 2005). This lawyer described his problems with the one-year rule:

> Some of the officials say "you can't prove you came in within a year." I made the argument that he did come in within one year; the burden of proof is the same as that for asylum. They can either believe them or give them an exception for the one-year rule.
>
> (McHaffey, 2005)

The exception McHaffey mentioned is one which allows applicants to apply if they can prove that the reason for the delay is a result of changed circumstances in the applicant's home country (as was the case for Tun, whom we described in Chapter 1), or "extraordinary" circumstances affecting the person, such as serious illness or mental or physical disability of significant duration.

Gloria, an old Liberian woman, arrived in the US several years ago, in terrible health, and applied for asylum beyond the deadline on the basis of exceptional circumstances which had made it impossible for her to apply earlier. Among other things, she had been forced by her persecutors to stare at the sun, which damaged her eyes. As a result she got cataracts and spent time in various hospitals in the US, and was way past the one-year deadline when she went to an asylum lawyer. The lawyer called the Deputy Director for the USCIS to say that the client hadn't been able to get help with the application because of her medical circumstances, and the Deputy Director made sure the hearing officer knew of the medical circumstances and heard the case, even though it was beyond the deadline.

Teinzin, whose story we will tell in the next chapter, is a Tibetan who came to the US on a false Indian identity document. He is another example of exceptional circumstances making it impossible to apply in time. He left his identity document on the subway in New York. He was afraid to go to the police or anywhere else for help because he had no proof of his immigration status, nor any proof of when he arrived in the US. His friend applied for asylum in New York soon after their arrival, but someone told Teinzin that he couldn't apply for political asylum because he had lost his identity document. The mental problems caused by his persecution in China worsened after he arrived in the US; he was ultimately hospitalized for several months and remained under psychiatric treatment after his release. When Teinzin finally reached a lawyer, the lawyer sought an extension of the one-year rule because of Teinzin's mental health difficulties. Fortunately, he was successful at the hearing stage.

Phuntsog, a Tibetan woman, came in on a false Nepalese passport, with a tourist visa, intending to return to Tibet. Tibetans don't have passports so they often travel on a Nepalese passport. While she was in the US, things got bad in Tibet and she was told by family members not to come back, so she tried to find some other way of staying. She extended her visa; it was approved, but it had expired three months earlier so the extension didn't work. By then other options were closed off because she was out of status (illegal), and the one-year deadline had expired. The officer who heard the case said she came in on a false passport, had never been in legal status, and so he denied Phuntsog's claim. The case has been referred to the court.

Sometimes, people get caught by bureaucratic problems. Maria had tried to claim within one year. She sent her application by overnight express mail; the authorities lost her asylum application and had no record of it, which happens quite often. They said they "think she has a one-year issue" and just sent her case to the court. Maria had kept the documents which showed that she had sent her application, so unless she sent an empty envelope, she had in fact filed in time. The judge agreed that she had tried to file in time and allowed her case to be heard.

In the UK, applications for asylum can either be made at the port of entry or direct to the Home Office after arrival in the United Kingdom. Legislation implemented in 2003, known as Section 55, meant that only those asylum seekers deemed by the Home Office to have claimed asylum "as soon as reasonably practicable" were eligible to make an application for public support. This did not apply to families with children, nor to decisions that would result in a breach of the applicant's human rights. Section 55 resulted in thousands of asylum seekers facing destitution. It also meant that asylum seekers would be very unlikely to reach a lawyer to advise them about whether asylum would be the best approach and if so, how to apply. However, a decision of the Court of Appeal in 2004 concluded that the way the Home Office was implementing the policy was itself in breach of the European Convention on Human Rights. The court said the government would have to make sure that an asylum seeker had some alternative source of income before denying public funds, effectively nullifying Section 55, so no one has since been refused support on these grounds. This effort to make the asylum process harder failed.

Even though the UK, unlike the US, does not have a statutory deadline within which an applicant must file, delay is often used as a credibility issue to deny the asylum application, as we saw above in Marthe's case. It is standard to question asylum seekers about why they did not apply for asylum immediately on arrival, even when they applied very soon after. Here is the Pakistani woman whose appeal we quoted from earlier. She applied after eight days in the UK:

R (representative):   So why did you not claim asylum as soon as you got to the UK?
AP (applicant):   You mean at the airport?
R: At the airport or the next day?
AP: The agent told me that if I told my story to anyone he would take me back.
R: Where was this?
AP: Inside the airport.
R: So why did you not claim asylum once you left the airport, the next day?
AP: My daughter was ill for three–four days.

The Home Office Asylum Policy Instructions to caseworkers include:

   . . . factors affecting credibility. The applicant failed, without reasonable explanation, to make an application for asylum at the earliest reasonable opportunity after their arrival in the United Kingdom, unless the application is founded on events that have taken place since their arrival in the United Kingdom.

(Amnesty International, 2004: 30)

The Amnesty International report goes on to quote from a refusal letter which shows how arbitrarily this "delay" is used against an asylum seeker:

Although you arrived in the United Kingdom on the 7 August 2002, you did not claim asylum until 12 August 2002. Whilst the Secretary of State is aware of disorientation resulting from your journey and arrival in a country where you did not fully understand the language, he considers your delay in applying to be unreasonable. He considers this had undermined the credibility of your claim. He must question why, if you felt to be in genuine fear of your life and wanted to seek international protection, why [sic] you would not have availed yourself or attempted to avail yourself of the protection of the United Kingdom by claiming asylum at the earliest opportunity at the arrival airport [sic], *irrespective of any lack of specific knowledge of how to accomplish this.*

(Amnesty International, 2004: 30; emphasis added by AI)

Here the Home Office refuses to grant asylum despite their knowledge that applicants have problems when they arrive which could prevent an immediate claim, yet another example of their efforts to use whatever excuse is handy to deny asylum applications.

The safe third country rule

Another way countries limit the number of asylum applicants is by requiring that an applicant seek asylum in the first safe country reached after flight. This makes intuitive sense, because the idea of shopping for the "best" country is contradictory to the need to flee to any safe country. In Europe, two treaties set up this principle in 1990, the Dublin Convention and the Schengen Treaty, part of a trend in Europe to present a united front on immigration issues in general. There is, of course, disagreement about how you decide whether a country is "safe." There seems to be some conflict between the 1951 UN Convention, which does not require a person to apply in the first safe country they reach, and the Dublin accord, which lists the criteria that give one country rather than another the obligation to hear an asylum claim. The UK also seems to be using this rule as another way of denying asylum:

> They say you're from a safe third country, and your credibility is doubted. It has been used even for countries not on the list. The failure to make a claim in a safe third country – this is about whether you get believed or not – the list included EA [European Accession] states. They are not paying attention to their own list.
> (Yeo, 2005)

Many applications are denied because the person chose the UK as the place for their application, rather than another country the adjudicator would have preferred.

> Worst of all is choosing Britain. A Sudanese asylum-seeker was severely judged because "the Secretary of State considered that your decision to claim asylum in the United Kingdom as a conscious decision to come to this country as opposed to any other country."
> (Asylum Aid, 1999: 34)

It is hard to imagine what this asylum seeker could do that would be acceptable to the authorities, since someone who flees persecution is likely to have some idea of where they will end up. The Asylum Aid report goes on to describe the way the authorities evaluate the decision when they describe a Slovak Roma asylum seeker who:

> . . . was taken to task for not having claimed asylum on the way through central Europe by bus. "Why not claim asylum in Austria?" he had been asked at his interview. Answer: "I wanted to go as far as possible from Slovakia." He explained: "I heard that this is a free country and the Queen wouldn't allow to happen here what's happening in our country."
> (1999: 34)

Deciding that an asylum seeker has chosen the wrong country can have terrible consequences.

> Two Tamils were sent back to Colombo as failed asylum-seekers. One had been turned away by the UK because he arrived via Germany. He was "bounced" back to Germany, who in turn sent him back to Sri Lanka. The other was sent back by Holland. Both had their travel documents impounded and were interrogated on arrival at the airport. Without documents, they had no chance of avoiding arrest by the security forces. Both were allowed into the country, but later each was stopped, arrested, questioned, and badly beaten.
>
> (from "Fairer, Faster, Firmer – A Modern Approach to Immigration and Asylum," Government White Paper, 9.7, quoted in Asylum Aid, 1999: 8)

The US Attorney General devised rules in 1995 which allowed an asylum seeker to be sent back to a country through which she had traveled to get to the US if there was a "full and fair" procedure for deciding the claim there, and the person would not face persecution, as long as there was an agreement between that country and the US. Until very recently, there were no such agreements, so the rules were not enforced, though a "bad" choice can be used as a credibility issue. One judge denied an asylum claim because the applicant had smuggled his way into several countries before coming to the US. The judge asked, "Why didn't you seek asylum in Nigeria or Belize?"

The first agreement, under the 1995 Safe Third Country Agreement, between the US and Canada, came into force at the end of 2004. Under this treaty, Canada is obliged to take back an asylum seeker who tries to get into the US via Canada, and vice versa. The country taking back the applicant is also committed to hear the claim. It is too soon to know how many people are affected by this new treaty, though one recent figure claimed that 11,000–12,000 people seek asylum in Canada after passing through the US (Migrations Wordpress, 2004). This is ostensibly a way of preventing asylum shopping; the effect is to make asylum more difficult. There have been several cases in which asylum seekers have been bounced from one country to another and ultimately returned home without their claims ever having been heard. This is in violation of international law, which forbids anyone being "refouled" (returned) to a country where they risk persecution. The Safe Third Country Agreement allows Canada, which has a higher rate of acceptance of asylum claims than the US, to do indirectly what it cannot do directly, i.e. use a tougher standard for adjudicating asylum claims (Macklin, 2005: 380).

Getting thrown out before you get in

Both the US and the UK have moved toward pressuring asylum seekers to claim asylum when they first arrive at the border. This was first initiated by countries in Europe in the early 1990s. New procedures in a 2002 UK statute are designed to identify "manifestly unfounded" asylum seekers when they first arrive, and send them back before they come into the country so they don't disappear into the woodwork or incur the time and expense of giving them a full hearing. If the authorities think the claim has no merit, the asylum seeker is sent abroad and can appeal from abroad, with little chance of success.

In the US, "expedited removal" was created by the 1996 Act (Musalo *et al.*, 2001). The legislation mandated the removal of anyone considered inadmissible because of some kinds of fraud, misrepresentation, or faulty documentation. The impetus for these provisions was the 1993 World Trade Center bombings. The law was designed to keep illegal aliens out of the country in general. The problems that have resulted for asylum seekers were a byproduct of these new procedures and so Congress added in some protections to ensure that *bona fide* asylum seekers were still able to claim asylum here. In 2003, only about 3 percent of those placed in expedited removal were asylum seekers (USCIRF, 2005: 9).

Someone who arrives in the US has to tell the immigration inspector at the border that she is seeking asylum, and prove before an asylum officer that she has a "credible fear" of persecution, before being allowed to stay and make a full asylum claim. If no credible fear is shown to the satisfaction of the officer, the applicant is deported. If credible fear is shown, the asylum seeker waits until the case can be heard by a judge. During this time, the applicant is detained. The report by the US Commission on International Religious Freedom (USCIRF, 2005) indicates that there is a lot of variation among different border posts about how expedited removal is being implemented. When a person makes a request for asylum, the immigration inspector must refer them for a credible fear determination. In 85 percent of the cases where a person made a claim for asylum, they were indeed referred, though of course, that leaves 15 percent of those who expressed a fear of return who were not interviewed by an asylum officer. However, the inspector has discretion not to refer the applicant when they believe that the fear claimed is unrelated to the criteria for asylum. But in some of the cases which were not referred, the applicants claimed fear based on religious, political or ethnic persecution, which clearly are criteria for asylum. In a few instances, the observers saw officers improperly encouraging asylum seekers to withdraw their applications. Of those who were referred after claiming credible fear, more than 90 percent were allowed in to make their full claim. Judges reviewing the denials allowed in many of those who were denied by asylum officers. So the system seems to allow in most of those who claim asylum at the border, though it does not address the problem of those who do not know they have to make the claim at this stage. Inspectors are supposed to read a three-paragraph statement to anyone about to be removed, which includes information that the alien should inform the inspector "privately and confidentially" if they have fear of persecution, because the US provides protection to those who face persecution, harm, or torture upon return. The USCIRF report shows that about half of the time this does not happen: "aliens are frequently informed of the penalties of Expedited Removal but not of the availability of protection if they fear being returned" (2005: 39). The report does not specify the language in which the paragraphs are read (when they are), but the director of the study told us that it was generally read in the language in which the interview is conducted, either by a bilingual officer or by an interpreter (Hetfield, 2005). Even if language is not a problem, a traumatized asylum seeker may not really understand what is expected of him, although those who did receive the information were seven time as likely to be referred to a credible fear hearing than those who did not.

A statute passed in the UK in 1999 made it a criminal offence to try to enter the country, or stay, using "deception." This was expanded in 2004 with a law making it a criminal offence to come to the UK without travel documents "without reasonable excuse," a statute whose provisions have been described by the leading author on UK immigration law as "draconian" and "surreal" (MacDonald and Webber, 2005: 818). The statute also set up what are called "Fast Track" procedures, which makes it possible for the Home Office to hurry through several categories of cases, including those in which the applicant has failed to produce a passport, cases which are perceived to lack merit, and those who come from "safe third countries." The last category fast tracks those who come from countries which the Home Office considers have no serious risk of persecution. This list is based on previous negative decisions by the Home Office itself, which illustrates the circularity of the whole business.

> There is a presumption that your case is clearly unfounded if you come from one of the countries on a list, though you can also be clearly unfounded from other countries as well. They are not using most of the lists at the moment. If you are male and from Nigeria, that is on the list, but not if you are female as they recognize that there are gender cases. They now make the lists more specific.
>
> (Yeo, 2005)

These "fast track" cases do not have a right of appeal before removal from the UK. Decisions are made in a matter of days and, not surprisingly, the vast majority of them are refused. Unlike other cases, everyone is provided with free legal advice, for what it is worth, given the speed with which the cases are heard and the fact that most of them are refused. The goal of the lawyer here is to get the case moved out of "fast track" into the normal process, so he has time to present a careful case (Ahluwalia, 2005b). The NGOs that provide legal assistance to asylum seekers are very critical of these new procedures; they argue that the results are not what the 1998 White Paper "Fairer, Faster, Firmer" intended when recommending them. Making the process faster is likely to make it less fair.

Detention

Both in the US and the UK, the use of detention for asylum seekers has recently increased. In both countries, the purpose is to avoid having people with unheard asylum cases disappear to live an undocumented life. The authorities in both countries justify the detention of increasing numbers of asylum seekers by claiming that they would abscond; research in both countries has shown that well over 90 percent of those who are released do appear for hearings (Fletcher, 2005). Ironically, it is much more expensive for a country to keep someone in detention than to parole them, even if the parole is extensively and expensively supervised.

It is clear that both countries are using detention for a deterrent purpose, in the hope that potential asylum seekers will decide not to come at all. In one survey of immigration officers in the UK, 25 percent of the respondents specifically stated that they detained asylum seekers either to encourage them to withdraw their applications or to deter others from making claims (Weber and Gelsthorpe, n.d.: 59). This is also evidence of the new punitive approach to asylum, especially in the UK, where it is justified because of the perception that most asylum seekers are bogus economic migrants abusing the system; the counterpart in the US is that they are perceived mostly as security risks.

In the US, the 1996 law requires that those who claim asylum at ports of entry to the US be detained throughout the initial stages of the "credible fear" process. In theory, applicants can then be released while they prepare for the full asylum hearing, but in practice this rarely happens, at least in some parts of the US. The Human Rights First report describes a consensus among lawyers in various parts of the country that asylum seekers are not being paroled, even when they have valid passports and proof of identity and ties to the community (Human Rights First, 2004: 29). In most cases, people are detained in jails or jail-like settings, though of course they have not committed a crime. In fact, there are many reports of conditions that are worse than for criminals, as they have none of the safeguards of those who have committed crimes (Dow, 2004). The decision to detain someone is entirely within the jurisdiction of the Department of Homeland Security and can't be appealed to a judge.

People are detained for months and even years in some cases. The report of the United States Commission on International Religious Freedom states that about 32 percent of asylum seekers are detained for 90 days or more, and some are held for much longer (USCIRF, 2005). For example, Beatrice Okum, a Christian from southern Sudan, was sold into slavery for fourteen years in Kenya. With the help of a friend, she escaped and arrived in the US in November 2001. On arrival, she was handcuffed, shackled, and brought to a detention center. Her detention triggered flashbacks of being in slavery. After five months in detention she was granted asylum and released (Lawyers Committee for Human Rights, 2002: 11). Fauziya, whom we met in the last chapter, spent sixteen months in various detention facilities before finally being granted asylum.

In Europe, with the exception of the UK, detention is rare. Other countries, however, seem to be even more punitive than the US and the UK. Australia has attracted international opprobrium for its mandatory detention program, and for its recent failed efforts to send asylum seekers to remote islands out of the country to lodge their claims from there (Squires, 2006). A recent E-brief from the Australian Parliament explains the mandatory detention of "unauthorised arrivals" as follows: "the primary reason for detaining boat people asylum seekers for as long as it takes to process their claims for protection visas has always been that it makes it easier to remove them when [sic] their claims are rejected" (Phillips and Milbank, 2005). As a result of intense political pressure, the government has recently made it possible for children and families to be free of detention while waiting for their claims to be processed, though detention remains mandatory for all other asylum seekers.

In the UK, as of February 2005, 1,515 asylum seekers were detained, and there are plans to expand the spaces to 3,000, in what have since 2002 been politely renamed "Removal Centres" (Fletcher, 2005). While these numbers don't seem huge, they are clearly larger than they would be if detention were only used for the purpose specified in the 1971 Act setting up the system. Instead, detention is a central part of the fast track process, a way of getting more applicants through the system and out of the country faster. It is also used for indefinite periods, and people (or their lawyers) are usually not told why they have been detained or when they will be released. In many cases, bail is set so high that there is no chance an asylum seeker can meet it. Fletcher describes the typical case of Clarence, from Zimbabwe, who was bailed by BID (Bail for Immigration Detainees), after he had spent seven months in a removal centre (2005: 30). He did what he was supposed to do: arrived in the UK on his own passport and claimed asylum at the airport. He was nevertheless detained then because he was considered "liable to abscond," though the authorities had no basis on which to make this claim; he had never been in the country before, and they knew nothing of him. His release was first opposed because he had a cousin who had not come forward as a surety for his release on bail, though there is no requirement that a person have a surety. Clarence was finally released at his second hearing, despite pressure from the Home Office to continue the detention.

Not surprisingly, the US does not keep numbers of those asylum seekers who are detained. The Human Rights First report on the detention of asylum seekers recommended that the Department of Homeland Security "should publicly release accurate and current statistics . . . *in compliance with US law*" (2004: 48, our italics). A *New York Times* article stated that in 2003, 5,585 men and 1,015 women seeking asylum were jailed (Bernstein and Santora, 2005).

Asylum seekers from Arab or Muslim countries are more likely to be detained without parole, though the specific policy Operation Liberty Shield, begun in 2003 to automatically detain asylum seekers from more than 30 countries, was terminated. Ironically, this policy targets exactly those people who fought against, and were persecuted by, the regimes the US sees as their enemies (Human Rights First, 2004). The Human Rights First report describes the case of two Christian women who fled Iraq and who were denied parole in Miami, even though one of the women had strong community ties. Her sister is a US citizen and her mother a US legal permanent resident; these are the variables which are supposed to be taken into account when deciding whether to parole someone (2004: 21).

Detention is problematic for a number of reasons. In the US, with its already spotty system of legal representation, the chances that an asylum seeker will be represented are much lower when they are detained. The jails in which asylum seekers are held are often far from the places where asylum lawyers are available, so a lawyer who represents a detained asylum seeker often has to travel long distances to see her client. Sometimes an asylum seeker is moved without anyone notifying his lawyer, which also makes representation difficult. The outcomes show the importance of representation; the study by the USCIRF shows that a detained asylum seeker without a lawyer has a 2 percent chance of being granted asylum, while one who is represented has a 25 percent chance. (USCIRF, 2005: 4.)

There are many psychological problems, too. A significant percentage of asylum seekers are suffering from PTSD. Spending an indeterminate amount of time being locked up with criminals has a seriously debilitating effect on the already fragile mental health of an applicant. A report by Physicians for Human Rights (2003) determined that 86 percent of detainees suffered from depression, 77 percent from anxiety, and 50 percent from PTSD. Now and then we hear stories of detained asylum seekers committing suicide; not surprisingly, the authorities do not publicize these cases, so it is impossible to determine how prevalent this is.

REAL ID

In 2005, Congress passed what is known as the REAL ID Act. The major purpose of this statute is to make it harder for undocumented aliens to get drivers' licenses. However, included in the statute were several changes in the law about asylum, though the final bill was much less draconian than originally. The fears of those who work with asylum applicants have not been fulfilled in the short time since the law was passed. The changes don't seem to have had much effect on the number of applicants deported. The statute changed the legal standards of reviewing claims; it requires an applicant to show that the ground on which they are seeking asylum is "at least one central reason" for the persecution. It also allows adjudicators to require applicants to provide corroboration for their claim, and allows the adjudicator to make a credibility denial based on a long list of "factors," including such things as the "demeanor, candor, or responsiveness" of the applicant. As we shall see in Chapter 4, it appears that this is already happening. What the law has done is to enshrine the practice, and perhaps to give justification to those hearing claims to deny them more readily.

The arbitrary system

We have already seen some ways in which the asylum system is arbitrary. Some of them, like the one-year rule, are arbitrary, but arguably necessary to deal with potential misuse of the system. The one-year rule also has exceptions to take care of those with special needs. More disturbing, however, are the various ways in which the system is arbitrary because of the differential exercise of discretion in decision-making by those who implement the system. Recent research examining the detention of asylum seekers in the UK shows vast differences in the reasons used to detain, and the purpose served by detention by different immigration officers, and at different ports of entry (Weber and Gelsthorpe, n.d.). In the US the study on detention at airports reports large differences in treatment of asylum seekers depending on the airport (USCIRF, 2005). Kennedy was the toughest place for asylum seekers; they were routinely shackled and had to undergo very personal interviews at public counters. Nearly five times the number who were allowed to proceed further were sent back immediately. By contrast, at Miami airport twice as many asylum seekers were allowed forward as were sent back. Judges also vary vastly in the rates of granting asylum. A recent study, by the Executive Office for Immigration Review, a Justice Department agency, found that from 2000 to 2005 refusal rates by different Immigration Court judges varied from a high of 96.7 percent to a low of 9.8 percent, hardly a reassuring example of the even-handedness of the justice system (Swarns, 2006).

Tensions between law and practice

In some areas of the law, the practice of law is more liberal than the law as it is written. In cases of negligence, for example, it is often possible for a plaintiff who has been injured to win a settlement out of court, even though she may not be able to prove that the defendant was negligent (an essential element of the legal claim). In the case of asylum law, however, it is the exact opposite; the law is more liberal than the practice. There are court cases in both the US and the UK which recognize that it may be very difficult, if not impossible, to prove the elements of the asylum seeker's story to the standards required in other areas of the law. Acknowledging this reality, court decisions (which are supposed to be followed under the rules of precedent) make it clear that the authorities should not demand such high standards. Nevertheless, this is exactly what hearing officers and some judges do. Asylum seekers are held to impossible standards of proof, and denied asylum. These denials can be, and sometimes are, overturned on appeal because of the existence of the cases allowing a lower standard. The problem is, however, that many, if not most, asylum seekers are not able to take their cases to a court high enough for this result. In the UK, one level of appeal has recently been eliminated, making it even harder to correct errors at lower levels. As we have seen, in the US, asylum seekers usually have no way to pay for such expensive legal representation, and in the UK, where reimbursement has in the past been available, the circumstances in which a lawyer can be compensated for taking a case on appeal have been reduced, further limiting the chances an applicant has of succeeding on appeal. In the US, Attorney General Ashcroft dramatically limited the role of the BIA (Bureau of Immigration Appeals), an appeal level between the Immigration Court and the Federal Courts, after 9/11. Federal Courts only take appeals on matters of law and not if an appeal is based on a claim that the authorities have denied the case unfairly on the facts.

In the UK, Tony Blair has made specific promises to dramatically reduce the number of asylum seekers. This promise came back to haunt him in 2006 when it was revealed that more than 2,000 "foreign criminals" were released at the end of their sentences, instead of being deported. As a result of the public outcry, news became available that some of them had already re-offended. According to the *Sunday Times*:

> The Home Office instructed immigration officers not to deport foreign convicts because of fears that they would claim asylum . . . this policy was implemented more than two years ago as part of a wider, undisclosed strategy to reduce asylum claims so that the Home Office could meet Tony Blair's target of driving down the number of applicants for refugee status.

> (Leppard, 2006)

It is clear that these changes are part of the policy of both the Home Office and the DHS to limit as far as possible the numbers receiving asylum, regardless of how many applicants have strong claims. Some scholars argue that this is a widespread phenomenon in which liberal governments circumvent the constraints of their constitutions to pass stringent enough laws by delegating power to the bureaucracies which enforce the laws (Cornelius and Rosenblum, 2005). The tension between the executive and judicial branch is seen in efforts by the governments to curtail the right of appeal in order to limit the asylum numbers. Lord Steyn, a Law Lord, argues that the 2004 statute, Asylum and Immigration (Treatment of Claimants etc.), in which a level of appeal was eliminated, was intended "in effect to oust the jurisdiction of ordinary courts to all but limited cases" (Steyn, 2006). We will see this process at work in the rest of the book.

The results of the changes: fewer asylum seekers

As we saw in Chapter 1, official and unofficial policy has been very successful in reducing the numbers of asylum seekers in both the US and the UK. In the UK, the Home Office releases numbers very publicly every quarter. Ironically, the public and media concern pre-dates the dramatic rise in the numbers of asylum seekers. The figures have gone up and down over the past decade or so, as much in response to the international situation as to any policy of the British government. In the 1980s asylum applicants numbered about 5,000 annually, but applications skyrocketed in the early 1990s, causing the concern which has developed a momentum of its own, despite fluctuations in the number of applications. From 44,800 in 1991 and 24,600 in 1992, they hit a peak of 71,200 in 1999, and an all-time high of 84,100 in 2003. Since then the Home Office has been trumpeting its "success" in cutting these numbers with regular bulletins. They show that only 25,701 asylum seekers made claims in 2005, and that number has been reduced to 5,850 in the third quarter of 2006 (Home Office, 2006).

In the US, the 1996 law sharply reduced the number of applications, from 116,877 in 1996 to 46,378 in 2000, and 62,872 in 2001; the figures for 2004 (32,682) show a striking drop. The post-9/11 drop can be largely attributed to policies which make it much harder for people in general to get into the country. These policies actually began before 9/11 but have accelerated since. In some cases, the reasons for the decline are country specific: for example, the number of Colombian asylum seekers has dropped significantly since new laws made it impossible to transit through the US on the way to another destination. Previously, many of them had claimed asylum en route to another country. Other reasons are more general. Since 9/11, the US government has been much more active in its control of the airports, where asylum seekers have often claimed asylum. It seems that people know it is more difficult now and so they are increasingly reluctant to travel with fraudulent documents or without documents, which, as we shall see, is often the only way they can flee. There is also some prescreening of travelers' documents at airports abroad. Other efforts to try to limit the access of terrorists to this country seem also to have had an effect on asylum application numbers. The US-VISIT program requires a biometric digital scan of visitors to the US, collected at consulates overseas and then verified on arrival. Increases in the budgets for enforcement and removal is another factor in the decline of applications, as is the increased use of detention, to the extent it is known abroad.

Conclusion

In conclusion, we can ask whether the difficulties in the political asylum application process are the inevitable result of managing a difficult situation or whether immigration policy is the result of political issues. The one-year rule in the US, for example, would seem to be politically neutral and non-discriminatory, but as we have demonstrated, it creates hardship for individuals who cannot prove when they entered the country or who did not realize that they needed to apply in that time period. The application forms and their requests for information are, in principal, also apolitical. However, asylum policies and practices are based on a conception of what an asylum application ought to look like. For example, applicants ought not only to be aware of political asylum as an option but also to know that acquiring asylum status requires declaring oneself immediately upon entry. This is the ideal, based on the understanding that certainly a year should be enough time for someone to find the necessary agencies or resources to make an application. Part of the problem with this ideal is that it assumes that information is regularly available to people needing asylum. Instead, navigating the immigration bureaucracy requires professional assistance, and not only is accurate information difficult to find, but also, in its absence, many other informal networks of information provide both helpful but also completely inaccurate information. New immigrants, but especially asylum seekers with few resources, depend on these informal networks for their daily survival, and not surprisingly, do not necessarily discriminate well between the accurate and inaccurate advice or information they find.

The asylum application requires answers to what seem to be simple identity questions, but these questions ignore the fact that the applicants are displaced people. The main feature that identifies their status is displacement, not having the ordinary means to establish identity, as we shall see in more detail in the next chapter. Instead of using the ability to establish identity as a criterion for establishing credibility, the asylum officials need to begin with the assumption of a before and after that will not be consistent. The application form can ask about a person's family configuration before the displacement, but the process needs to be able to account for the partial or total dismantling of that configuration and its replacement by new familial structures and obligations. For many people who experience catastrophe, the ordinary structures of social life are destroyed. Political turmoil or persecution changes the options available and, more often than not, presents the necessity of making impossible choices. Asylum officials evaluating applications know this, but in the process of asking simple questions about identity, they sometimes resort to their own assumptions about what a person would do under normal conditions and fail to account for the actual choices facing people fleeing persecution.

Some of the misunderstandings and practical problems in the political asylum application process can be attributed to the wide gulf between the cultural experiences of the applicants and the culture of the immigration bureaucracy. For example, one application was sent back because it was not typed. For the asylum applicant the problem is not only finding the means to type the application but more importantly knowing that such bureaucratic documents ought to be typed.

Similarly, some asylum applicants miss notices of hearings because they change addresses; moving frequently is a fact of life, a part of the culture of asylum applicants who depend on the goodwill of others for shelter.

Perhaps the central problem for asylum applicants is the criminalization of what is understood as "illegal entry." Individuals who arrive at the border without the necessary documentation or visa status or, worse, with fraudulent documents, are quickly categorized as drug traffickers or potential terrorists. Entering without proper documentation for economic reasons is also a crime. Requests for asylum are read as attempts to avoid prosecution for the illegal entry. We are not suggesting that it is not possible to identify typical candidates for asylum. To the contrary, our research has identified several common dimensions of the asylum applicants' experiences; we are suggesting that current practices are misinformed in their assessments.

3　Are you who you say you are?

Teinzin's story

Teinzin, whom we met in Chapter 2, is an asylum seeker from Tibet, which is now part of China. This is how he tells his story:

I come from a village in Eastern Tibet. My family is semi-nomadic, raising livestock and farming. Before the Communist Chinese entered Tibet, my family was rich and well-respected. When the Chinese invaded our country, there was huge discrimination by the Chinese against the Tibetans. They treated us badly and said we were anti-Communist for favoring His Holiness, the Dalai Lama. The Communist Chinese arrested my father and uncle for demonstrating against the Chinese occupation. They were sent to prison and tortured. Finally, they were released, but they had to report to court twice a month. Because of my father and uncle's case, the Communists wouldn't let me marry a Tibetan woman. The Communist Chinese have never given the rights and opportunities to Tibetan people that they give to Chinese people. My family is devoted to the Buddhist religion and believe in His Holiness, the Dalai Lama. But in Tibet we do not have religious freedom; the Chinese government represses the Tibetan people's faith and trust in their spiritual leader, and they forbid the Tibetan people to follow their religion.

October 1st, 1999 was the forty-year anniversary of the "Liberation of Tibet" by the Communist Chinese, and the fiftieth anniversary of the founding of the Communist Chinese Party. The Chinese authorities made our entire town gather together, and three officers from the Public Security Bureau gave lectures denouncing our spiritual leader, His Holiness the Dalai Lama, and demanding that the townspeople realize that the Tibetans should be grateful to the Communist Chinese. The town authority asked me to say what I thought about the meeting, but instead of saying that I loved the Communist Chinese, I could not bear to hear the way they denounced our spiritual leader and I began to shout, "Long live His Holiness the Dalai Lama!" and "Free Tibet!" The Chinese policemen began to shoot their guns in the air. They arrested six of us; we were put in a police van and driven to the Public Security Bureau.

When we got there, they put us in individual cells. On the first night I couldn't fall asleep from the terror and worry about receiving punishment. I worried that I would never see my parents and relatives again, and that they might persecute my family for my guilt. The next day, they took me again to the interview room, asked me to sign a paper. "Do you know you did a bad thing, made a mistake? If you sign a paper admitting this, we will release you, you will go home." Then I thought, if I sign that paper that means I agree Tibet is not an independent country, then His Holiness would be bad. So I refused, and then they started beating me. They took a piece of metal and beat on my head, and then I lost consciousness, and I fell down. When I woke up, they kicked me, on the back, the hip, everywhere. Then I thought if I didn't sign the paper they would kill me. So I signed the paper.

After I signed, they dragged me to my tiny prison cell, which had only a disgusting mattress with bloodstains on it. My head and back were continuously bleeding from their torture, but they didn't provide me with any medication or take me to the hospital. That whole night I had terrible pain from my wounds and could not sleep from the pain and fear. That night, many times I thought of committing suicide. My whole body was numb. I was hungry and frightened and I was shivering from the cold. I thought I might die soon. I felt like my life was in real hell.

I was detained for two weeks. Every day they fed me very little. They gave me Chinese steamed bread, one small steamed bread and hot water. Sometimes twice a day, sometimes once. Always the same thing, and the whole day I was very hungry. On October 14, 1999, in the morning, I was released. On the day of my release they had me sign a "Promise Paper" and ordered me not to leave Tengchen County in the future. They gave me a "Release Paper" and told me to give it to the People's Authority of Chungpo Town, my village. My elder brother came to take me home. It was October 14, 1999.

When I got home my body was sore everywhere. On that day, my friend came to visit me. He was with me in jail, but he got out earlier. We decided we couldn't stay under Chinese domination; we would have to escape to India. I stayed in my home town about eighteen days. It was a very difficult decision; it meant leaving family, brothers, sisters, town, etc. Then in November, 1999 we left and escaped to India. To escape from my home was one of the hardest and saddest decisions in my life, but to have a safer future life, to live without constant anxiety and fear, this was the only choice for me. I had become "an ex-political prisoner, guilty of being a counterrevolutionary."

When we left, our destination was India. I didn't have any documents because when I got in jail, the police took all my documents and said I shouldn't leave the country. I didn't need documents, though, because we went through the mountains; at the border with Nepal, we didn't go any public way, we went round, so the guards didn't see us. After several days, walking and taking buses, we crossed into India.

We arrived in Delhi, India, on December 11th in the early morning. The next day we continued our journey to Dharamsala in northern India where the Tibetan Exile Government is situated. We stayed in the Tibetan Reception Center in Dharamsala for five days. On December 15th, 1999, we received a holy audience with His Holiness, the Dalai Lama.

On December 18th, my friend and I were sent to Bylakuppe, Tibetan Camp Number 3, in southern India. Living in India without legal papers was very difficult. The Indian government does not give any legal status to Tibetan arrivals. I stayed three years in India, working as a dishwasher in a Tibetan restaurant.

A friend told me that I might get political asylum if I went to the US. So, I bought a false Indian Identity Certificate from a broker, through one of my friends. I got a visa at the American embassy in Madras (Chennai) in my name. The person who sold me the identity document went with us to the embassy. When we got there, they asked him "Why are you going to the US?" He answered the Consul: "They are going to do religious dances." I didn't have to say anything.

Someone who was going to the US bought a ticket for me and my friend. We arrived in New York on December 31, 2002. When I arrived, I stayed with a friend for about a month. When they said we couldn't stay any longer, we went out looking for somewhere to rent. People said I should take my identity document with me and I lost it. We traveled by subway, and it was in a bag. I left the bag on the subway. I didn't go to the police; I didn't know how to do it. I was also afraid because of my immigration status.

My friend applied for political asylum, but I didn't, because someone told me I couldn't as I had no identity document to prove who I was. I worried a lot. I was very sad and depressed. I thought they would send me back to China or India. If I were sent back, the result would be either the Chinese would kill me or put me in prison until death. Wherever I went in Tibet, they would find me; they know I am a person who escaped from my country.

When I started to be sick, depressed, and everything, one of my friends from my town, he lives in Vermont, came to pick me up, and took me to hospital. I was in hospital about a week, then I went out of the hospital, taking medicine. I'm still living at my friend's house in Vermont.

As we saw in Chapter 2, Teinzin had two problems with his asylum claim: he applied after the expiration of the one-year deadline, and he had no identity document to prove he is who he says he is. Teinzin did receive asylum at the hearing stage. His case is an example of the "extraordinary" circumstances in which it is possible to get asylum even if the deadline has expired. These circumstances are his psychiatric hospitalization and subsequent mental health problems. We will talk more in this chapter about his second problem, not having identity documents.

The importance of identity in the asylum process

Identity is central to any asylum case. In fact, one person we interviewed asserted that identity is one of the most crucial issues, especially after 9/11 (Berthold, 2004). In this context, asylum seekers, lawyers, and the immigration authorities have a common goal. They all need to prove that someone is who they say they are and that their stories of persecution are true, all in a world without evidence (Daniel and Knudsen, 1995). People are asked to produce identity in a system that produces ignorance, a system that erases identity systematically and then asks for identity that itself obliterates who they are (Bohmer and Shuman, 2007). In this chapter we tell the stories of people whose journeys often required them to compromise traces of their identity: people who pitched their documents en route to conceal their identity from pursuers; people who left them behind in their rush to escape; people who never had any documents; stories about illegal use of documents.

The applicants themselves find the whole idea of needing documents to prove identity incomprehensible. For them, identity is about much more than one's name on an unforged document. It is about how they formed the political identity that led them to flee, why they adhere to the religious beliefs that got them into trouble, how they identify themselves as a member of a particular ethnic group that is persecuted because of it. Their names and identifying characteristics are a small part of that identity. In other words, identity is a matter of reputation and relationships rather than a bureaucratic record. In their attempt to prove their identity to the immigration officials, they sometimes refer to reputation and relationships, and these references are sometimes misunderstood as efforts to avoid addressing the officials' inquiries.

For the authorities, names and documents are central to the process of proof in a claim for asylum, and those who do not have the appropriate papers suffer because of it. As one asylum lawyer put it:

> The need for identity proof is based on an assumption that everyone has access to written documentation. The system is biased in favor of countries that have documentation and also against applicants who have fled without either, concealing their identity, adopting a different identity, or not having documentation of identity. Recently there have been a lot of untraceable cases coming out of Africa, you can't confirm how they arrived in the US, you could [previously] assume an I-94 [a visitor's visa] for Ethiopians, Afghanis, you could assume a boarding pass, that all created records. But, lately [there has been a problem with] not just Somalis, other Africans . . .
>
> (Quinn, 2002a)

Traveling with false documents

The classic entry narrative causes the greatest problem in trying to prove you are who you say you are. We have heard this story more times than we can count. A person finds someone in the country they are fleeing who arranges for someone else to bring them into the US on a false passport, or the person is somehow smuggled in without a passport. Once they are successfully past the immigration authorities at the airport, the "helper" melts away taking the passport with him and the asylum seeker is alone, without any record of their arrival. For example, Mohamed, a Mauritanian, was one of the many people who fled to refugee camps in Senegal after an uprising in 1989. After he left the refugee camp, he spent a number of years in Dakar, Senegal. When he was able to amass enough money to pay a "fixer," he bought a ticket to the US via Lisbon. He was brought into the country by someone who presented the false passport to the customs official and then disappeared, taking the false passport with him and leaving Mohamed to fend for himself. He made his way to Ohio and claimed asylum. He could prove nothing about himself; not who he was, when he came, how he got to the US, even whether he was indeed Mauritanian.

The entire process of people moving from one country to another without legal documents is complex and murky. Many people who flee persecution use "agents" to help them. In fact the role of the agent is so common in asylum cases in the UK that the appeal hearings we attended took it for granted. This is another illustration of how complex the asylum issue is; often the same people who help genuine asylum seekers flee persecution also provide the means whereby others (economic migrants) can enter the country illegally. These traffickers are in business and don't care why a person wants to leave, only whether they can pay the fee.

The result of using others to help flee is that a person who comes to the country as Mohamed did, has nothing to tell the authorities about the name on the passport, or the name of the person who brought them in, as they were intentionally kept unaware of these basic facts to protect that person. Because of this ignorance, anything the applicant may tell the authorities about their identity, or about details of their arrival, is simply more of their uncorroborated story and becomes a major barrier to their asylum claim. It provides material for the authorities to use when they claim that the applicant is lying, which is a reason to deny them asylum.

Peter, a Cameroonian, did not have his passport when he fled because the army had been looking for him and had ransacked his house, taking most of his belongings and his identity documents (including his passport, driver's license, and party membership card). All he was able to find was his birth certificate, which was inside a book where he had used it as a bookmark. Peter also had his national identity card with him. He could not get a replacement passport from the government as that would have alerted them to his intention to leave and risk him being killed, as other members of his family had been. In any case, he could not leave the country on his own passport, as he knew his name would be on the government's list and he would be arrested when he presented his passport to the authorities at the airport when leaving the country. With the help of a friend and political colleague, he managed to buy a doctored diplomatic passport from the son of a diplomat. The passport cost Peter a lot of money, some of which he had himself, and some of which he received from his political organization. The passport had been altered to show Peter's photograph; he also had a visitor's visa to the US. The person from whom he bought the passport gave him a preaddressed envelope and insisted that Peter mail the passport back as soon as he arrived in the US; otherwise his friend, who had been the intermediary, would be in trouble. He was met in Washington, DC by someone who had been told of his arrival. Peter stayed with this person for several days until he was put on a plane to Los Angeles to live with his contact's brother. It was this person in Los Angeles who first told Peter to apply for asylum. Until then he had no idea that he would have to do this. When he applied for asylum, he could not prove who he was or when he arrived. He was denied asylum at his hearing, and finally, after getting little help from an unsatisfactory lawyer, he found another lawyer, who helped him prove his identity with the birth certificate and other documents he later obtained, as well as statements by family members who were also in the US.

Identity documents and cultural difference

Many people from Third World countries do not have the kind of documentation we take for granted. Even if they do, it may be impossible for them to get hold of them after they have fled. Many people cannot safely contact anyone back home to help them get documents, for fear that they would be endangering loved ones. After great effort, we persuaded Henri that he had to try to get hold of the birth and death certificates of his wife and children, as well as his marriage certificate. We had tried to get them through the International Red Cross, who can help with documentation in some countries. But they did not have an office in the Central African Republic, so they couldn't help. Finally, Henri asked a friend to get him the documents. Later, Henri learned that the friend had disappeared. He may have been killed. Henri worried that he might have been responsible for his death.

John, another Cameroonian, also escaped on a borrowed passport. His only resource through which to obtain documents from Cameroon was a friend in the US who had family back in the Cameroon, but he wouldn't let John contact them to get hold of some identity documents out of fear for their lives. So John had no documents proving his own identity to show those who couldn't (or wouldn't) make a decision without such information. The film *Chasing Freedom* presents a fictionalized account of an Afghani woman who arrives in the US without documentation and is put in jail (Court TV, 2004). The film documents and legitimizes her fear that any attempt to contact relatives who could help her to prove her identity will jeopardize their lives.

But for those who escape persecution who have no other options, a false passport (or sneaking in without any documents, like Mustapha, though this has become increasingly difficult after 9/11) may be the only way of getting out and in. If they are being politically persecuted, they may be unable to get a passport, as was the case with Peter. When Chan, Tun's wife, decided she had to get away from Burma to escape persecution, she did not have a passport and was convinced that the Burmese government would not issue her with one. So she contacted her friends in Burma, and they bribed Burmese Immigration officials to issue her a Burmese passport. She used that passport to travel to the United States on a valid student visa. This passport was "official" in the sense that it came from the right bureaucracy, but "unofficial" in that it wasn't obtained in the normal way, but through bribery of a bureaucrat.

Even if people fleeing persecution can get passports, they may be unwilling to draw attention to their plans to leave, fearing (usually rightly) that this could lead to further persecution, maybe even death. When one's life is in danger, sneaking away in the dead of night may be the most sensible thing to do.

One lawyer told us of particular problems he has with Afghan clients:

> Afghanis – no one has a birth certificate. One judge had never done any Afghan cases, no birth certificate, no school certificate, no bank account, nothing I can get. I send the person to the Afghan consul to get them a birth certificate. One's age is not important, but one's nationality, identity is – if the Afghan consul says he is Afghan.
>
> (Siman, 2002)

There is often a class bias here. People with more education and greater resources can find ways of coming to the US or the UK on their own passports and a visitor's visa, a student visa, or a short-term business visa, as many of the people we have met have done. They have been able to convince the consul in their country that they are genuine visitors and do not intend to overstay their visa. Being able to convince the consul depends on such things as whether they have money, a plausible reason for coming, family in the destination, a place to stay, and a return ticket. They must look as if they are not coming to immigrate or to claim asylum (either to the authorities of the countries they are leaving or to the consul who grants them the visa) but for the purpose on the visa: to visit family, attend a conference, or to do business. None of these people has identity problems because they can come in on their own passports with valid visas.

Getting a visitor's visa also depends on where the asylum seeker is coming from. The poorer the country from which they come, the harder it is to get a visitor's visa. In those cases, having a relative already there may even make it harder to get a visa since the consul may believe that they intend to use the visitor's visa as a back door-way to immigrate illegally. Ironically, it is just these impoverished countries which have been involved in the sorts of civil wars that make it more likely that someone needs to flee persecution. In addition, diplomatic officials in the field have a lot of discretion to deny a visa when they decide whether someone is likely not to leave when it expires. The British Home Office recently produced a report examining the behavior of their consuls in denying short-term visas to people wanting to visit Britain (Lindsley, 2004). They list such a variety of reasons people are denied a visa that it is clear that anything that strikes the consul as unusual, or different from "normal" behavior (as defined by the consul) can be enough for a denial. For example, if someone has never traveled before, if they don't have an itinerary, or don't have specific detailed information about tourist sites (or if they do), or if they don't know anyone, or if they come from a country where people have often overstayed their visas, or if they plan to visit someone who has overstayed their visa (even legally, for a job). Officials also make judgments about the appropriateness of applicants' plans; whether their business plans look good to the consul may be the deciding factor in their getting a short-term business visa. One applicant said he hoped to obtain enlightenment at a religious conference, but was refused a visa because the cost of the trip was not considered commensurate with the benefit he would obtain (in the consul's opinion)! Some applicants for student visas were turned down because the consul thought they could just as well have studied at home, or that the expense of the study wasn't worth the benefits they would get. One applicant for a visa for medical treatment was turned down because he was not sufficiently informed about the details of the planned treatment. There has been no similar public report of the actions of US consular officers in the field, but it would not be surprising if some of this arrogant second guessing without information goes on there, too, given the anecdotes one hears, especially from applicants from poor countries.

Victoria, a Sierra Leonean, was lucky to be able to get a visitor's visa. She had watched her family being killed by the rebels and was living in terror that she would be the next victim. She came to the US on a visitor's visa to attend a conference organized by the Episcopal Church. She had spent several months in hiding, during which time her church made the arrangements so she could escape from Sierra Leone. They provided the money and the visa (and the excuse) so she could come legally to the US. They were also able to convince the consul that attending the conference was a legitimate reason to apply for a visa.

Tun and Henri both came to the US on student visas. For Tun, it was an extension of the studies he had pursued on short courses both in Scandinavia and in the US. He was able to convince the consul in Thailand of his bona fides, despite the fact that he acknowledged that he had a forged passport. Henri's student visa was arranged by members of his political organization as a way to get him out of the country to escape the death threats he was under. Before arriving in the US, he had never even heard of the small university in the northeast where he was to study.

The validity and legality of documents

Recently, there has been great concern by the immigration authorities about the validity of documents that are used to prove identity as well as credibility. This is especially true of documents from particular countries, like the Dominican Republic, where none of the documents produced are considered valid. The report about the granting of visas to the UK indicates that the view of the British High Commission's Nairobi Visa Section is similar to that of US officials, who argue that Somali documents are completely unacceptable (Lindsley, 2004). The report, by contrast, states that documents issued legitimately before the collapse of the Somali state in 1991 must be acceptable. The Nairobi Visa Section also insists that Kenyan marriage certificates must be presented for all marriages that take place in Kenya, and that there is no reason why the applicant should not be able to present one. The report points out that, on the contrary, there might be many reasons why a Somali refugee would not have an official marriage certificate. So, not only do people need to have identity documents, but the documents also have to pass official muster. The authorities have tests they use to authenticate documents, but they can't always tell one way or the other, as the system depends on having something with which to compare the document.

Peter, the Cameroonian who escaped on a borrowed diplomatic passport, cleverly kept a copy of it. His second lawyer submitted it as evidence of identity. The Department of Homeland Security sent it and his party ID card off for authentication. The problem in cases like this is that the authorities have no template with which to compare the party card; in certain countries there are no exemplars, so it comes back "inconclusive." So Peter can't use the only document he has to help him prove who he is because the State Department has no way of authenticating it. His passport was obviously no help to prove his identity as it was admittedly fake. Fortunately Peter was so compelling as a witness in court, and the expert testimony of a therapist was so strong, that he succeeded in his asylum claim.

What has become really clear is that the system is stacked against people who use methods that are seen as illegitimate, even if those are the only means of escape. Some judges see it negatively, but in fact the claim that trying to get hold of authentic documents before fleeing could jeopardize one's safety should bolster an application rather than the reverse. If the only way a person could leave was by concealing his identity or disposing of documents, it could be evidence that he was more likely to be in imminent danger of persecution.

There is a risk of being charged with fraud for using someone else's passport. If someone comes to the US on a false passport, the case is immediately referred to the court, without the more informal hearing with an asylum officer. Using a false passport used not to be a particular problem either in the US or the UK, as the authorities recognized the reasons it was necessary, but now, with the general tightening up after 9/11, it can become a bigger issue. At the court hearing the applicant needs to explain why she used a false passport. Though it isn't a bar to asylum, it may come up later when the person applies for permanent residence. In the experience of one of the US lawyers we talked to, the USCIS invariably approves the application as being "in the public interest," which is what the law says is required to waive the bar caused by fraud (London, 2004).

Asylum applicants in the UK are now not so lucky. In 2004, as we saw in Chapter 1, a law was passed which makes it a crime to come into the country without a passport, or with a false passport, unless the person has a "reasonable excuse" for doing so. This is supposed to prevent people who come to the UK from deliberately destroying their passports before they arrive, as well as those who claim to come from a country other their real country of origin, as part of a false claim. This new law is seen by those who represent asylum seekers as yet another effort to severely cut back on those granted asylum, by making the assumption that anyone who comes into the country using false documents is a "bogus asylum seeker." In fact, this is a violation of the 1951 UN Convention, which specifically forbids "the imposition of penalties for illegal entry [normally requiring false documents], provided asylum-seekers come direct, present themselves "without delay" to the authorities of the country of arrival, and "show good cause" for their illegal entry (Article 31).

One of the lawyers we interviewed in London estimated that between half and three-quarters of all UK asylum seekers don't have passports (Grewall, 2004). Many asylum seekers destroy documents because they have been told to do so by those who have helped them escape. For those who have destroyed their documents, we were told by a London barrister:

It would appear that airline officials/immigration officers at the point of departure are under instructions to photocopy all documents, and these are then produced when documents are destroyed/taken back by agents, and used to undermine a claim that a person is from a particular country or of a particular age.

(Ahluwalia, 2005a)

This means that they can be deported to the country on the passport they presented to the airline when they departed, regardless of whether that is their actual country of origin. It emphasizes the fervor of the British authorities who assume that applicants are bogus and that they should be sent back at all costs. This, too, is in violation of international treaties, which prohibit sending people back to a country other than their own.

Even when applicants do have a "reasonable excuse" to enter the UK on false documents, they must present that excuse by pleading not guilty to the criminal charge, which will result in a court hearing in a Crown court, a higher court than is usual for similar criminal offenses. Clearly, without good legal representation, an applicant will have little chance of proving that their explanation is a reasonable one. A couple of months after the law came into force, it was reported that already 80 people had been charged and 20 convicted. As one lawyer wryly pointed out: "If Mandela had escaped he'd have had to do it by illegal means . . . if no one had heard of you, you could leave on your own passport" (Grewall, 2004).

A false passport is one obvious way of getting to the US if you are fleeing, but a remarkable number of people manage to arrive without any documents at all (though fewer since 9/11). David, a Sierra Leonean client simply walked ashore at the Port of Baltimore without anyone catching him. He was a stowaway on a ship, and the captain had told him that he would turn him in to the authorities when they reached Baltimore. To avoid tipping the captain off, David left the bag containing his belongings behind but was smart enough to take his birth certificate with him when he waded ashore. "I kept it here," he said proudly, patting his shirt pocket. Mustapha, whom we met in Chapter 1, also arrived without any documents whatsoever. As we saw in Chapter 2, this has become much harder since 9/11 in the US, and since the various new policies and laws have been implemented in the UK.

Having a passport that is not yours may also cause identity problems. Fauziya Kassindja, whom we met in Chapter 1, came to the US on someone else's Nigerian passport, which she had bought from a friend in Germany. As soon as she arrived here, she told the INS officer that it was not her passport and that she was from Togo, not Nigeria. Because she spoke English, rather than the French which is typical of people from Togo, and because she was confused and didn't draw the Togolese flag correctly, the INS decided she was not Togolese, but Nigerian, as the borrowed passport claimed. She did in fact have an identity document with her, but she was not asked for it when she arrived in Newark, nor did she know enough to provide it to them. Her ID documents were later lost in a riot at the detention center, along with other material that could have helped her in her claim of who she was, including letters and family pictures. Fauziya's story is one example in which identity is part of a general problem that we see again and again. The authorities expect asylum seekers to tell them certain stories, and when they don't hear them, they are likely to decide that the person is lying and is not who she says she is. We will talk more about lying in the next chapter.

Dhundup, a Tibetan monk came in on a false Nepalese passport. Tibetans do not have passports. As one lawyer told us "if you have status in India you can travel on a refugee document – in Nepal, they have to travel on a Nepalese passport – they are all false in some way" (Berger, 2005). Dhundup's lawyer found ingenious ways of proving that he was really who he said he was, by calling on the Tibetan community. They could not say anything about Dhundup's persecution, because they had all left earlier, but they did know who he was and accepted him as one of their group. Dhundup's lawyer was able to give the asylum officer a photo which had been on the front page of a local newspaper in Vermont showing Dhundup leading a prayer meeting with the other exiles from Tibet. Berger also contacted the Tibetan government in exile in New York who spoke to him at some length over the phone in Tibetan. The official said that no one who was not Tibetan could speak Tibetan that well or know all the local information that Dhundup clearly knew, which meant that he was indeed Tibetan and not Nepali as his false passport said.

David, an asylum applicant in the UK, had a problem proving that he was from Burundi. He had fled to Britain via South Africa. When he arrived, he produced his ID card to prove his nationality. He had arrived on a South African passport but explained to immigration officials that it was false. The Home Office refused to accept that David was in fact from Burundi and that he had escaped on a route that eventually took him via South Africa.

Proving identity

People from some countries have special problems proving their nationality. In the case of nationals from Afghanistan and Pakistan, Liberia and Nigeria, and Kosovo and Albania, the British authorities assume that someone claiming to belong to the first of each pair of countries in fact belongs to the second. The belief is that in the former countries things are bad enough to make getting asylum likely, but in the latter, things are calm and asylum is therefore unlikely. No doubt this happens, but the assumption of deception is part of the focus on asylum seekers as "bogus" economic migrants. The countries change, of course, but the concern remains. In one case, the sole ground for considering an applicant Ghanaian and not Liberian as in fact he was, was the arbitrary decision of an Immigration Officer. The Home Office "usually fall back on questions to tell if they come from where they say they do . . . 'Are you a Kosovan?' There is a list of questions for officers to use . . . They have tried piloting by language experts, but it is too expensive" (Yeo, 2005). The British authorities are also trying to use technology to determine which country someone is from, like biometric testing. This is a system of comparison, so it doesn't work unless there is something with which to compare it, generally the person having tried to enter the country before.

We say that it is understandable and acceptable for someone seeking asylum to arrive with false documents, or no documents, but then we make the whole process much harder in practice. This is especially true now that a claim has to be made within a year after arrival in the US. How can you show when you arrived if you came without any identifying documents? Sometimes this problem becomes surreal. Dieudonne came to the US from the Democratic Republic of the Congo (DRC) in 2002 but at his hearing the asylum officer accused him of being in the US in 1998 and 1999. It turned out that someone had been in the US and used his name and the address of his brother, which was what convinced the INS that in fact Dieudonne had come to the US before 2002, and that he was not only outside the one-year time limit but was also lying. Dieudionne actually came into the US on the borrowed passport of a Canadian diplomat, and, as requested, he sent the passport back to its rightful owner as soon as he arrived in the US. He had flown on an airline (Air Afrique) which had since gone out of business so they had no records which could corroborate the story. However, his story of persecution in the DRC was so horrific that the officer tried to help by asking him to provide information which only someone who had been in the Congo rather than in the US could have known. The asylum officer had been in the Peace Corps and knew a lot about the area. Dieudonne described a rail strike which took place in the capital, Brazzaville, that he would be unlikely to have known about if he had been in the US at the time. Unfortunately, even though the officer was convinced that his identity had been stolen by the person who was here in 1999, he couldn't give him asylum because he needed more evidence to convince his superiors, and so the case was referred to the court for a hearing. To compound the irony of Dieudonne's case, he decided to return to the DRC before his case could be heard in court. He had a terrible story of persecution as a Tutsi: several family members were raped and killed; he was beaten on a number of occasions, imprisoned and tortured, and finally escaped after spending three years hiding in a basement. Despite his history of persecution he was very homesick and distraught that he could not find out the whereabouts of several family members. He had won a claim for the return of some property from the current government and had decided that it was safe enough to go home. We don't know how he has fared since his return.

For many people fleeing Somalia, there are special identity problems regarding the authenticity of documents, which we discussed earlier. Somalis come from one of the countries where there has traditionally been very little documentation of status, like births, deaths, and marriages. They do not consider birthdays significant in the way we do, and many do not know exactly how old they are. For this reason, refugees from Somalia have routinely been given a birth date of January 1. Not only has Somalia traditionally done without identity documents, but also the country really doesn't exist as a political entity at the moment, nor has it since 1991. Thus even those documents which might exist in Somalia are unavailable to asylum seekers. In addition, during the turmoil the majority clans frequently went through the public records office and vandalized it, so that people would no longer be able to use records to claim title to property. Many Somalis have been denied asylum because the authorities do not believe that they are who they say they are, even though the oral testimony of an applicant supported by oral testimony of third parties is supposed to be sufficient proof of identity under asylum law. Instead, the authorities believe that they are all lying about identity, the applicants and the witnesses alike, and that all documents are forged. As one US lawyer put it: "the judge says, 'I am not going to put much stock in the testimony of a clan member, get evidence from someone in the country.' The judge disregards people who are not family members 'I am a distant relative.' To me that is identity." (Quinn, 2002a).

This skepticism regarding Somali identity is shared by the UK authorities, who seem to assume that all Somali asylum seekers are bogus. Here is part of an appeal by a Somali man to the AIT in London, which we observed in May, 2006: *HO* is the Home Office representative, *AD* is the administrative judge, and *AP* is the applicant.

HO: Do you have proof of your relationship to your brother, any proof?

AD: You mean by way of documentation?

AP: I have my brother's documents that he was allowed to remain.

HO: That is not quite what I mean. Do you have documents that link you as siblings?

AP: My brother is my brother and when I came to this country I met him, he took me to the Home Office.

AD: I think you need to answer the question. Do you have any documents linking you to your brother?

AP: What sort of documents do you mean?

HO: Like birth certificates with both parents' names on it?

AP: No, our country has broken down, we fled, all those things were lost.

HO: Have you carried out DNA tests to prove you were brothers?

AP: We did not do that yet.

HO: Why not?

AP: We were not asked to do it.

HO: So is there any way you can prove you are related to your brother?

AP: My brother is my brother and I did mention he was my brother. I'm ready for a DNA test if a DNA test is required.

The expectation that someone would have an expensive DNA test to prove what they already feel is patently obvious illustrates the disconnect between how the authorities perceive identity and how asylum seekers do.

We noted above the Nairobi Visa Section's view that all their documents were assumed to be invalid. Also, the Home Office works to detect Somali asylum seekers from East Africa, who they believe are "posing as citizens of other countries, or actually hold other citizenship, and who are attempting to travel to the UK on genuine passports that have been issued with visas" (Lindsley, 2004: 19). The assumption here is that this has to be stopped; nowhere is it considered that some of the Somalis may be genuinely fleeing persecution.

One therapist, who works with tortured asylum seekers, described a Somali woman client, called Fatima, who testified at four separate court hearings, for a total of 10 hours, much of it focused on her identity (Berthold, 2004). The questions related to minute details about a whole range of issues. In one way she was lucky because she had been an employee of an NGO in Somalia and her employer was now also living in the US. Fatima was tortured because she was working for the NGO, which was active on behalf of minority individuals and women, a position that made her a target of the warring clans. Fatima's employer came to court to testify in person and also testified on the telephone to support Fatima's claim that she was who she said she was. At the trial, the employer was grilled about minute differences in the story. "What was the street number?" (Fatima said they don't have street numbers in Somalia), "What color was the wall?" Red. "Was it a fire engine red or an orange red?" (They don't have such distinctions.) "Exactly how was the room organized?" The judge didn't think she was who she said she was (even after all this) but he ultimately gave her asylum, although begrudgingly. It is even more difficult when the Somali brings in a relative to testify because as we have seen, the authorities assume they are all lying about their identities.

The authorities look askance at applicants who have no documents or those who pitch their documents en route; what is an act of survival for the person fleeing persecution looks like a deliberate act of deceit to asylum officials. Even though officials understand that disposing of documents may be necessary to elude captors, in the West, a person without documents is immediately under suspicion. It is not only a matter of not being able to put ourselves in the mindset of those who flee persecution (in whose experience documents are used *against* individuals by authorities). A person fleeing persecution may consider herself to be safer if she is caught with no evidence as to who she is. Once she reaches an asylum destination, the lack of documentation puts her in danger of being incarcerated, or deported, or both.

One lawyer told us about the USCIS: "the service doesn't believe that a person doesn't have documents when they enter . . . a judge said he didn't believe that they would throw away their illegal entry documents" (Quinn, 2002a). Of course, as with so much in this area, there is the alternative story of someone who throws away identifying documentation so that it cannot be proved where they come from when the time comes to deport them. The change in British law, criminalizing the presentation of false documents on arrival discussed above, is a response to recent stories in the UK of "bogus asylum seekers," which revolved around applicants discarding their documents for this reason. Such narratives, while doubtless sometimes true, reinforce the view that asylum seekers are simply economic migrants masquerading as those seeking refuge from persecution. In New Zealand, an Algerian, Ahmed Zaoui, who claimed he was persecuted, threw away his documents in the toilet of the plane on which he arrived several years ago. That action contributed to the view that he was a terrorist who has been expelled from several European countries rather than a genuine asylum seeker. The case, which received extensive publicity in the New Zealand media, has been in and out of the courts for several years and has yet to be fully resolved (*Attorney General* v. *Ahmed Zaoui*, 2005).

Identity problems can arise in more subtle ways. Because foreign names are unfamiliar to immigration officers, many refugees end up with incorrect names on their documents. Fauziya Kassindja's name was misspelled early in her encounter with the INS; from that point on, all the legal documents on her case spell her last name Kasinga. For an immigrant, the effort to regain their correct name can be difficult and costly, and may not be worth bothering about. It does, however, add another dimension to the many losses suffered by asylum seekers when they flee their homeland.

Identity issues affect applicants differently. For example, as we mentioned, Tun's passport was avowedly false, but he did not have any identity problems in his asylum application. He bought a Burmese passport in Thailand in his own name. When he applied for a visa, he met the US consul both in Bangkok and Cheng Mai, and told them at the outset that the passport was fake, which did not prevent them from issuing him a visa to study in the US. It is hard to know why the consul was willing to accept his story about needing a forged passport, when other applicants have had trouble. It may be that the consular officer was knowledgeable about the political situation and sympathetic to Tun's cause and that he knew quite well that he might be helping someone to claim asylum. It may be simply be that Tun appeared educated and convincing.

The issue can also affect people in the same position differently for no apparent reason. As we discussed earlier, Mustapha didn't have a passport, but he wasn't questioned about whether he was who he said he was, nor was he detained. For Fauziya, the issue was important because it contributed to the authorities not believing her initially, and therefore putting her in detention, even though at the time she did have some identifying documents other than the Nigerian passport she used to get in. Once she was stuck in the detention system, she needed to prove other issues, as we will see in later chapters: whether she was telling the truth, whether the events she described actually happened to her, and whether they fell into the category of persecution.

From the Department of Homeland Security's point of view, identity issues can justify the detention of asylum seekers, even though, in many of the cases where people are detained, identity is not in question. Asa Hutchinson, the Department of Homeland Security's under-secretary for border security said that initial detention was often necessary to establish the identity of refugees traveling with false papers, to make sure they are not a danger (Bernstein, 2004). It is apparent that it is used for a number of purposes, not all of them authorized by department policy and the law. Weber and Gelsthorpe, in their study of UK detention practices, describe identity as a "particularly vexed issue" as a basis for detaining asylum seekers (n.d.: 48). They report that some officers advocate detaining applicants so their identity can be established, while others think it is pointless (n.d.: 48).

Identity issues can merge into credibility issues, which we will deal with in the next chapter. Not only is it a question of: "Are you who you say you are?" but also "Did you really belong to X political party?" which implies both that a party ID card is fake and that the applicant was lying about belonging to the party.

Many applicants find this concern for identity very hard to understand. They ask: "What is the big deal?" "Why are they trying to force me to contact people over there?" "Why do they make me do this?" They say: "This is me," "You know, they don't understand, things are done differently in our country, we don't have computerized systems . . ."

Having one's identity questioned can cause psychological distress, in addition to the general distress of the asylum process. As we saw, some people are afraid to contact their families or friends back home for fear of causing danger to them. There is also an intense sense of guilt, responsibility to people back home, and an unwillingness to burden them further, or put them at greater risk than they have already been under. Henri feels this guilt constantly, and it is reinforced by the remaining members of his family who tell him that they would not have been injured or in exile were it not for his activities. The possibility that a friend has suffered because of Henri's need to prove his story only adds to his guilt. Some people who are persecuted because of ethnicity find that the questioning of their identity brings forward enormous pain, churning up generations of discrimination, and prejudice. It can call into question identity in a much deeper sense than what the immigration authorities are investigating. One can assume that the whole experience of being tortured and fleeing one's country makes a person reflect seriously about life and their life choices. For many people, the persecution they suffer precipitates a crisis of identity about who they *really* are.

Longman (2001) writes of identity problems as they pertain to ethnic labeling. He describes a young Rwandan woman whom he calls Claudette, who grew up as a Hutu, with all that involved. During the Rwandan genocide, it was discovered that her grandfather had been known as a Tutsi before he moved to the area where Claudette had been raised. He had received an identity card stating his ethnicity as Hutu, which he passed down to his descendants. As a result of this becoming public knowledge, Claudette's family became the targets of ethnic violence and several family members were killed. Her "new" identity as a Tutsi is suspect, as she and her family had enjoyed the benefits of being Hutu before the genocide. Now she says: "I do not really know what I am. I do not know what it means to be Tutsi" (Longman, 2001: 346).

Identity crises are particularly problematic for those who are persecuted for their religious beliefs, who may have a crisis of faith as a result of their persecution, a crisis further exacerbated by the whole process of seeking asylum. Berthold has found that those who have been tortured because of religious belief or political affiliation do better if they are able to retain or reclaim their identity after the torture. But some people have their faith called into question and may lose their faith; that which used to be the source of enormous strength and support is now gone (2004). One example was Daniel, a Nigerian Christian, whose father had a limb hacked off in religious rioting and then died. Daniel was tortured for engaging in religious protest. He still identifies as a Christian, but he can no longer pray or go to church because it triggers traumatic memories. So his identity as he defines it himself is not the same as it was before the persecution, for reasons that are different from Claudette's but no less significant. This framing of identity, however, is of no interest to the immigration authorities.

Conclusion

Many of the problems we have described are a matter of cultural or national differences in documenting identity. Many cases of so-called "fraudulent" documents can be justified by the need for survival (not only for themselves but for others) in the face of discrimination and persecution. Understanding the problems of the lost identity of people who have suffered political trauma, and the larger issues of reputation and dignity, would also help to repair some of the misunderstandings that are currently built into the political asylum review process. However, the larger issue, more difficult to resolve, is the criminal-ization of people who enter the country without the proper documenta-tion. As we have noted, criminalization is more explicit in the UK than currently in the US, but in both countries, someone who enters without proper documentation is an "illegal alien." Such persons have "broken the law" and thus are suspect from the start. No amount of crosscultural understanding about identity documentation or greater awareness of the ways that political persecution compromises the maintenance of documents or the possibility of gaining legitimate entry to another country can overcome the association between the lack of documenta-tion and criminality. We can point to 9/11 as a moment in which this association was intensified, but 9/11 did not create the problem. Maintaining secure borders and monitoring terrorism is a justification for closely examining the applications of people claiming political asylum, but such monitoring is not the same as categorizing those people as criminals *because* of their lack of documentation. Political asylum policy has equated the problem of establishing identity with a criminal act. In its simplest form, the production of fraudulent papers is "fraud." But this over-simplification overlooks the fact that creating false papers to survive is quite different than creating false papers for some monetary gain or to make a fraudulent asylum claim. Is our justice system unable to distinguish between these? Shouldn't our efforts be directed toward establishing the validity of the claim to have experienced political or religious persecution? We have to ask our-selves why the proof of identity plays such a large role in our inquiries, and whether the demand for documentation is an adequate or fair way to address the credibility of applicants' claims. In giving proof of identity such importance, have we not created the very system of fraud that we are attempting to monitor? Why do we connect the question, "Are you who you say you are?" with the more important question, "Did this really happen to you?" As we will see in the next chapters, even this second question is fraught with difficulties, as we try to establish whether what happened was indeed as terrible as the applicant says it was or whether, if it was terrible, such a horrible thing could have happened.

4 Did this really happen to you?

The problem of credibility

The story of Fauziya Kassindja, introduced in the first chapter, says a lot about the problem of credibility. In her book, *Do They Hear You When You Cry?*, she describes her life in Togo and her escape to the US via Germany (1998). Fauziya was very close to both her parents, who were unusual people in a number of ways. They were both of mixed tribal origin, he Koussountu and Tchamba, she Fulani and Dendi. Theirs was a love match (though the marriage was officially arranged by Fauziya's mother's parents at their daughter's request, itself atypical). Usually marriages were arranged without consulting the woman. Fauziya's parents were both devout Muslims and, under Muslim law, he could have taken up to four wives. He chose not to. He also decided that the widespread practice of "*kakia*" (female genital mutilation – FGM) was unacceptable. When he was young, he apparently saw it done to his sister, and asked why it was done. " 'It's tradition. That's what our ancestors did. That's what we do.' Which wasn't a good enough reason for him" (1998: 23).

> A lot of fathers extinguish any sign of independent thinking in their daughters, but not my father . . . He was always interested in my opinion . . . And he taught me early that I had the power and right to express myself, to make my own choices.
>
> (1998: 46)

Fauziya's upbringing was different in another way, too.

> Like many Muslim girls, my sisters and I were all sent to
> *madrasah* beginning at around age six, to receive training in
> our religion . . . If they could afford only a secular education
> for some of their children, parents would send their sons, not
> their daughters . . . My parents, however, were strong
> believers in educating all their children, in both *madrasah* and
> secular school.
>
> (1998: 46–7)

Later, when Fauziya was 14, she went to an English boarding
school in Ghana, since she had begun her education in English, rather
than the more typical French, which was the language of instruction
in secondary school in Togo. After a little over a year, she was called
out of class to the principal's office. "Fauziya, please sit down. I've
just gotten a telegram. You are wanted at home. You have to leave
right now" (1998: 85). When Fauziya asked why, he was reluctant
to tell her, but finally he told her: "I'm very sorry to have to tell you
this, Fauziya, but your father has died" (1998: 85).

After the funeral, Fauziya's uncle called her and her siblings
together at his house for counseling and advice, as is traditional when
a man dies. He said: "Your father is dead. He's dead and he's spoiled
you. Especially you, Fauziya. He spoiled you the worst. He treated
you like some fancy ornament he couldn't stop admiring. Well, that
stops now. There'll be no more of it" (1998: 89). Fauziya's uncle and
aunt had never approved of her mother, because she was of a
different tribe, and had kept pushing her father to divorce her, or
at least to take another wife. "The two brothers became estranged
over an incident involving female circumcision – *kakia* – which both
my parents abhorred and both my father's siblings believed in and
had had done to their own daughters" (1998: 76).

Fauziya went back to school, but when she came home for the
summer, her mother was not there. When she asked where her
mother had gone, her aunt told her: "She went to be with her family

in Benin. I'm staying here while she's gone" (1998: 92). In fact, her mother's departure was not temporary, as Fauziya had been led to believe.

> Under tribal law, everything my father had owned, now belonged to them [the aunt and uncle], his house, his vans, his money, everything. Even Babs and I, the only two children left in the house, were now theirs. They'd allowed my mother to remain in the house for four months, ten days, in accordance with tribal law. Then they'd given her a share of his money – the widow is supposed to get one third – and they'd told her to go.
>
> (1998: 95)

Fauziya tried to find out where her mother had gone, but when she asked her older sister, Ayisha, she wasn't sure.

After the summer, Fauziya went back to boarding school for a year, which turned out to be her last. By the following summer, her aunt had found a suitable man for her to marry, a man who was 45 years old, and who already had three wives. Instead of going back to school, she was to be married, after she had been circumcised so that she would be a suitable bride. Fauziya refused to marry this man, and couldn't believe that it would happen in the face of her adamant opposition. She went into denial. "As long as I kept saying no, she'll wait. I clung to that hope. I honestly believed it, until the morning I woke up and saw the dresses and jewelry laid out on the bed" (1998: 105). The marriage was to take place before the circumcision, which was to be a couple of days later. This gave Fauziya and her older sister, Ayisha, time to arrange her escape. Her mother had given Ayisha some of her money so Fauziya and Ayisha could leave. On the evening of the day before she was to be circumcised, they left in a car which took them to the border between Togo and Ghana. They went to a "spot where people cross illegally through the forest. We could have crossed legally. But Ayisha was thinking ahead. She knew my aunt and uncle would search for me and she didn't want any guard to remember seeing us" (1998: 124). Fauziya flew out of Ghana to Germany with the help of a man whom Ayisha had paid to provide a ticket and to get her through immigration when they arrived in Düsseldorf. After she arrived, the man said: "Well, that's it . . . You're on your own now. Good luck" (1998: 133).

> The concourse was vast, modern, clean, crowded. I'd never seen anything like it . . . Everyone was dressed in heavy clothing . . . I was wearing a thin, short-sleeved cotton dress . . . I was cold . . . Not knowing what else to do, I wandered along, looking in the shop windows . . . all I saw was a sea of white faces, and all I heard was German.
>
> (1998: 135)

Finally, after she wandered around, for a while, a woman whom Fauziya had encountered in one of the stores, smiled at her. "She'd smiled at me three times now. I had to try to talk to someone. Maybe she could help me find some African people." With some difficulty, Fauziya managed to explain her situation to this stranger, who, when she realized Fauziya had nowhere to go, invited her to stay at her house.

She stayed with Rudina, the German woman who had offered her hospitality, for several weeks. Rudina fed her, gave her money, and encouraged her to go out. Finally Fauziya started taking the *Strassenbahn* (the streetcar) to a local mall. On one of her trips on the *Strassenbahn* she met a Nigerian, called Charlie, with whom, after some initial reluctance, she struck up a friendship. He was "the first black person I'd spoken to. And no black person had ever approached me or spoken to me" (1998: 145). They met regularly for several weeks, and one day she told him her story. When Charlie asked her if she had claimed asylum, she initially thought he meant that she was crazy and needed an "insane asylum." He explained what asylum was, and they talked about where she could go to get asylum. She didn't want to stay in Germany because she didn't speak the language. Because she had relatives in America, she eventually decided to go there to seek asylum. When she pointed out that she didn't have a passport, Charlie offered her his sister's which she eventually bought from him for $600. He also got her a ticket and told her that when she arrived she should ask for asylum and tell them about her relatives. "My teachers at school said it was a great country. They said people believed in justice in America. If I went there and I told them what had happened to me, surely, they'd sympathize" (1998: 152).

When Fauziya arrived at Newark airport, the reality was very different. Rather than simply accepting her story, and letting her go to her relatives as she had expected, they kept her aside, fingerprinted her, refused to allow her to contact her relatives in New Jersey, and in general terrified her. Finally she was interviewed and asked to tell her story, which she did, minus the part about FGM because she was too embarrassed. "How could I explain *kakia* to someone who'd probably never heard of it?" (1998: 172). She was asked if she spoke French, and when she said she didn't the officer assumed she was not from Togo, and she didn't tell him that she had gone to school in Ghana. An officer asked her to draw the Togolese flag, which she initially got wrong. "That's not Togo's flag," the officer told her. She replied: "I made a mistake. The star goes in the other corner." "You don't know your own flag?" (1998: 175). The officer decided she was probably from Nigeria, the country on her false passport. Fauziya was told that she would have to go to prison before she could talk to a judge, which is exactly what happened to her, in chains and handcuffs. Various indignities followed at the Esmor Detention Center in Elizabeth, New Jersey, where she was taken: strip searches, having to wear prison clothing, eating food she was not used to and which violated the rules of her religion. When she finally got access to a phone, she couldn't call her uncle because she didn't have the number. She reached a cousin, Rahuf, who began the process of getting her a lawyer. Her uncle, whom she never spoke to, in fact didn't want to help her stay in the US. She was finally able to contact an immigration lawyer, who later handed the case over to a law student, Layli Bashir, who ultimately became her savior. After Fauziya had spent several months in Esmor waiting for her court hearing, there was a riot there. In the rush to escape, she put her most precious possessions, including her ID cards, in an envelope in her bra. The envelope was taken from her for safekeeping (and never returned) during the move to Hudson County Correctional Center, her new place of detention. After several weeks in a maximum security prison, Fauziya was moved again, this time to a minimum security dorm in York Correctional Center. She stayed there only a few days, when she was moved yet again, to Lehigh County prison. During this period before her hearing, she had several health problems, spent nineteen days in seclusion, had only occasional contact with her lawyer and never knew when her hearing was to take place. It did finally take place in late August 1995, months after she had arrived in the US, when it was denied on the grounds of lack of credibility. By this time Fauziya no longer wanted to fight for asylum. "I just had to get out of prison. That's why one of the first things I'd done after returning from my hearing was to write out a request to see the INS counselor, Natasha. All I wanted was for her to tell the INS to send me home" (1998: 395). By then, others, including Fauziya's lawyers, were determined to continue the fight on Fauziya's behalf, so they filed an appeal and enlisted the help of an asylum expert, Karen Musalo. This was when the case became the *cause célèbre* we talked about in Chapter 1. The story hit the media; it was on the TV news, and was written up in newspapers. Many people became involved in the case. In the meantime, however, Fauziya was still in prison, and was in fact transferred once again, back to the maximum security unit at York Connectional Center, while she waited for her appeal, this time sharing her cell with a convicted murderer. Her lawyers had tried to get her paroled, but had failed. Meanwhile, her emotional and physical health deteriorated. Finally, in April, 1996, she was paroled and went to live with the mother of Layli, her lawyer, until her appeal before the BIA on May 2. On June 13, 1996, the BIA granted her appeal for asylum. Fauziya was finally free.

The importance of credibility

Ambivalence toward asylum makes itself known in how hearings are actually conducted and what is expected of applicants. Even though case law both in the US and the UK permits informal evidence and allows for the granting of asylum based only on the applicant's story, asylum hearings are dominated by a search for the "truth" as perceived by the official hearing the case. The recent passage of the REAL ID Act in the US has validated this search; the law allows adjudicators to require corroboration of otherwise credible testimony, and allows them to deny asylum on a number of factors related to credibility, including demeanor, plausibility, and inconsistencies. In the UK, as we have already seen, the Home Office is very skeptical of the credibility of asylum seekers, a skepticism which is shared by the immigration judges who hear appeals (Jarvis, 2003). An applicant can't win an asylum case unless the story has the three Cs: corroboration, consistency, and chronology. It also has to sound plausible to the Western ear of the asylum officer or judge.

For many of the people involved in the asylum process, credibility is the crux of the matter. How can the officials tell whether applicants are telling the truth when they themselves are the only source of information about who they are and what happened to them? A search for truth, of course, occurs not only in the asylum process but in many parts of the US and UK justice systems. The criminal law, for example, is all about whose story to believe: the defendant's or the state's. Officials believe, like most people, that they can tell if someone is lying, even though the research in this area shows otherwise (see e.g. Ekman and O'Sullivan, 1991; Vrij, 2001). The process of deciding if the story is to be believed is very complex but, of course, essential. This necessary process goes on, despite research which shows that judgments about credibility are extremely fallible (Schooler *et al.*, 1986).

Corroboration

The paper trail

We saw the importance of paper in the last chapter as a way of proving identity. Here we see that paper is the classic kind of "objective" evidence that reassures us that a narrative is "true." A British report argues that without it, a person doesn't have much hope of getting asylum, even though the law allows for such a possibility:

> Documentary evidence to support the asylum claim is, in practice, not an option but a pre-requisite. The standard of proof is thus already set at a level that is hard to achieve in circumstances of flight, and often well-nigh impossible at long-distance. It can be extremely hard for asylum-seekers to obtain any sort of documentary evidence from often war-torn or unstable countries where mail may be monitored and official records of [for instance] police activities are more or less non-existent. Indeed, if an asylum-seeker were to come equipped with all the necessary documentary evidence, he or she would might [sic] be said to be more, not less, suspect.
>
> (Asylum Aid, 1999: 23)

This irony has been noticed by the Italian authorities, who don't bother with paper on the assumption that it is too likely to be forged (Furlan, 2005). By contrast, officials in the US and the UK rely on paper; the authorities are aware of the risks of forgery, but believe they have the ability to tell whether a document is a forgery or not.

Producing documents that show he was indeed arrested when he says he was puts an applicant in a far better position than if he just says he was arrested, but doesn't have any document to prove it (a much more common situation). The officer hearing the story has to connect political problems in the applicant's homeland with the actual applicant who applies for asylum. As one writer on political asylum put it:

> The basic facts in any particular case are highly elusive. The adjudicator has to decide what happened in a distant country, but usually only has two imperfect sources for judging what happened to the applicant or others similarly situated. First, general human rights reports on conditions in the country of origin can provide genuine assistance, but they rarely mention the applicant or the precise events at issue in the individual claim. The second source

is live testimony, but quite often the only witness to the central personal events now available in the country of haven is the applicant himself or herself.

(Martin, 2000: 3)

It is rare that there is much written corroboration of the applicant's claim. Most countries from which people flee persecution don't have the kind of press that reports details of political activism. It is only in those unusual cases where someone is well known that there is likely to be a written record.

Dev was one of those rare cases. When preparing his asylum claim we were able to put together an extensive paper trail in support of the application. Because he was a political activist in a small country, Bhutan, we were able to gather material from a variety of sources, some about him directly, and some about the general condition of his ethnic group, the Nepali people in Bhutan. There was a long history of persecution of these people, many of whom had been expelled, and human rights groups had been documenting their plight since the government began its policy of discrimination against ethnic Nepalis in the 1980s. So we had documents attached to Dev's application which went from Exhibit A to Exhibit Y, as well as three affidavits from people corroborating Dev's story. Among the documents, we had several different types; each category designed to prove different parts of his story, from the personal to the general. First, there were Dev's personal documents, such as his citizenship ID card, certificates for his academic record, his marriage certificate, birth certificates of his children, his Red Cross ID card as a refugee in Nepal, which proved the basic facts of his life. In addition, we submitted documents supporting his story about how he came to the US (his travel document, his I-94 form). The second category of documents was those supporting the parts of Dev's story which related to his family, to prove that they also had been persecuted; these included his father's citizenship ID, a number of letters from family members to each other in refugee camps on Red Cross message forms, and letters from Amnesty International to several family members, which included the fact that he was adopted as an Amnesty Prisoner of Conscience in February 1992 when he was in prison. The next level of documents supporting Dev's application was articles in newspapers which specifically mentioned Dev or his family. We were able to get all this because Dev was a fairly well-known activist. We had an interview of Dev published in the *Bhutan Review* and a letter to another ethnic Nepali from a village headman, ordering her to leave Bhutan for the same reason Dev's family was ordered to leave. The final, most general level of supporting documents is the kind that is available in all cases: articles about the conditions of ethnic Nepalis in Bhutan and in the Nepalese refugee camps in newspapers and in reports from human rights agencies. In addition to all this paper, we also had the three affidavits written especially for Dev's application, two from people working in the area with NGOs and one from a fellow student activist, stating that Dev's story was indeed true.

Amazingly, all this paper was not enough for the asylum officer. She asked for more evidence of two aspects of his application. The first was a detailed list of all the places he had lived since 1990. Dev was very nervous at the hearing and had difficulty responding to questions, which apparently made the asylum officer skeptical about whether he was telling the truth. He had forgotten to mention one or two of his many addresses in his written application. The officer also wanted to know why he could not return to Nepal, and what his legal status was in Nepal. So we had to scurry around to get all this information in the one week we were given. We then sent a package to USCIS with the address list and an additional statement from Dev as well as a letter from someone who had done extensive work for several NGOs and the UNHCR (United Nations High Commission on Refugees) who knew Dev personally. By a fluke, we also managed to get help from a student who was spending the summer in Nepal. He was able to get us a letter from the former Vice-Chairman of the Nepal Bar Association detailing the legal status (actually the lack of it) of Bhutanese refugees in Nepal. Ironically, part of Dev's case depended on the absence of paper as proof. In his application, he described how in the 1990 census all his family members were declared illegal immigrants because (according to the government) they didn't have enough evidence of residence in Bhutan before 1958, even though they had been living there for more than three generations. A few months later, the government confiscated all their properties and seized all the documents of ownership. They were also ordered to surrender their citizenship cards, which was equivalent to surrendering their citizenship. Even though they refused to do this, they were nevertheless stripped of their citizenship and forced to leave Bhutan. Of all this, they had no documentary proof; the government had taken it as part of the persecution. After a few anxious months, Dev was granted asylum and began the process of bringing his wife and children over from their refugee camp in Nepal. He was lucky in having a dedicated group of lawyers working on his case who were able to marshal all this evidence to prove his claim. He now has a green card and is living with his family in the southeast US; the children are in school, and both he and his wife are working.

An applicant who is famous enough that his activities are reported in the local press, or better still, in human rights reports, will have little trouble convincing the authorities of the credibility of his claim. Hilton Fyle came to CRIS for help after he had claimed asylum in Maryland. A quick search of the web provided all the corroboration we needed to support his claim. He was a Sierra Leonean journalist who spent a number of years as a correspondent and announcer for the BBC's Africa Service. He left Britain after twenty-one years with the BBC to return to Sierra Leone in 1994. Hilton was the owner and publisher of the weekly newspaper, *1 2 3, Legal Action*, in 1996 when he was charged with "seditious publication" in connection with a story in the paper that alleged that justice officials had accepted bribes to drop a fraud case against a former foreign minister and a businessman. In 1998 he was charged and convicted of collaborating with the rebels and sentenced to death. He was released by the RUF (Revolutionary United Front) rebels, along with the several other journalists with whom he was imprisoned while their sentences were appealed. All this information is available in many sources on the web, including a report by the International League for Human Rights and the Committee to Protect Journalists. In these reports, he is named specifically and his actions described in detail. So Hilton had no trouble getting asylum at his hearing.

Cases like Hilton Fyle's are the model against which judges and asylum officers measure the typical claim. However, Hilton's is far from the typical claim. In the typical case, an applicant who has suffered persecution has no paper he can produce to support his story of persecution.

In the UK, applicants with uncorroborated claims face a stark problem. The report by Asylum Aid describes several cases in which a lack of corroboration was a reason for denial of an application.

> An Iranian asylum-seeker was informed that the Secretary of State accepted human rights reports of *"systematic use of torture by the security forces, deaths in police custody, disappearances and so-called extra-judicial executions"*. The refusal letter nevertheless goes on: *"However, given the documents make no mention of you, the Secretary of State is not satisfied that you had demonstrated a well founded fear of persecution in Iran."*
>
> (Asylum Aid, 1999: 25)

In a similar vein, an Ethiopian learned that reports and letters carry no weight, because the Secretary of State "*does not consider these generalized reports to verify the events that you allege to have affected you personally*" (1999: 25).

One of the most frustrating aspects of preparing the typical asylum claim is trying to obtain some evidence from a source other than the applicant to corroborate the claim. As we have seen, most applicants can't connect their persecution to published documents. Also, many asylum seekers don't understand the need for external support for their stories. They describe events they know happened, and they assume the listener will believe them. They often resist the efforts of lawyers or community assistance workers to get them to obtain external evidence, perhaps because they are offended by not being believed or because they are afraid of putting others in jeopardy. Others don't understand what corroboration means and, when asked for evidence to support their story, they produce materials that don't actually support their claim. When we asked Mustapha for letters or affidavits from other people who could corroborate his story, he produced a photograph of the docks, from where he apparently made his escape. He carefully showed us the place on the photo where he climbed over the fence to reach the ship on which he stowed away to Brazil. He also asked out of the blue, at the end of an interview "Don't you want to see the video?" The video turned out to be a promotional video of the nonprofit camp where he spent some time in Sierra Leone before he left. Neither of these pieces of "evidence" did anything to support his story of persecution and escape because they added nothing that would make it more credible.

By contrast, more sophisticated applicants have no trouble understanding what is needed. They often arrive at the office clutching a file of newspaper clippings or other documents. Assis, a freelance journalist from Gambia, came into the office armed with a pile of papers, which were newspaper clippings about the situation including references to himself; he was a dream applicant from the point of view of the lawyer helping him apply. Of course, there is always the risk mentioned in the Asylum Aid report that such a person will look "too well prepared" and therefore not be believed, which clearly happens in the UK and perhaps also in the US, though we have not heard of it specifically. Here we have another example of the Catch 22 quality of asylum policy: if you don't have enough evidence to support your claim, you are denied; if you do, you risk being told that you must be lying because you have too much corroborating documentation!

Even if the applicant understands what is required, it is often not possible to get hold of supporting documentation that is good enough for the authorities. Allaya, an Iraqi, was afraid to return to Iraq because she was being targeted as a result of her closeness to the Americans in her job as a translator. Her brother emailed her a letter that had been thrown over the fence at her family home. The letter included such terrifying phrases as:

> God's curse be on those who cooperate with the Americans . . . They should stay in America . . . We are preparing the torture and revenge for them to create an example for others once they come back from there . . . May God have them in the fire of hell and in its deepest spot. Otherwise the honorable resistant mujahideen will be there waiting to murder them.

Allaya was named as one of the targets in the letter, which, however, was unsigned, and her brother couldn't tell her exactly who had left it. So, it is very good evidence in support of Allaya's story, if the authorities were willing to believe the letter was authentic. We can assume they did, as Allaya was granted asylum at her hearing. No doubt, the deterioration of the security situation in Iraq in the months before the hearing, as well as the murder of a number of translators, also bolstered Allaya's claim.

The authorities, in fact, often conclude that the documents produced are not good enough or not authentic, as we saw in the last chapter with identity documents. The Asylum Aid report describes a particularly egregious case:

> A Ghanaian asylum-seeker was asked by the Home Office to supply the arrest warrant that he knew had been issued by the police in his own country. He succeeded in obtaining a copy. The Home Office contested its validity on the basis that its form did not comply with what the Secretary of State would expect, and it was completed by hand, not typed. It took an expert witness (who required a fee) to point out that the form of the warrant was typical, and the local magistrate who filled it in would be unlikely to do so on a type-writer.
>
> (1999: 23)

This case illustrates how difficult it is to correct a misimpression once the authorities have latched onto it. It leads one to wonder how many cases are denied because the authorities continue to stick to their original impression, or the applicant is unable to marshal the forces to override the initial view of his case.

The appeal of Hina, a Pakistani woman whose case we observed in London in June 2006, illustrates the difficulties of convincing the authorities of the validity of a document. The document at issue here was called a FIR, which was submitted as evidence that Hina's husband had charged her with adultery and running away from him. The Home Office representative went to some length to argue that it was not a valid document. First, they disputed the content of the document and pointed to what they saw as an inconsistency.

> In her SEF, her interview, she stated that there were charges of adultery, running away with someone, they've been told to the

mother, it seems to fly in the face of what is actually said in the FIR, that she left and took possessions. The charges she claimed seem to be different from the FIR.

Her lawyer responded:

> As for the adultery issue, the words in the FIR [are] "I have no doubt that my wife has gone away with another person." Normal words are used in the FIR; they never actually say adultery. The words are consistent with what the applicant knows.

Second, they questioned the validity of the document because it was a translation and because: "There is no evidence of an envelope." The immigration judge asked: "Why was a translation given to the mother when she got the document?" to which Hina's lawyer responded:

> She was told to produce a document so she told her mother. Why did she send her mother to get the FIR? I imagine it would be very traumatic to get it. The applicant was told she had to provide evidence of these charges by the asylum authorities otherwise the Home Office wouldn't believe her. It was the lesser of two evils.

In Henri's case, certificates of the deaths of his wife and children, and his father, were important pieces of the paper trail, which is why we spent a lot of time pressuring him into getting them, despite his great reluctance. We had to show that his family had indeed died to support our argument that they had died because of his political activities. After lots of problems we managed to get hold of a number of certificates of birth, death, and marriage, as well as a wedding photo.

In addition to its use as an identity document, a passport can be used to corroborate the story. At Henri's hearing, the officer kept asking for chronology about when Henri got his passport, who filled out the forms, when he got the visa, who was involved in that, where he was when he got the passport. The officer wanted to know how he managed to obtain a passport in 2001 when he had been involved in three coups in 1996, and had been imprisoned and tortured then. So the question about the passport was a way of trying to prove whether the story Henri had told was true and the circumstances under which Henri got his passport was information which could contribute to this truth.

Sometimes the need for documentary evidence becomes ludicrous. In the UK, a Colombian applicant whose claim included three attempts by the police to kill him, and whose friend was killed, was told "*you have not produced [name of friend's] death certificate*" (Asylum Aid, 1999: 24). One wonders how he could ever be in a position to provide that documentation.

In the US, there is an elaborate procedure for the authentication of documents in general, but, as is so often the case, there are special problems when this is applied to asylum cases (Wiebe and Parker, 2001–2). Asylum law recognizes the difficulties of authentication; nevertheless the authorities often ask for verification. One of the ways documents are authenticated is by sending them back to the country of origin, for the embassy there to check on their validity. The embassy usually has their local employees do the job, on the ground that they attract less attention. While it may be true that a local attracts less attention than a consular officer would, the risk of disclosure and resultant danger to the applicant's family remains a serious problem. The embassy attempts to keep information confidential but they cannot provide guarantees, especially when the name of the person is essential to the verification of the document. In addition, asking a government which tortures its citizens to authenticate documents supporting a claim of persecution is unlikely to result in reliable evidence. In the case of S, an investigator from the US consulate in Cameroon, took an arrest warrant with the applicant's name on it to the local State Counsel for verification. The State Counsel claimed that the document was false and asked that the applicant be deported so he could be prosecuted for forgery (Wiebe and Parker, 2001–2: 430).

Experts and associates

Another way in which an asylum seeker's story can be verified is through the word of others, either those who know the applicant personally or experts who know the situation in the country from which she comes. Sometimes, a fellow activist or associate is available to say that indeed the things that the applicant says happened to her did happen. The associate may already have been granted asylum for similar activities, which adds credibility to the evidence.

Some lawyers feel strongly that evidence from others can be very helpful. One lawyer told us:

> I want to bring witnesses . . . Many judges said, "I don't believe anything they say; I won't grant asylum." It's very hard to overturn that. I would insist on bringing witnesses. One judge who hates granting asylum . . . the client was giving testimony, I brought the client, and his aunt who knew of the events, she gave evidence under oath . . . I was able to get asylum granted. If you have a good expert, good witnesses . . .

> (Greenberger, 2002)

As Greenberger implies, good witnesses can help a case by introducing someone with credible knowledge about the situation.

We all tend to respect the word of an expert. Those who hear asylum cases are no exception. In the initial hearing, it is very rare to have experts testify in person. In the UK, the SEF is filled out within a few days of the initial interview to determine eligibility for benefits, so there is less chance that someone will be able to provide either documents or expert support for their claim in such a short time. As one lawyer we interviewed said: "They rarely have documents with them, and it is almost impossible to get expert evidence or country information, so they get denied" (Yeo, 2004a). In the US, where there is no hearing for benefits because there are no benefits, an applicant has a year after arrival to complete the form. If the applicant finds her way to a lawyer during that time, it is possible that the application may include a letter from an expert in the written material attached to the application form.

In the last chapter, we described the case of Dieudonne, who escaped from the Democratic Republic of the Congo, and who had trouble proving his claim when he first arrived in the US. He had a powerful story of persecution as an ethnic Tutsi, which was supported in general by an expert who wrote a letter on his behalf. The expert, a college professor, attached evidence of his expertise through his scholarly publications, and wrote a letter about the general situation of Tutsis in the DRC. He was careful to clarify his role in this way: "I have been asked by Attorney — to comment specifically on the treatment of ethnic Tutsis in the DRC recently. I have not received a fee for writing this letter, and I cannot comment on [Dieudonne's] case in particular." He then discussed the situation in the DRC for several paragraphs and concluded as follows:

> It is my expert opinion that should Dieudonne go back to the Democratic Republic of Congo, he would be in immediate physical danger. The DRC is in the throes of a civil war. The violent conflicts have taken on an ethnic dimension, where Tutsi such as Dieudonne are subject to persecution by virtue of their ethnicity.

This sort of evidence seems to be very helpful in corroborating the general part of an applicant's story. In this case the expert was able to argue that the very fact that Dieudonne was Tutsi was evidence in support of his fear of persecution, even though he did not know him personally. Usually the expert doesn't know, or know of, the person who is claiming asylum. Dev was an exception, as we saw above, and some of his documents came from people working professionally in Nepal. As is the case so often, the authorities in the UK are skeptical about the use of experts. We were told of one well-respected expert who prepared a report for a son claiming asylum, but the court held that it couldn't rely upon it for a claim by the mother (Ahluwalia, 2005b).

The big problem with experts in the US is expense. Many lawyers we interviewed made it clear that their clients could not afford the several thousand dollars in fees charged by some experts. It is an art to be able to find experts who are willing at least to write a letter, as did Dieudonne's expert, without charging a fee; in the case of a court appearance, it is more difficult to find someone good who is willing to testify for nothing. In the UK, there is some money available for experts in cases approved by the Legal Services Commission (LSC), so it is easier to use them, though often there are delays in finding someone who will provide the expertise for the limited amount available from the LSC (Ahluwalia, 2005b).

When it is possible, lawyers may use both evidence from associates or relatives and from experts. Fatima, an Iranian woman, fell in love with a Pakistani journalist and got pregnant. Her brother and her father threatened to kill her by stoning. She fled to the Emirates, where she had another, more sympathetic, brother who sent her to the US to a friend. In her asylum claim, her lawyer used a letter from the brother in the Emirates, written to the friend in the US, which Fatima had brought with her. In it, the brother said that she'd be killed if she went back to Iran. The lawyer also got an Imam to write a letter simply stating the law, which says that she could be killed for being unmarried and getting pregnant. The Imam was a rather unusual kind of expert, but he was in a unique position to provide essential information supporting Fatima's claim.

One asylum lawyer told us experts were often crucial:

> One judge, who doesn't like giving asylum, he makes up his mind pretty much in advance, won't listen to anyone (me included) but listens to experts. "Mr. —, is it plausible that extremists in Pakistan would do such a thing?" [The expert says] "I think it is totally crazy, but they do it all the time." [And] if I start out with the judge saying, "I believe him, but he's from Mexico . . . " [I say] "Let us finish . . . " [the judge says] "No, he's from Mexico . . . " [I say] "Will you listen to my expert?" *Then* I got asylum (the guy had been in the military). The expert said: "If he goes back, they will kill him."

> (Greenberger, 2002)

Medical experts can provide essential corroboration for asylum seekers. If someone has been tortured, there are generally scars. A doctor can make it clear that such scars fit the story of what happened. As one lawyer in London said:

> It is important to get it documented. The Home Office has a culture of disbelief; it is shifted if they have a way of showing scars etc. Lay people don't know enough to know why. How would we know it was not an appendix scar? Some things don't come about any other way; there is no other reason for various forms of felacca on your feet, or cigarette burns. The Home Office can hardly assess if you've had torture on your private parts.

> (Grewall, 2005)

Our observations in the appeal tribunal in London illustrate the problems of medical evidence. On several occasions the applicant was asked why he did not have medical evidence to support the claim, in circumstances where it would be unreasonable for a person to have it. The authorities (particularly in the UK) may not believe the medical evidence, but its absence may be seen negatively. For example, Wei, a Chinese asylum seeker, whose claim rested on her persecution for practicing Falun Gong, was asked why she could not provide medical evidence to support her claim that her husband had been tortured by the authorities to such an extent that he couldn't walk. In his submissions to the judge, the Home Officer representative said: "There are no documents whether the husband is imprisoned for five years, none about the medical conditions. He has been to the hospital, doctors have been to the house, there is no written evidence." This is another example of culturally based assumptions: that a person who goes to a doctor or hospital in China will have written evidence as they would if they had gone in the UK.

Even if the torture has not left direct scars, a doctor can say an applicant's current health problem is likely to be related to earlier abusive treatment (Good, 2004: 358). The other area in which medical testimony can corroborate a claim is in evidence about Post-Traumatic Stress Disorder (PTSD), a psychological condition suffered by many victims of persecution. Often a description of the PTSD symptoms suffered by an asylum applicant supports their story that they did suffer persecution. For example, Teinzin, whose story we told in Chapter 3, suffered mental health problems. We decided to get a psychological report detailing his PTSD to strengthen his case, both to support his claim of having been beaten by the Chinese police, and also to support his explanation of why he couldn't apply for asylum earlier.

One therapist who works with survivors of torture, described her role as an expert for a woman with PTSD who received sympathetic treatment in court.

> She was in the top ten of 500 cases I have had in terms of psychological consequences . . . She has flashbacks, dissociates . . . The lawyer and I worked together; we had to teach her techniques to keep her grounded. The lawyer met with the judge before; she [the

applicant] didn't have to testify, I testified at length, the judge even left the room at one point [to make it easier for the applicant], the judge allowed her to casually answer questions to convince the attorney for the USCIS. We had the client waiting in the other room, she wouldn't have been able to tolerate staying in the room, she was terrified of men, especially black men – the judge was an African American. We were very concerned about her chances in court, because she was not able to be an effective witness. I had to explain how her memory had been affected by the torture experiences – she had dissociated during the experience – how the impact on her memory could complicate her ability to remember some of the details (which were important to the USCIS), give a coherent account. There has been so much research in the area, on traumatic memory versus nontraumatic memory, how the brain works – it is a hot research area. I am able to utilize this as well as my clinical findings.

(Berthold, 2004)

A psychologist who was asked to serve as a witness to an asylum seeker's state of trauma wrote a letter in support of his claim. In it she confirms much of the same kind of account given by the asylum seeker himself, which she uses to illustrate his symptoms of PTSD:

Mr. M's discussion of his current life situation including the fact that he experiences a depressed mood most of the day, every day, accompanied by markedly diminished interest in almost all activities, such as dating, friendship and socializing. He notes a decrease in his appetite – for example, at the end of the day he will wonder, 'Did I eat today?' He experiences daily insomnia, going to bed at 10 or 11pm, but not falling asleep until 3 or 4am, then, waking up suddenly at 7 or 8am . . . He feels like he never sleeps. He reports a loss of energy during the days . . . He is experiencing intense survivor guilt, guilt that he's alive and his family is dead, and feels that he should be doing more with his life as the only one left, yet he feels paralyzed by his current situation and symptomatology. This is beyond a simple grief reaction. He is experiencing a diminished ability to concentrate, which causes clinically significant distress and impairment in his social and educational functioning. Mr. M is experiencing regular, recurrent and intrusive distressing recollections of the traumatic events he experienced during the war in his country, including images, thoughts and perceptions of events and scenes he saw and experienced. He experiences recurrent distressing, vivid dreams and nightmares of the events as well as regular fearfulness that he is about to be violently attacked.

(Burstein, 2004)

Medical testimony can be very powerful corroboration; it is not, however, a guarantee of success. The authorities may claim that the injuries could have been caused in some other way, despite the doctor's report. The Asylum Aid (1999) report gives examples of circumstances when even the strongest testimony by the most respected medical experts has been ignored or not believed by the Home Office in the UK. For example, in a Kurdish case where the medical evidence of injuries and scars was accepted the refusal letter stated: "*the [medical] report does not state that any of these injuries could be solely attributable to torture or mistreatment which means that they could have been caused by any number of other ways.*" Similarly, a West African whose beatings in detention had necessitated four months' hospital treatment was told by the Home Office that his injuries "*could have occurred in another way*". The special adjudicator, however, agreed with the examining doctor in finding that, "*the multiple injuries to his legs, resulting in scars in the same place meant that he was injured again and again in the same place which is totally consistent with the Appellant's claims that he was beaten and tortured*" (Asylum Aid, 1999: 21).

In another example, the doctor was discredited, even though he was a member of one of the most respected organizations in this area in Britain, the Medical Foundation.

"*He [the Secretary of State] also notes that Dr — appears to have no experience with Turkish asylum seekers and states 'descriptions of conditions in Turkish Gendarme stations given to me by other asylum seekers,' his knowledge is therefore based on hearsay.*" Only the Home Office could argue in the same breath that a doctor had "no experience with Turkish asylum seekers" and that this same doctor had received descriptions of detention in Turkey from other asylum seekers. As to the hearsay argument, if this is the case, then all evidence provided by a patient to his or her doctor is hearsay.

(Asylum Aid, 1999: 20)

It is important to remember that this is all taking place in an environment where strict legal rules (like the ban on hearsay evidence) are not required. The Home Office often claims that the psychiatrist did not spend long enough with a patient to be able to write a convincing report, though usually they spend what is considered in the profession an appropriate amount of time. It is unfortunate that one medical expert was recently found to have provided a report on a patient he had not seen, the kind of bad judgment which gives the Home Office support for its skepticism of all medical experts (Ahluwalia, 2005b). This denial of expert witness testimony is astonishing considering the fact that the asylum officials make their own assessments based on hearsay and a "sense" of whether someone is lying or telling the truth.

The need to find that the whole claim is made up can outweigh the medical evidence, as was the case in another example from the Asylum Aid report:

A 24-year-old Iranian was arrested for protesting about the execution of his brother. He was held for six months, tortured continuously and released when it became clear he had no connection with his brother's activities, and then only on payment of a bribe by his father and on signing an undertaking not to participate in political activity. The fact that he had a report from the Medical Foundation detailing signs of injuries entirely consistent with his story did not deter the Home Office from its assertion that he made it all up.

The Secretary of State took into account the medical report . . . However, he is not satisfied that this provides evidence in itself for recognition as a refugee under the 1951 Convention and the 1967 protocol relating to the Status of Refugees. Furthermore, given the view taken of your claim, the fears described in the report are not considered to be well-founded.

(Asylum Aid, 1999: 21)

The authorities clearly fear that once they accept medical evidence, they have to recognize that the claimant is telling the truth. The authorities differentiate between medical evidence about past events and medical evidence about future needs for treatment (Barnes, 2004: 354-5). Many judges seem to decide whether the story is true based on what they see as inconsistencies and implausibility, and then decide that the medical evidence is not therefore to be relied on, a process one judge described as "putting the cart before the horse" (*R (on the application of Virjon B)* v. *SSHD*, 2002).

Country reports

Paper documentation connects the narrative as presented by the asylum seeker with what is going on in the applicant's homeland, through the use of country condition reports. Both the lawyers who prepare cases and the officials who judge them rely heavily on reports from various sources. The major sources are the US State Department Country Condition reports (which are relied on by people both in the US and the UK, and even in Italy), the CIPU reports (put out twice a year by the Country Information and Policy Unit of the Home Office for 35 asylum-producing countries), Amnesty International country reports, Human Rights Watch, and sometimes other more specific reports. All these reports have the benefit that they are accepted as legitimate by the officers and judges who hear the applications. Their use is limited by the fact that they are not, with the exception of the CIPU, written for the sole purpose of supporting asylum claims, so sometimes they don't have the necessary information. Sometimes, a country hasn't been evaluated during the relevant time. They are also unlikely to help except in generally supporting specific claims, because, as we have seen, the asylum seeker himself is not usually mentioned in the report. Of course, not being included in a country condition report does not mean that the person's story is untrue. In fact, as the Amnesty report points out about the situation in Iran:

Political activists who are 'low-level' in the sense of having no national or international profile, may be at an increased risk of torture or ill-treatment in detention, because the details of their treatment are less likely to become publicly known.

(2004: 19)

Recently, in the UK, the government has been putting out what are known as Country Guidelines, available to lawyers on the website of the Immigration Appeal Authority. They are:

. . . [a] new system of factual precedents – if the tribunal does a thorough job on a particular issue, they notify the NGO in advance, take information from lawyers, and then do a factual precedent. It is quite dangerous; you can't appeal, and then everyone is stuck.

(Yeo, 2005)

So if an issue has already been addressed by the tribunal, lawyers are expected to use the guidelines and explain why they believe that, in the current case, the Country Guidelines case should not be followed. The Immigration Authority considers these guidelines to be binding on subsequent cases, despite the caution with which some of them have been greeted by the Court of Appeals (Yeo, n.d.: 15). The Country Guidelines have the benefit for the authorities of facilitating evaluation of later cases from the same country, and if they are good, they can be useful for everyone. They have been criticized, however, as being sometimes out of date, relying on unsourced, incorrect, or inappropriate evidence, or describing a situation as more certain than it really is (Yeo, n.d).

Lawyers in the US believe that the State Department reports are sometimes unduly kind to friendly or allied regimes, which means that they don't report the human rights abuses that are claimed by the applicant. Similarly, concern about the validity of the CIPU in the UK was so great that the Immigration Advisory Service did a study of the reports (Yeo, n.d.). They found that the CIPU used information selectively and out of context, without sources in some cases, and that they painted an inaccurately positive picture of human rights situations in countries where serious violations are taking place. Despite these difficulties, reports are an invaluable source of third party corroboration of the asylum seeker's story, especially in the post REAL ID world in cases where no other paper is available.

Consistency

The devil is in the details: checking and rechecking "facts"

One of the hallmarks of the US and UK legal systems is that a story, to be credible, must be consistent. Many a criminal has been convicted because his story was not consistent. Either he told it differently on different occasions, or the details he gave did not match details available from other sources (Becker, 1997: 180; Einolf, 2001: 150; LaCapra, 2001: 66). Likewise, a rape case often results in an acquittal because the victim told her story differently on the several occasions on which she was questioned. Legal authorities assume that normal people with normal memories can remember details consistently, and that, if the details they give differ, they are lying. Because this belief is so firmly entrenched, much of the asylum hearing, both in the US and the UK, involves checking and rechecking the story for consistency. This focus exists despite research which has long shown that retold stories change with each retelling (Cohen, 2002: 298).

Einolf refers to an interview with a Judge Gossart who talked about evaluating credibility:

> . . . particularly in cases where no documentary evidence is available to support a claim. "A person can be a truthful witness, or an untruthful witness who's very good at being untruthful. For example, I can tell you a story. And if I tell you a story that makes sense, and I tell it in a very convincing fashion, because I'm good at that, I can make a successful claim of asylum. So there's a lot of things that come into play."

> (Einolf, 2001: 162)

This judge places emphasis on consistency as one of the most important things to examine.

He examines both the consistency between the applicant's oral testimony and written statement, and the consistency between the applicant's testimony on direct questioning and cross examination. He listens carefully to an applicant's explanation of perceived inconsistencies in testimony. "If the person can readily give an answer as to the inconsistency and explain it in a plausible way, that certainly enhances someone's credibility. But if they change their testimony, if they vacillate, if they act unsure, or they just avoid the question with vagaries, well, that's going to call into question their credibility."

(Einolf, 2000: 163)

Not all judges are as careful as the one quoted above. In one case, the judge himself confused the deaths of the applicant's father and husband, both of whom had died in Latvia as a result of anti-Semitic violence, and then used his mistake as evidence that the applicant's account was inconsistent (Bernstein, 2006).

The checking and rechecking of facts is based on the assumption that truth telling is connected to remembering information, including numbers and dates, clearly and consistently, a questionable assumption even in the case of those who have not had to flee persecution. Research has shown that the memory for details like dates and times is notoriously unreliable (Caruth, 1995: 8; Einolf, 2001: 150; McIntyre and Craik, 1987). In Wei's appeal, much was made of whether she began practicing Falun Gong at the beginning or the end of April 2005. She was asked in court when she began to practice and she replied the end of April. After checking whether she was sure, the Home Office representative told her that, in her witness statement, she had said it was early April, a difference which the Home Office representative called a "key discrepancy" in his final submissions to the court, despite the fact that it was hardly central to her claim and there was some evidence that this was a translation problem. Another example of problems with details is seen in the film *Well-Founded Fear*, in which the applicant is asked how many people were in the car in which he was abducted. He gives the number (without including the driver), but the officer assumes he is lying, because elsewhere the number had included the driver (Robertson and Camerini, 2000).

Sometimes applicants are caught out because they express themselves differently than their questioners. One telling example is given in the Amnesty International report as follows, quoting from a refusal letter:

> The Secretary of State notes that there are significant differences between your various accounts, and that these cast doubt on the credibility of your claim. In your statement you claimed that your husband had kept the documents about [organization] in the house. However when you were interviewed on [date] September 2002, when asked about the documents, you claimed that your husband had hidden the documents in the back yard.

The report comments: "It is clear that references to a person's house could include the back yard" (Amnesty International, 2004: 20).

One US lawyer told us about the ways in which the authorities use language as a way to trip up applicants:

> Asylum officers try to use their knowledge against someone – they might use a slang term that is not always used. I had a client, a Sierra Leonean, the claim was based on nationality . . . This officer thought she could test credibility, that she knew about stuff. He was a very light-skinned Lebanese who was born and raised in Sierra Leone, a Christian. The officer used his Christianity . . . "You should know the name of the school." He said it was called "Roman Catholic School." She said, "No, they have names, like St Augustine." We had to go to the Internet to show that it was really called Roman Catholic School. She said, "If you're Catholic, you must be going to church here, you need a certificate from the pastor that you have been attending." The officer is trying to show he is not credible, because she didn't want to give him asylum, based on views which were both inaccurate and intrusive.
> (McHaffey, 2005)

In the UK, in particular, checking for discrepancies seems to be part of the effort to limit the number of successful applicants by discrediting as many as possible, rather than to determine credibility. For that reason, hearings focus extensively on details. Below is a transcript from an appeal hearing in London, which provides an illustration of this process of checking for detail. *HO* is the Home Office representative, *AP* is the applicant.

HO: About these detentions, in question 16 of your interview you said you were detained in 1994, but according to your statement, it was 1998.

AP: I don't remember what I said in the interview.

HO: My friend [the applicant's lawyer] asked you to explain if the first detention was in '94.

AP: Yes, it was 2–3 hours.

HO: The question was then repeated in another way and you said: "I didn't regard it as a detention, it was only a couple of hours."

AP: Yes, that's why I didn't mention it.

HO: Where do you draw the line about detention.

AP: I suppose I am concerned about at least a day.

HO: According to your statement all your detentions happened after you'd done your military service?

AP: Yes, but I don't count the ones only for a few hours.

HO: In your interview, q. 17, the occasion in '98, you claim you were one of 16 detained. Do you remember that?

AP: What year is that?

HO: 1998.

AP: We were 9–10 people, I don't remember.

HO: You give the date as 21 March, possibly following Navros.

AP: Yes, we were on our way back from Navros, I was driving a lorry.

HO: You were asked how many people were detained with you, and you said 16.

AP: I don't remember that . . .

HO: In your statement, q. B7 you said everyone else at C was released, I was taken to C . . .

AP: Yes, my village station.

HO: Yet in C 17 you say you were all released at the same time.

AP: In the interview.

HO: Yes, q. 59. Were the 16 all released with you? You said all of us.

AP: I don't remember.

Here the Home Office representative is clearly engaged in trying to prove that the applicant's story is a fabrication by questioning the number of times the applicant was detained, the dates of his detentions, the number of people who were with him. The applicant is trying, for his part, to explain away the discrepancies in the story which he has told on two different occasions.

   This transcript is a classic example of the kind of questions asked of asylum seekers, and is based on the (invalid) assumption that, for a story to be true, it must be told the same way each time. Many people, especially those who have suffered trauma, remember things somewhat differently each time (Herlihy *et al.*, 2002). The assumption that someone will be able to remember all the addresses where he lived during a time when he was of necessity moving around a lot, as Dev was asked to do, is not even a cultural construct, but a matter of the extent of memory. As we saw in Chapter 2, the level of detail expected of an applicant is more than anyone could reasonably be expected to remember. The Asylum Aid report puts it this way:

   The more traumatic (or "genuine") the asylum-seeker's experiences, the less he or she is likely to have all the details neatly arranged, ready for interrogation. Yet men and women who have seen their family killed, who have been detained, or lived for months in hiding, are expected to arrive in Britain with the perfect recall that many people cannot achieve with all the props of a modern office. The Home Office's obsession with dates remains as unforgiving as it was when Asylum Aid produced the first *No Reason at All*. Since then, asylum-seekers have continued to be asked to exhibit feats of memory that would normally demand a scrupulously maintained diary. Whatever they say in their initial interview will dog them throughout the whole process and they will be cross-questioned at the appeal stage often many years after the events they are asked to recall.

(1999: 29–30)

It is also possible to argue that the absence of minor discrepancies is an indication of lying, rather than the reverse. Speaking of the Home Office, the Amnesty report says:

> . . . they ignore the wealth of objective information which shows that minor discrepancies in the accounts given by asylum seekers are to be expected, and in some cases actually support the view that an applicant is telling the truth about his or her experiences.
> (2004: 29)

Another aspect of the credibility determination is what the person does *not* reveal. For many asylum seekers, some things are just too terrible to describe, at least in the early stages. One of the characteristics of Post-Traumatic Stress Disorder, a psychiatric condition which affects a significant percentage of asylum seekers, is impaired memory and inability to concentrate (Cohen, 2002). People, especially those suffering from PTSD frequently remember more as time goes by (Cohen, 2002). As one lawyer put it: "With PTSD people rearrange things in their minds, have difficulty remembering" (McHaffey, 2005). For them, the authorities question is, "Why didn't you talk about this sooner, if it is so important to your claim?" But they couldn't have talked about it any sooner as they only just remembered it. In fact, the expectations of consistency and providing accurate details may be more than even a person familiar with the Western legal system could manage, let alone an applicant from a very different culture who may be suffering from PTSD with its characteristic memory lapses.

In addition to the problems of PTSD, asylum seekers may simply not know what is important. One US lawyer told us:

> No matter how well you prepare your client, there are always surprises . . . They leave out incredibly relevant facts . . . It comes up that the guy's sister was gang raped. "Why did you never tell me?" "It wasn't about me."
> (London, 2003)

It is just those "surprises" which make the story harder for the authorities to believe. The following case we observed of a Kurdish applicant in London shows the ways the authorities will pick on information the person failed to mention as evidence that they are lying: Here, again, *HO* is the representative for the Home Office and *AP* is the applicant:

HO: In paragraph 7 of your statement, you thought your father had been involved with an organization but you didn't know which organization, is that correct?

AP: Yes.

HO: In your interview you thought your father had been involved in Haddad. How did you find that out?

AP: From my uncle.

HO: The one you stayed with in Turkey?

AP: Yes.

HO: If you knew that then, while you were staying in Turkey, why did you not include it in your statement?

AP: I don't understand.

HO: You said you found out while staying in Turkey that you found out that your father was something to do with Haddad.

AP: He didn't tell me that directly. They were talking.

HO: You heard it then, why did you not include it in your statement?

AP: I couldn't think at the time because of my age.

Here the applicant is forced to come up with a reasonable explanation of why he did not initially mention his father's political involvement. There are many perfectly understandable reasons why he did not do so, but the Home Office representative is arguing that the only explanation is that his case is a fabrication. One of the lawyers we interviewed in London pointed out that an asylum seeker might simply have more information at the later hearing. "[He said] 'I don't know how much the agent charged my father,' then later he says the agent charges £5,000 – they were asked by the solicitor to find out in the meantime" (Ahluwalia, 2004).

For Fauziya, describing FGM (and anything sexual) was so difficult that, as we saw, she did not mention it in her initial contacts with the authorities. She is not alone in her reluctance to talk. Many women seeking asylum have been persecuted because they are women, and have suffered such horrors as FGM, rape, domestic violence, sexual slavery, forced marriage, forced sterilization, or fears of honor killings. They feel personal shame about their experiences and may have already suffered social stigma as a result of what has happened to them. So for them to talk freely about their experiences is very difficult and, for many, simply impossible. Not being able to talk about a traumatic experience is, in fact, one of the hallmarks of PTSD. One therapist said that she is sometimes the first person to whom a woman who had been tortured spoke about a rape or other sexual abuse, and that may occur only after a number of sessions. She tells the story of a client who was gang raped on several occasions, but never included that information in her application, nor in her initial interview. In court she finally talked about it. When asked "Why now?" she said that if her family found out, especially her husband, she would have to kill herself (Berthold, 2003).

The unwillingness of women to talk about their sexual persecution may be exacerbated when the interviewer is a male stranger, perhaps accompanied by a male interpreter. The woman fears that the interpreter, who may come from her homeland, will reveal her "shameful" secrets to her community, or, worse, her family, who do not about it. The Lawyers Committee for Human Rights describe the case of Jane Doe who:

> . . . fled Albania after being gang-raped by masked, armed men. She arrived at the Boston airport in May 1997 with invalid travel documents and she was put into expedited removal. Traumatized by her recent experiences and unassisted by counsel, Jane was too ashamed and afraid to explain to a male Albanian interpreter – provided by the INS – what had happened to her. Without even being allowed to apply for asylum, Jane was deported under expedited removal.
>
> (2002: 6)

She was not even given the chance to explain why she was seeking asylum. It was not until her case was picked up by the *New York Times* that she was finally allowed to apply for asylum. She was one of the lucky ones.

Many applications are refused because someone who failed to mention something early on brings it up later in the process. In the UK, new details provide the impetus for denying a claim on the grounds that it is not credible.

> The Secretary of State notes that during interview you failed to mention rape. The Secretary of State also believes that it would be reasonable to expect that you would have mentioned this at the earliest opportunity. Furthermore the Secretary of State concludes that the fact that you did not undermines the veracity of your claim.
>
> (Amnesty International, 2004: 36)

The fact that someone did not mention something, especially of a sexual nature, may be a result of inadequate interviewing. The Asylum Aid report describes the situation in this way:

> The most common complaint, by men as well as women, is that they never got a chance to tell the full story (at the initial interview). In answer to the accusation that they did not divulge a relevant piece of information during the interview, the answer is: *"but he never asked."*
>
> (1999: 65)

Marthe, the Cameroonian woman whose hearing we excerpted in Chapter 2, was asked why she didn't mention that her escape had been announced on the radio in her initial statement. She replied, rather perceptively: "When you are giving a statement through questions, sometimes details can go unnoticed and you don't dwell on them."

Some of the problems with discrepancies are caused by bad translators. This is a bigger problem in the US, where finding translators is a more haphazard process than it is in the UK. Applicants in the US bring their own translators to the asylum hearing, and their skills can vary a great deal. In the UK, the court provides translators and there is a more organized system for certifying them. Our experience as observers in many asylum appeals in London showed that the system works pretty well. For example, an Arabic-speaker will be assigned an interpreter who speaks the same kind of Arabic. Judges are also usually quite careful, for example, checking to make sure the translator and the applicant can understand each other.

This is not the case in the US, where the onus is on the applicant or her lawyer to provide a suitable interpreter. One lawyer said:

> I hate translators – you have to use them sometimes. I'd never want to go in cold with a translator at the interview because you are asking for trouble. People get referred [to the Immigration Court] because the interpreter didn't translate something properly. For example, I had someone who was Cambodian, I had a translator who was Cambodian-American who didn't know the legal language, didn't know slang. The officer was from somewhere else and had a thick accent. The case got referred because no one understood each other. At court I had a much better interpreter and I told the judge about this and he won.
>
> (McHaffey, 2005)

Anker's study of the asylum process in the US found that the use of bad translators led to misunderstandings that affected the outcome of the case because they made the applicant look as if he was lying. In one case, the interpreter said that the applicant was "released" from his job, but he had said that he was "fired," while in another the interpreter said that the applicant's "uncle" had been killed when she had actually said "grandfather." The translator later used the word "grandfather" and the judge used the interpreter's error as evidence of the applicant's lack of credibility (Anker, 1992: 511–12).

Translation problems are connected to cultural differences. One of the lawyers we interviewed said:

> It is surprising how messed up it will be, if you go through a translator – the assumption that language translate exactly, and it doesn't. One of the biggest things, not so much language difficulty as cultural differences embedded into language. [For example people] use Ford to mean automobile . . . an American thinks of Ford . . . a certain history . . . may not be important to a Chinese. Americans may base a decision on [the] basis of cultural baggage.
>
> (Quinn, 2002b)

Translators also help cases of course, not only by directly translating the language but sometimes, as Susan Berk-Seligson reports, by translating the applicant's responses into a more formal (and therefore more credible) register (1989: 89).

The different ways people identify relatives is an example of both a linguistic and cultural problem. Many other cultures have different systems for identifying family members, as well as different ways of assessing family connections and obligations. For example, someone might be called a brother, when in our system, he would be a cousin. For many Somalis, whose families were decimated in the war, children have been taken in by relatives and raised as family members. Such children might be technically nieces or cousins of their "parents" but they are called son or daughter. Dev shows a sophisticated awareness of these differences when he said in a supplemental statement: "I hid myself in my mother's cousin's house (culturally, I refer to him as my uncle) for about three months." Most people don't explain the differences as Dev did and as a result may look as if they are lying when they describe their relatives "incorrectly."

Chronology

Many asylum officials expect stories to be told in chronological order, but, for some cultural groups, narrative does not work that way. Assumptions about chronology can be another source of misunderstanding in the asylum process. One experienced UK asylum lawyer said: "Getting a sequential story, from the average person, I have no trouble. 10 percent don't understand the concept. I also got a theory . . . that people from the former Commonwealth – they think the British Government knows it anyway" (Grewall, 2004).

Kot (1988) describes what she calls "powerless speech," which she argues Central American refugees used in the asylum hearings she examined. This speech is hesitant, insecure and vague and may be interpreted by the authorities as untruthful (1988: 8–9). At his asylum hearing, Mustapha provided a rambling account of his life in Sierra Leone during the time the rebels were fighting there. The officer kept asking him questions like "What happened then? Was that before you went to Freetown? How long were you in the hands of the rebels?" At one point, she looked to Carol for help, but she couldn't enlighten the officer, as she had had exactly the same problems with the sequence of events. Even after several interviews with Mustapha, we were never able to clarify his story. We kept asking him questions about what happened when, which he simply didn't answer. Clearly, he didn't think that way.

The Home Office apparently has the same experience with other Sierra Leoneans. One officer told us:

> Some people have no idea whatever, can't respond to specific questions, you have to ask it in various ways. I had a Sierra Leonean, he had been abducted by the rebels. How long were you with them? How many seasons were you with them? Why are you asking me about seasons? He said he didn't know what a year was. He had previously said that something took a year and two months . . . just give me an indication. Some cultures don't deal with dates, but could pinpoint something else, tie it in with something else – if they went to school when it was.
>
> (Avery, 2004)

It appears that the officer actually thought the applicant was lying, checking for what she viewed as inconsistencies, despite her perception that the inability to tell a chronological story is a cultural failing.

One attorney gave this example of the problems with chronology and her techniques for dealing with it:

> Afghan clients are often not educated, [one] knew nothing about the Western calendar, it's very hard to get accurate dates, doing the affidavit. The worst thing I could do [was to get dates that were inaccurate] because the officer will use it to impeach his evidence. I had one guy, with a poor memory, no dates. I don't put dates, don't put in an affidavit and the officer said how can I follow the client if I don't have dates – the person went to the supervisor who said you have to do it [interview him]. [I] don't want to give reasons for them to impeach his evidence.
>
> (Greenberger, 2002)

One British adjudicator said she took the problem of those nationalities which do not think in chronological terms into account. She said: "Some people are not familiar with dates, so we do seasons. How many wet seasons, how many dry? Especially those with different calendars, like the Ethiopians, it makes it quite difficult – we record their calendar dates and our calendar dates" (Avery, 2004). Whether this technique results in a "Western" version of events is another question. Even when a group does not have particular problems with chronology, there can be misunderstandings about dates. In our observations of UK asylum appeals, dates were often discussed in the Iranian cases, caused by differences in the way dates are calculated in Iran and the need to transpose them into dates in the Western calendar, while simultaneously translating from Farsi to English.

Presentation: do you behave like someone telling the truth?

Another way the authorities decide if a story is "true" is by judging the way the tellers present themselves. This is called demeanor in the law, and it is supposed to be a significant indication of credibility. Judges pride themselves on being able to tell whether someone is lying by watching how they behave when being questioned. Immigration judges in the UK who were questioned about what factors they considered important in determining credibility said that they considered demeanor significant, and even in a couple of respondents, determinative (Jarvis, 2003: 9). The problem is that assessments of whether someone is lying are notoriously unreliable, even when the teller is from the same culture as the listener. They are also based on cultural notions of appropriate self-presentation. We assume that an honest person is more likely to look someone in the eye when telling their story. In other cultures, looking someone is the eye is considered rude, especially if the person is someone in authority.

One lawyer we interviewed in London had a clear view of the difficulties of relying on demeanor:

> . . . [it is] not supposed to be the reason you refuse. Adjudicators are more aware of cultural things – eye contact, not answering

questions directly. You think you know they're [applicants are] telling the truth. Showing respect – they [adjudicators] now know different people do it in different ways; just because they [applicants] are not looking at you, [it's] not that they're not showing respect. Someone looks shifty, when someone is giving evidence you'd expect them to act in a certain way, either forcefully, with weight of anger [at their treatment] behind them, or be demure or upset emotionally. With interpreters it makes it doubly difficult: you're not hearing the person, you're hearing people in a language they don't understand. We understand people by their choice of words, language . . . if you don't have it you could be relying on the voice of the interpreter, the words used. It is doubly difficult to make judgments – the interpreter comes across as a bit shifty, you translate that to the person. Showing emotion – it depends on what the decision maker is expecting to see; there is the danger of going overboard – if someone is overly emotional the adjudicator thinks it is overkill, beyond that it's forced, there for show. Could be a cultural, gender thing. It is very stressful in court, so much is at stake you are not 100 percent sure about what is going on – could work both ways – overly keen to please, or merely aggressive, or too restrained. You look quite happy – you look fine, if you haven't been persecuted enough.

(Nolan, 2004)

Clearly, even when the authorities know about the cultural differences in demeanor, they still use Western ideas of appropriate self-presentation to judge credibility, and are expressly permitted to do so in the US under the REAL ID Act.

The connection between demeanor and "truth" is tellingly illustrated in this report from a US lawyer:

I always tell my clients the story of my two Salvadoran clients that were caught together but were on opposite sides of the political fence. One had a great case [his father was murdered] and was on the side of the guerrillas. The other had family in the military and had a terrible case. The one that had the horrible case was a great witness. He answered the questions without hesitation, he always looked the person asking the questions in the eye and he did not fidget. He sat upright and answered with sincerity. The judge liked him. Even though he lost, the judge found him credible. The other client slumped in his seat and just looked at his hands. He kept twisting his fingers and never looked anybody in the eye. He should have won, and I had a great expert witness, but he lost. In other words, demeanor is the "key to credibility."

(Hurwitz, 2002)

Some officers and judges say they have learned to take into account these cultural differences. In an interview, an asylum adjudicator in the Home Office in Britain described the process of determining whether someone is telling the truth as follows:

Part of it is common sense, part comes with experience, part comes from the demeanor. You have to be very careful with that, certain nationalities have different demeanor – some cultures don't make eye contact, either generally or with women. You can't always use that – your initial instinct – this person is very shifty. If they have a fear of persecution, they have a fear of authority – we are authority. It can be quite an intimidating process.

(Dunford, 2004)

The problem with the use of common sense, a very highly valued attribute among judges, is that it, too, is based on cultural assumptions (Kot, 1988).

How something is said is closely related to what is said. One US attorney tells his clients how best to present their story (both content and presentation) so as to have maximum effect for the officer or judge:

I explain what refugee means; whatever they ask, say "I am afraid to go back," stress fear. I tell them, never volunteer anything except maltreatment suffered by you and your family. If you do it say it in a way the judge will feel it. "They hit me," say what part of the body was affected, what they hit you with, how that affected you emotionally and physically, then and are there remnants of that now . . . "I have nightmares . . . backaches."

(Greenberger, 2002)

It is another way in which lawyers need to "educate" the applicant in the expressing of "suitable" (i.e. acceptable to Western ideas) emotion when describing the story. Telling it "too calmly" will be bad for the claimant in the interview because the interviewer will be less likely to believe an account that is not accompanied by "suitable" expression of the trauma being described. As one attorney put it:

> Clients are stoic. I tell them this is not the time to be stoic; this is the time to show emotion. I had a client who made a joke of everything, he used to laugh all the time, this is how he handles stress . . . and this doesn't work [in court]. He was so grim-faced after I told him not to make a joke of everything.
>
> (Quinn, 2002a)

On the other hand, telling the story with "too much" emotion will also have a negative impact because the interviewer may dismiss the claimant as simply hysterical. Some asylum applicants use language that is very dramatic and therefore "unsuitable" for our legal system. For example, one person wrote in her application: "I don't want to live in fear any more so I'm begging you to please grant me asylum so I can live in peace once more." Another said: "with the above claim, I humbly put my fate in you regarding your noble task to consider my request." Dev described how he had forgotten to include an address in the list of the many places he had lived, which was picked up by the asylum officer at his hearing: "It was an accidental mistake. I prayed the immigration officer for forgiveness." This manner of speaking sounds very foreign and insufficiently legal to us, but is normal speech for many contexts, including, in many instances, meetings with authorities and bureaucrats in other cultures, and, possibly, the kind of interrogators faced by victims of persecution. Some applicants make the mistake of using extreme language, which diminishes their credibility. In the hearings we observed in the UK, several asylum seekers used the word "torture" to describe what turned out to be routine minor beatings by the police during a demonstration. Showing the "appropriate" level of emotion is an issue in courts generally, as Conley and O'Barr (1998) have shown in the case of rape trials; as always, in asylum cases, the possibilities for misinterpretation are more extreme because of the cultural differences (Conley

and O'Barr, 1998). Spijkerboer argues that perceptions of emotion also
have racial and gender overtones. In his study of the Dutch system of
asylum, he concludes that "black women are supposed to be more
emotional than white women and that the display of emotion sufficient
for a Bosnian woman is judged as insufficient for a Zairian woman"
(Spijkerboer, 2000: 65).

Demeanor includes also the need to look suitably serious. Attorneys
always tell clients to dress like the stereotype of a librarian when they
come to court. One attorney told us about his client for whom this was
particularly important as she was prone to wearing flamboyant clothing.
He told her to dress in a somber way, perhaps in black and white. She
arrived for the hearing in black and white leopard skin pants, yet
another example of the cultural misunderstandings we see so often in
this area (Quinn, 2002a).

So, is the story plausible?

Administrators and judges include in their definition of credibility a
sense that the event itself must be plausible, so they can believe it.
However, the way they decide a narrative is plausible is very closely
connected to Western ideas of what is likely and what is not. One UK
lawyer we interviewed defined credibility this way:

> Whether it's believable, whether it's believed. The Home Office
> might accept everything they say but not the persecution. The use
> of the term "credible" has been expanded to things the decision
> maker doesn't understand, rather than things that are not credible.
> Most refusals are on the basis of not credible. It is stretched to its
> limits.
>
> (Yeo, 2004a)

Some people who work in the system distinguish between the
applicant's credibility and the plausibility of the account. The same
lawyer told us:

> The distinction I drew was, I think, between plausibility and
> personal credibility. This is one of my legal bugbears – I accept

that adjudicators can dismiss cases on the basis of personal credibility where there are good reasons to doubt someone's account
(an extremely problematic exercise, but a necessary one, I accept)
but I take the view that adjudicators should not, other than in
exceptional cases, start ruminating on what is and is not plausible
in a culture they know nothing about with actors who are not
necessarily rational, as an adjudicator sitting in the UK might
define rationality at least. We regularly see decisions where the
adjudicator has taken a view on plausibility without reference to
country information or anything else. I've seen cases dismissed
because the prosecutors apparently would not have tortured the
person so horribly (forced to drink acid, mouth and throat was
fused together and had been operated on several times in the UK),
they would just have killed them, or because a persecutor would
not use a machete to kill family members because the screams
would be so noisy: shooting them would be quieter and easier.

(Yeo, 2004b)

Einolf also distinguishes plausibility from credibility. He defines
credibility as: "whether it is likely or possible that a series of events
actually happened" (2001: 152). He mentions two officers who have
had previous experience in the Peace Corps. These officers articulate
the nature of their assessment based on this experience. As one lawyer
put it:

. . . and to be able to listen to someone describe something that
another person would think unbelievable, but to know that you've
seen it is worth a lot of weight. Another person, not having had
the opportunity to go down that road, would rely more on a rigid,
legalistic way to deal with it.

(2001: 153)

The problem here is that experience abroad is not a requirement for the
job of asylum officer or judge, so others do not have the experience to
recognize that the unreasonable can be reasonable. The other officer
mentioned by Einolf who had refugee experience said: "We rarely use
plausibility as a ground for referring an asylum claim. They teach us

that in the training. Implausible has to be really implausible, like 'I saw someone six miles away and recognized his face.'" Despite the training of which he speaks, many other judges do indeed use a sense of plausibility as the basis for their decisions, something expressly allowed by the REAL ID Act. This is not to say that there is no place for a judge or officer to assess whether the story is likely; the issue is the extent to which the behavior is culturally connected. Gita, an Iranian woman whose case we observed in London in July 2006, claimed that she had communicated in code with her sister in Iran. Here is an interchange between the immigration judge (*IJ*) and the applicant (*AP*):

IJ: Do you have a computer of your own?
AP: Yes.
IJ :   These messages were sent when?
AP: Until the time she was arrested.
IJ :   Are they still on your computer?
AP: No.
IJ :   Why not?
AP: Because I changed my computer.
IJ :   You don't need to lose messages when you change computers.
AP: I thought this was better.
IJ :   Let's hear about the code. How did you and your sister agree on a code between you?
AP: From the contact we had between each other.
IJ :   But you said, you spoke in coded messages, for example, you talked about going to the boutique If you send a message like that, how does the other person know what it means?
AP: She knew what it meant.
IJ :   How?
AP: Because we are aware of the routine and activity in Iran and the timetable; for example, I knew she was going to meet someone. I would send a message, if she was supposed to meet a person at 7 o'clock, I'd say "Did you go shopping?"

The difficulty here hinges on how participants used, recognized, and learned their secret code. The applicant's response to the question of how the sisters knew what the code meant is insufficient. The applicant explains that they were aware of each other's schedules, but this doesn't answer the judge's question. This story doesn't hang together. Gita claimed she was able to communicate with her sister in code but was unable to explain satisfactorily how she and her sister knew what the code was, or even why she was engaged in this email correspondence, of which there was no external evidence. The judge didn't need to know about the situation in Iran to decide that people can't communicate in code unless they both know the nature of that code.

Stories of the horrors of persecution are by definition implausible; trauma is defined as out of the ordinary and a disruption of everything ordinary. Such descriptions simply do not lend themselves to the kind of cold logical presentation expected by the law. Sometimes what has happened to someone is truly incredible, and so officers may be unwilling to believe that the ghastly story is true because "we don't treat people like that in the 'civilized' world" and they can't imagine how it might be possible in the applicant's homeland. McDonald and Webber, authors of the leading British legal text on immigration put it this way:

> Since it is not in the nature of repressive regimes and societies to behave reasonably, the strange or unusual cannot be dismissed as incredible or improbable . . . and decision-makers should constantly be on their guard to avoid implicitly recharacterising the nature of the risk based on their own perceptions of reasonability.
> (2005: 815)

Far from understanding the circumstances from which asylum seekers come, the Amnesty International report takes the view that the behavior of the authorities in the UK amounts to a kind of second-guessing of the quality of decision making of applicants and their persecutors:

> Where asylum applicants have made decisions or taken actions which diverge from those that the Home Office would consider wise or rational, denials of credibility can be put forward in Refusal letters which have no basis whatever in fact or in law.
> (Amnesty International, 2004: 36)

The situation is less extreme in the US; however, we have come across numerous situations in which the officer or judge has based a decision on her view of what is likely rather than what could have happened in the particular situation of the asylum seeker. This is contrary to the law of asylum. Judges are not supposed to substitute their personal speculations for the facts themselves. The next section will show the ways in which officers and judges do exactly that.

The assumptions of those making judgments

Asylum officers and judges make a variety of assumptions about the narratives they hear to determine whether they are credible: (1) assumptions about the motivations of applicants, (2) assumptions about the behavior and beliefs of the applicants (including the legitimacy of their fears), (3) assumptions about the motivations and behavior of the persecutors, (4) assumptions about appropriate knowledge of applicants, and (5) assumptions about the likelihood and meaning of the help many asylum seekers have received, especially to help them escape (Shuman and Bohmer, 2004). These assumptions are based on officials' ideas of what sort of narratives are plausible, which in turn are based on their cultural values, rather than an understanding of the world of the applicants. As we shall discuss in Chapter 6, the by-product of the asylum process is the reliance on stereotypes and binary oppositions between us/them and civilized/barbaric. Ironically, exotic cases are sometimes more convincing than those reporting more familiar experiences.

Assumptions about the applicants' motivations

Sometimes the authorities deny an application because they don't accept the applicant's reasoning in getting involved in political activity in the first place. This form of "second-guessing" is truly remarkable when one considers the purpose of asylum. One Home Office refusal letter said this: "If you were in genuine fear of the authorities due to your political activities, you would not have continued to associate with people who might bring you to the adverse attention of the authorities" (quoted in Amnesty International, 2004: 22). The report continues as follows:

In countries such as Bhutan with repressive regimes, opposing political activities are always carried out in a climate of fear. Political activists – referred to by the government in Bhutan as "anti-nationals" – continue to face discrimination and danger of arrest, exile or imprisonment . . . Amnesty International is aware that, traumatic as they often are, unjust actions by the authorities of a country can result in a strengthened resolve of individuals who continue to fight the system in place. Also individuals react differently to threats – some shrink, some fail to register the threat, and some are galvanised into action.

(Amnesty International, 2004: 22–3)

The people whose stories we have told, like Dev, Henri, and Tun, all knew perfectly well that they ran a risk by continuing their political activities. They did so because they believed in their causes.

Assumptions about the behavior and beliefs of the applicants.

Marie, from the Democratic Republic of the Congo, applied for asylum in the US. She was a local secretary of a political party who was chosen to go to a conference in South Africa to be a community representative at a time when the Congo wanted to look good, because the government was in the midst of some peace negotiations. She had been previously arrested, raped, and beaten badly. At her asylum hearing, the judge was skeptical about Marie's claim because of her professional situation. She had trained as a nurse in the Congo. A short time later she went to work as a volunteer at a hospital. The judge thought it was implausible that, after her arrest and rape, given also that she was very poor, she would volunteer at the hospital, rather than work for pay. She was indeed impoverished, but she volunteered in the hope that it would lead to a job. At the hospital, she reasoned, she would get training in malaria prevention (which might make her more employable). She would also get free testing and she wanted to have her blood drawn. She believed (!) that if you suffered from high blood pressure, you needed to get your blood drawn. This is an example of a situation in which the applicant made a perfectly reasonable decision, given her position at the time, and taking into account her cultural values and beliefs. The judge apparently wouldn't have made that decision in similar circumstances so he decided it was implausible.

Amir, a young Iranian man whose case we observed in London in May 2006, claimed that he distributed anti-government leaflets and CDs to fellow university students. He said he was caught by the police at a demonstration and they found the material in his bag. The Home Office representative asked Amir: "When you saw that the special forces came and started arresting people, didn't it occur to you that you should have dropped the bag with the incriminating evidence in it?" The representative's question makes sense with hindsight in the comfort of the courtroom but does not take into account Amir's actions in the face of danger.

In the case of Abdul, an Afghan man, the US judge found the story implausible because the applicant had said his brother was in a prison hospital, and he didn't even know the name of the hospital; nor did he go to see his sick brother. In Afghanistan, the name of a hospital is not common knowledge as it is in the US. Since the client's family members were all in jeopardy, it isn't surprising they didn't go and see him. They clearly decided it was more important to protect themselves from persecution than to visit their sick brother, a decision that the brother would no doubt have endorsed, even though the judge did not.

In another case, the judge in California said to a Ukrainian asylum applicant: "You were arrested on trumped up charges, sent to jail for five years, get out, [you're] dealing with a new government . . . you're telling me someone tampered with your car. Why would a vandal do that?" The judge defined it as vandalism, because that is what it would most likely be in the US but it is not the same to a Ukrainian. As his lawyer said: "You read Dostoevsky [and about the] *Gulag* [and] you begin to understand paranoia. What is a reasonable belief? That of a person who has lived in Russia, or a judge who lives across the world?" (Quinn, 2002a). To the Ukrainian, it was perfectly reasonable to assume that tampering with his car was part of the persecution he was suffering in his homeland.

One of the US lawyers we interviewed told us that, in her opinion, the people who faced the greatest skepticism from judges were women who were not believed about actions they took vis-à-vis their children. Judges apparently find it implausible that a woman would leave her child behind when she fled, though this may have been her only hope of getting out. Sometimes, the opposite behavior is considered implausible, such as when a woman takes her children with her, thus subjecting them to risks the judge thinks are too great (London, 2003).

Fatima was raped by the military in a fundamentalist Middle Eastern country. As a result of the rape she gave birth to a child, which, under Sharia law, could result in her death, so she gave birth in private, very quietly. She was part of a music group that played music on political themes. Two weeks after the birth of her child she went to a neighboring country with the music group. The US judge found it implausible that Fatima would travel so soon after she had had a child, even though she did so because she was terrified that the birth would be revealed if she said she couldn't join her group on their trip. To her, the behavior, and the beliefs on which it was based, were perfectly reasonable, though not to the judge.

The UK authorities seem to be particularly narrow-minded in their evaluation of credible behavior toward family members, especially children. In one refusal letter quoted in the Amnesty International report they said:

> You also claimed you had five children. However upon your release from detention you made no attempt to find them before you left the country. You seemed quite happy with the idea that they all got separated. You were quite content to make good with the only child that you claimed was kept by neighbours. Again it is unlikely that the neighbours would keep your child for an entire year after the rest of her family had deserted her and compounded with the fact that you also had an uncle who you were in obvious contact with [sic].

The report points out that:

> This paragraph is laden with subjective judgments. Implicit is a suggestion that the applicant is a "bad" mother, although even if she were proved to be such, that would be irrelevant to her asylum

claim (in fact, three of this applicant's children were adults and not living with her – a fourth child went missing).

(Amnesty International, 2004: 36)

According to British cultural attitudes, the idea that a neighbor would take in a child seemed impossible, even though at that time in Uganda it happened frequently.

Fauziya's court hearing is illustrative of the problems we have with cultures that are very different than our own. She describes her court hearing in her book, telling how the judge took over the questioning at various points of her testimony, firing questions at her about her family and her personal history (Kassindja, 1998: 351–71). Was her oldest sister circumcised? Why not? How had her father prevented that? Where was her mother at the time? Why didn't she prevent her from being circumcised? Why didn't she just say "I'm not going to be circumcised?" The judge couldn't accept that it was possible for her father to prevent her from being circumcised, even though it was a long-standing practice of her tribe, but that she couldn't prevent it herself. The judge also wanted to know why her mother or sisters couldn't protect her.

And how old was I when my aunt pulled me out of school and told me I was going to be married and be circumcised? Seventeen? And she told my mother? My mother was in the house? No, no, she wasn't there. She'd been sent out of the house. So where was she living? I didn't know. I didn't know but my aunt knew? How did my aunt know? So my aunt got together with my mom and told my mother what her plans were for me? Why did she do that? . . . Did my mom have to give her permission? . . .

Later, the judge asked how she avoided circumcision after she was married. "Hadn't I said that no man in my tribe would marry an uncircumcised female? I tried to explain. He cut me off. 'That doesn't make sense.'" Fauziya's lawyer tried to explain that she hadn't yet slept with her husband as she wasn't circumcised. Later, the judge asked her why she had to leave to avoid circumcision. "Had I ever thought of going to the government or the police for protection? They wouldn't have helped me, I said. But did I ask them? They couldn't have helped me, I repeated. But did I ask them? No" (1998: 359). She was asked why she hadn't sought asylum in Ghana, the neighboring country where she had gone to boarding school. The attorney asked if Fauziya could have run off and lived with another tribe, which didn't believe in FGM (1998: 361). Fauziya described the questioning:

> Why hadn't they circumcised me immediately after the wedding? I tried to explain that once I'd been married under Islamic law, I'd become my husband's property . . . So why hadn't I tried to escape before the marriage? "Because I didn't know when the marriage was going to be held. It was impromptu."

The judge jumped in again, wondering how it could have been impromptu when there were "fancy clothes and fancy jewelry and laylay designs on my legs" (1998: 361). Fauziya tried to explain that she didn't believe that her aunt would really marry her off, as we explained earlier. She was apparently in denial, and even a Westerner might be willing to accept this passivity from a 17-year-old who had recently lost her father, whose mother had been driven away by her father's family, who had the right to all her father's property including his children. We are not suggesting that the actions of asylum seekers actually do make sense to Westerners upon further reflection but that many circumstances are beyond the comprehension of the asylum officials and that their limited knowledge of other cultural life experiences is an obstacle to determining the plausibility of an applicant's choices and behaviors.

Fauziya's experience shows also the ways in which people's actions are accepted to the extent that they can be comprehended in terms of Western mores. It is not plausible, to Western thinking, that a young woman could be pulled out of school and married against her will to someone almost three times her age who insisted that she undergo FGM. That she could become property when she was married is an idea that is already two centuries out of date in Western law. That her mother could simply be thrown out of the house she had shared for many years with her husband, as well as lose any control over her children, may seem too outrageous for the asylum officials to believe. That she couldn't get help from the police in Togo or refuge in Ghana may be difficult for a middle-class Westerner to understand. There are many people in the US, particularly minorities, who don't believe the police will help the downtrodden rather than protect the powerful. That Fauziya could keep hoping that her marriage and the FGM wouldn't happen seems understandable (especially in a teenager) but illustrates a passivity which does not conform to Western contemporary ideas that, if a situation is bad, one should leave it (not that this is always possible in the West). It is exactly like the difficulty many people have in understanding why abused women stay with their abusers, rather than leaving them. In Hina's case the Home Office representative (*HO*) made clear his western views in the following excerpt for the testimony:

HO: If your husband remarried in August 2005, you went to the police, you made enquiries at a women's shelter, why didn't you leave your husband then?

AP (applicant):   I did go to make enquiries, there was no result. So then I tried to continue living with him as long as I could, but his behavior didn't improve.

HO: This is what I don't understand. He hated your daughter, has remarried, he beat you. What was the point continuing to live with him?

The representative clearly thought that a husband taking a second wife should have been the trigger for Hina to leave him, but Hina left later, only after she had made an escape plan to go to the UK.

These examples illustrate the ease with which officials judge the behavior of others by expecting them to behave as they would. There are many other examples of this assessment of how a sensible person would behave. Kot described a judge who refused to believe that a Salvadoran was telling the truth when he described staying at home to avoid forced conscription. The judge thought that he could easily have been found at home, so it made no sense to hide there. In fact men were usually rounded up in public meeting places, so avoiding them was a sensible way of avoiding forced military service (1988: 11).

Assumptions about the motivations and behavior of the persecutors

The authorities even second-guess the behavior of those from whom the applicants are fleeing. A Home Office refusal letter to a Jamaican asylum seeker read as follows:

> You claimed that the gun men came twice. You claimed that they had said that they will come next day [sic] and so you fled to a friend's place with the children. However, the Secretary of State considered that the gun men would not have taken a chance if you had previously escaped from them. He also noted that there was a group of gun men and considered that they could have easily kidnapped you and the children at the time.
>
> (Asylum Aid, 1999: 21)

Here the authorities are using their perceptions of what "reasonable people" would do to deny the claim of an applicant, even though there is empirical evidence that the behavior of the applicant's persecutors did actually happen in Jamaica. By definition, persecutors are not "reasonable people."

The Asylum Aid report quotes from another case in the UK in which a man was refused asylum:

> You state that the men drove you to a place one-and-a-half hours away and told you to run before they opened fire on you. The Secretary of State . . . considers that if the men intended to kill you they would have done so straight away, rather than give you a chance to escape.
>
> (1999: 39)

How can an applicant respond to this?

Spijkerboer also finds that the authorities attribute motives to persecutors, which, he argues, vary depending on the country of origin of the applicant; presumptions were used to deny asylum applications of those from certain countries, most notably Zaire. "The purported incredibility is based entirely on presumptions on how things go in a country like Zaire in the eyes of the decision maker during a detention period and an escape" (Spijkerboer, 2000: 101).

Assumptions about appropriate knowledge of applicants

The authorities often check on information which they believe the applicant should have if their story is really true. The Home Office officers, in particular, pride themselves on using their knowledge of the applicant's homeland to check whether he is telling the truth. One officer said:

> An example: in certain countries we'd be aware of the geography, so we ask where is the nearest postbox, what color are the post-boxes, etc., things people who were genuinely from that area, things that they should know.
>
> (Woodhurst, 2004)

One wonders how the officers can have this level of detailed knowledge about the many countries from which applicants come. We asked a barrister how they could reliably ask these sorts of geography questions and received this response: "They get information from travel writing. For example, the Iranian Christian cases, they have pictures of churches. The people are asked to describe the inside of the churches" (Ahluwalia, 2004). The Home Office also asks other things about the country where the person says they come from, including banks, and other places in a particular town. The barrister said "Why ask about a bank when people keep their money under the bed or in a bag? Or ask a woman about something when women never leave the house?" (Ahluwalia, 2004). Applicants have problems when their questioners have fixed ideas about what a resident of a particular place should know about that place, itself a cultural expectation.

In a case shown in the film *Well-Founded Fear*, the officer questioned an applicant who claimed she was persecuted because she was an Anglican. She was asked who was the head of the church, and she said, the Bishop of Gibraltar is the head of the Romanian Anglican Church. The official said she was wrong, that everyone knows the

Archbishop of Canterbury is the head of the Anglican Church, and denies her claim; she's later proved to be right and is granted asylum on appeal (Robertson and Camerini, 2000).

Cultural expectations guide many of the knowledge questions asked of asylum seekers. For example, in one Kurdish case we witnessed in London, the following dialogue took place between the Home Office representative and the asylum seeker:

HO: According to your statement and your interview you actually attended the Hadep building, but in your interview you didn't know the address of it. Why would that be?

AP: There was a party building in N . . . I knew the building, I knew where it was, I didn't have to know address. It is like in this country I know where my friend lives, I don't have to know his address.

The underlying assumption is that someone who goes regularly to a building knows its address. The asylum seeker, by contrast, quite reasonably points out that he can go to a place without knowing the address. This is even more likely to be so in countries where street addresses are less often used. The Home Office representative is trying to discredit the applicant by implying that, because he doesn't know the address, he is lying about his connection with the political organization.

When Marie, the Congolese woman whose case we mentioned above, was asked questions at her court hearing about the political party for which she worked, and other political details, she was unable to answer. For example, she didn't know the year in which her party was founded. The judge found it implausible that she was politically active but didn't know specific facts about her country. However, in developing countries with lots of violence, it is not uncommon to find people who are very unsophisticated about political issues. They get involved on a local level and aren't kept informed about the broader issues; there is no free press and lots of secrecy. In fact, her ignorance is entirely plausible, even though it may not be characteristic of a political activist in the developed world. Again, however, the authorities believed that someone who was politically active should have certain knowledge, and someone who did not must be lying.

Assumptions about the help from third parties.

Here again the authorities use their own view of what people would do to help others, by assuming that someone would not be willing to take risks to help a friend or relative, or even help a stranger out of altruism. We saw this assumption at work in the case of the Ugandan who took in her neighbor's child. The Amnesty International report quotes a refusal letter:

> The Secretary of State looks at the manner of your escape from hospital. You have stated that your cousin who also happened to be a doctor at the hospital helped you to flee. He is of the view that if your cousin had overheard that you were going to be killed, he would not have played a role in your escape which invariably would implicate himself.

(2004: 23)

And again:

> The Secretary of State has further considered your claim that whilst in detention that one of the guards had asked what he could do for you. You claim that you had given your parents' address to him, and to inform them [sic] that you were in prison. The Secretary of State finds it particularly difficult to accept that this guard would have asked that question, or more importantly would have helped you in such a way. As such he has doubts about your credibility.

(2004: 23–4)

All second-guessing; all unsubstantiated.

Here is an extract from a case we heard in London, where the lawyer representing Gina, a woman from Ecuador claiming asylum is trying to counteract the assumptions about helping others held by officials. *R* is the legal representative for the applicant, *AP* is the applicant, and *AD* is the administrator.

R: Carry on. Explain how you were robbed . . .

AP: There were a lot of people when I stopped to look at a McDonald's, they pushed me, they took the suitcase from me.

R: Where was that?

AP: Now I realize it was around Piccadilly.

R: What day was that?

AP: 5 June, 2002.

AD: The same day you came here?

R: Did you tell the police?

AP: I remained afraid, I screamed that I had been robbed, but no one helped me.

R: You say you met a gentleman who spoke Spanish and he accommodated you?

AP: Yes, he helped me a lot.

R: What was his name?

AP: Maria Martinez and the husband is Felipe.

R: Why would complete strangers help you?

AD: How can she answer the question?

R: She can't.

AD: She can't go into their mind. You have to rephrase the question.

R: I'll rephrase it. Did you know these people before coming to the UK?

AP: No, never.

R: Where did you meet these people?

AP: When I was robbed.

R: Were they from your city?

AP: No, they were Spanish.

R: Were they Christians?

AP: Yes, Catholics.

R: Did you pay them?

AP: No, everything had gone.

R: They kept you in their house for three months without any payment? Do you know why they would do this?

AP: They said to me it was because they were Catholic.

R: Are you saying they were just good Christian Samaritans?

AP: No, good people in every sense [the translator didn't use the word Samaritan].

R: Do you still maintain contact with these people?

AP: No, more or less for one year, they went to Holland.

The lawyer is trying to frame the behavior in terms the court will understand: people do help others out of religious conviction. In his closing argument, however, the Home Office representative said:

> I also ask you to find the good Samaritans' lack plausibility. If they had put her up and made such an effort to accommodate her why wouldn't they help her with the appeal? She only claimed asylum after she was arrested for traveling without a ticket on public transportation.

He is not contesting the fact that the applicant could be helped by strangers, but rather questioning the consistency of their behavior. This questioning is a way of placing their actions in a context of what appears to him to be the appropriate behavior of the third parties. By his logic, a person who gives a home to a stranger would also help them with their asylum application.

We are not arguing the validity of the case; in fact this case seems to us as well to have too many inconsistencies and implausibilities. But the same kind of questioning undermines cases that seem plausible. For example, Henri was questioned at his asylum hearing at great length about why someone would let him escape from the Central African Republic to Cameroon. He described how an "enemy" (someone from the current leader's party [Patasse] helped him cross the border. It was clear that the officer couldn't understand why an "enemy" would help someone. In fact, as Henri told him over and over, he was also a childhood friend. In that society, long-standing friendships trump party affiliation. Similarly, the Asylum Aid report describes the case of : "J.L., for instance, was allowed to get away by Zairian soldiers who had captured him on orders, because he spoke in Tshiluba, their language. But shared loyalties are not a motive the Home Office recognizes" (1999: 41).

We've heard it all before

One of the problems facing the authorities is when to believe a story that they have heard before. On the one hand, people who are persecuted are often treated similarly so the stories sound similar. On the other hand, there is the possibility that asylum seekers share stories which they believe (or are told) are likely lead to success. As one lawyer put it: "A lot of the same stories are starting to come out. Obviously you get successful with one client and the client has shared the affidavit, so the new affidavit looks similar" (Hohenstein, 2002). As Kai Erikson (1976) discovered in his study of flood victims whose stories too closely resembled each other (according to the insurance company that reviewed their claims), trauma victims often draw on collective memories to describe their experiences. On one hand, asylum seekers are expected to report a story of societal persecution rather than individual trauma, and, on the other, they are challenged for representations that appear too similar to others' stories. Attorneys who represent asylum applicants say that for them, deciding whether the story is a fabrication is the hardest part of their job. One attorney told us that the applicant spends one hour with a paralegal, after which the attorney has to decide whether to believe a person. She thinks about 1 in 150 is lying. Recently three Ethiopians in three days all told exactly the same story: " 'After 15 minutes, my father said "Down with the government."' We called them back in. How is it possible that all three of you have exactly the same claim? They kept saying 'It happened to us. . ..' They didn't speak English . . ." (London, 2004).

The difficulty the authorities have in believing applicants is shown in the description by a former member of the Refugee Division of the Immigration and Refugee Board in Canada:

> I recall one claimant whose story struck me and my colleague as consistent and plausible. His demeanour was confident, his testimony was straightforward, and he held up well under questioning. The only problem was that his written story happened to be plagiarized word for word from that of a claimant I had heard a few months earlier.
>
> (Macklin, 1998: 138)

We asked officers in the Home Office how they reacted to stories they had heard before and got these replies: "If a person makes a common claim I don't think that has an impact. In Zimbabwe it is membership in the MDC. I wouldn't look more or less favorably on it [if I had heard it before]" (Avery, 2004). From another officer:

> It depends on the merits of the individual claims, for example, the Jamaican labor party – people have said they were an active member, so you ask who was the candidate at the campaign you worked on . . . If they don't know . . . it helps to have heard it before, the more you deal with it, the better you know what to ask.
>
> (Woodhurst, 2004)

Lawyers tell us that many people who in fact have good claims don't use them because they are duped by someone who assures them that "you will only get asylum if you say you were raped . . . tortured with electric shock . . ." So they tell the story they think is more likely to be believed, even though it is a lie, and even though their own story may be good enough. One lawyer, quoted in Bernstein (2006), said: "A lot of these people, if you look behind the foolish lies they're telling, they really do have a case. But the lawyer they go to adapts their story to conform with the pattern. . .." The big problem for a lawyer who later represents such an applicant is that they start with a client whom they must admit to the judge is a liar, and then provide a reasonable explanation of why they lied. A former Immigration Court judge told us:

> A good adjudicator can spell out what was not credible in the story. Sometimes, which is unfortunate, the applicant often had a good story but was told to follow the script, then you throw in corrupt lawyers connected to smugglers . . . so the Chinese lost cases . . . I still see them from years ago. As judge I did what I could do . . . Judges often complain that they don't have enough latitude, but you have to know how to make it work.
>
> (Joyce, 2003)

Many judges, however, assume that "once a liar, always a liar," and it is very difficult to convince them that *this* time the applicant is telling the truth.

Applicants can be caught between a rock and a hard place. The authorities may base a decision on the idea that "this story is so weird that I can't believe it." However, the application can be denied because of exactly the opposite thinking: "I've heard this story before, so it can't be true this time as well." And they might be right; there is always the possibility that an applicant has made up the story.

Ironically, one recent case, which was later revealed to have been fabricated, occurred at a time when the FGM claim on which it was based was relatively new, though very much in the public eye. Adelaide Abankwah arrived in the US in 1997, the year after Fauziya Kassindja obtained asylum, with all the attendant publicity we have described. Adelaide claimed that she belonged to a small tribe in central Ghana, and that she was supposed to assume the role of queen mother of the tribe (Kratz, 2002: 320). Becoming queen mother apparently required a virginity test and marriage to someone selected for her by the tribal elders. Because Adelaide was not a virgin, she claimed that she would have to undergo FGM as a punishment. She came to the US and was detained; she had a number of asylum hearings, culminating in an appeal to the Second Circuit Court from the decision of the BIA denying her application for asylum. During that time, her cause had been taken up by the magazine *Marie Claire* and various organizations, as well as receiving widespread media coverage and support from politicians and high administration officials. Adelaide won her appeal and was granted asylum by the BIA in 1999. More than a year later, further INS investigation revealed that her claims were fraudulent and that her identity was fake. She turned out to be someone called Regina Norma Danson, a former hotel worker, rather than a prospective queen mother of her tribe (Kratz, 2002). Her former employer said: "Her whole story is a complete lie . . . She left because she wanted to go to the United States" (Kratz, 2002: 334). Because the case received so much publicity and support from politicians, the investigators have been reluctant to prosecute her for fraud (Kratz, 2002).

Conclusion

The successful asylum story is one that fits into the framework of credibility and truth telling; the successful lawyer is the one who is best able to get her clients to tell a story that is perceived as "true" (credible, plausible). Credibility is often measured by coherence. That is, being who you say you are is a matter of presenting a consistent identity – a mother is a person who would do x and y but not z. An official would do one thing, not another. But trauma disrupts coherent identity by interrupting ordinary life. Trauma victims are faced with impossible choices that can't always be explained by narratives that attempt to sustain a coherent identity between before and after or even between the period of persecution and the present. Rather than recognize that categories of ordinary life are disrupted, we generalize about people and their practices; for example, someone who sells arms is an arms dealer, not to be trusted. Narrative can create coherence out of the chaos of experience but narratives are based on the available ideas shared in a community and can appear to be "stock stories" rather than personal accounts (Shuman, 2005). Narratives about trauma will inevitably have gaps, unexplainable parts.

Some things are too ghastly for the immigration authorities to bring themselves to believe so they decide the person is lying. "This didn't happen to you because it is too awful to happen to anyone." One attorney has found that it is sometimes easier to convince a male judge that a story of gender violence is true, than a case in which a man is tortured (London, 2004). One can speculate that the judge does not need to put himself in the place of the female victim, and so does not need to distance himself from the horror as he does in the case of the male victim.

The asylum process can be seen as one in which the authorities try to make sense of the senseless. Using the traditional "tools" of evidence is not the way to determine credibility. The way to get there is through greater cultural understanding of how trauma is represented and of the limits of representation, credibility, coherence, and corroboration. The law, however, doesn't do that but rather sticks to its traditional tools, even in the face of evidence that these tools don't work. We saw that people aren't very good at detecting liars; similarly, the tools we rely on so heavily in our legal system, such as lie detector tests and eye witness identification, turn out to be to be inaccurate at telling whether someone is lying. There is some evidence that the best technique for detecting lying is the use of minute changes in facial expressions which to some extent is a learned skill (see e.g. Ekman, 1985). However, there is no evidence that hearing officers and judges have learned this skill, nor do they believe that they need to do so. It is also less likely to work across cultures where the cues may be different.

We do not claim that people don't lie to get asylum; it is apparent from our research that they do. We believe that, as the asylum system is currently set up in the US and the UK, it is appropriate that only genuine asylum seekers should be granted asylum. However, current methods for determining credibility do not serve the goal of correctly identifying genuine asylum seekers. According to many of the lawyers who assist asylum seekers, credibility remains the most common reason for refusal of asylum claims. (Franklin-Houtzager and Williams, 2004). Instead of measuring credibility by identifying inconsistencies in stories of trauma that, all evidence suggests, are bound to contain inconsistencies, and evaluating the likelihood that what an applicant states could have happened, we suggest that asylum officials learn to recognize the cultural differences in reporting on trauma and that they rely more on knowledge about practices of persecution in each site of political turmoil, rather than assuming that such practices follow the logic of the asylum-granting country. The best measure of applicants' credibility may be their ability to sustain an extensive account of what happened.

We are not optimistic that such changes will ever take place in the asylum process in the US and the UK. Implementation of such changes would require a complete rethinking of the laws of evidence and the way courts operate, not to mention a re-examination of the legal system itself. It would also fly in the face of the efforts to justify lower grants of asylum in both countries. Instead, the two countries are going in the opposite direction: moving toward even greater reliance on the same "tests" of credibility we have discussed in this chapter.

5   Politics gets personal

What counts as persecution

Tun's story

Tun, first introduced in Chapter 3, is from Burma (he refuses to call it Myanmar) and has had a long history of political activism in his country. He came to the US on a student visa, having convinced the consul in Thailand that he was for real, despite the forged passport he was using. He received asylum in the US and is now working in Washington to improve the situation in his home country. Here is his story:

When I was a physics student at the Rangoon Institute of Technology, in 1988, I saw the government's violent treatment of peaceful student demonstrators. One student was killed by the riot police that day. Later I marched with hundreds of students in a peaceful protest against the government's brutal treatment of students. Soldiers and riot police stopped and massacred unarmed student demonstrators without warning. After, I helped organize a secret student union [unions are outlawed by the Burmese government] in my home township, working with the All Burma Federation of Students Union [ABFSU]. I worked with many other activists and groups to prepare for the 1988 People Power Uprising, known as the "8888 Movement." Our goal was to replace the military regime with a democratic form of government. I helped lead a march of thousands of people to the Shwedagon Pagoda in Rangoon, as part of an uprising against the government. That evening, government soldiers attacked the people who marched, killing thousands in Rangoon alone. A few weeks later, the military staged a coup and continued to crush pro-democracy protests and organizations.

After the coup, I went into hiding for several weeks, then returned to my hometown, even though it was dangerous. But I had to keep working for democracy in Burma, by organizing and educating students in Rangoon for the pro-democracy movement. My parents were occasionally summoned by the military and questioned about what I was doing; the soldiers told them to make me stop my political activities.

In 1991, when I was a third year student at Rangoon University, I organized a peaceful student demonstration at Rangoon University to honor Daw [Daw Aung San Suu Kyi], the 1991 Nobel Peace Prize Winner. I was so inspired by her that I decided not to continue my degree in physics then, but instead to work full time in politics. The military junta crushed the demonstration, arresting and imprisoning hundreds of students.

I knew that my activities were risky because the military regime was so brutal. They always respond by violence. As a human being I was afraid. I wanted to honor Daw; my friends and I really wanted to demand the regime to release all the political prisoners.

As a result of my activities, I had to go underground. I knew for sure that I would otherwise be arrested. My friends got arrested, and were imprisoned for 15 to 20 years for participating in the demonstration. As a leader I would probably get 20+ years. I didn't want to leave my family and the prospect of getting a PhD, but it would be too dangerous to stay. I really loved my father and mother (especially my mother) and my brothers, but because of Daw Aung San Suu Kyi, I left everyone behind. I was afraid at first, but later I was very proud of what I did. In April, 1992, I left Rangoon University to go to the jungle and join the Democratic Party for a New Society [DPNS].

After I went underground, the authorities came to my parents' house and confiscated my photocopy machines, my typewriters, my notes and all my belongings. They also arrested my brother-in-law instead of me, though he knew nothing about where I was or what I was doing. They tortured him. My father was also tortured by the intelligence service in an effort to find out where I was hiding. He was investigated several times a week. Once, he was summoned four times during the night; no sooner had they let him go than they called him back. In 1993 I secretly went back into Burma to carry out the DPNS non-violence programs in Rangoon, but it was too dangerous there, so I went into the areas of Burma that were not controlled by the military regime, mostly the areas controlled by ethnic minorities. These groups had been fighting for equality since 1948. I didn't know where to go; I was with my friend. But I didn't feel safe with us being together. He didn't want to take a risk living with me. I didn't know where to go. I stayed hidden. Most of my friends got arrested because they tried to go to another place. They got arrested in the bus station.

While I was in hiding, the regime also arrested my teacher and friends instead of me. My teacher was jailed for five years. I almost gave myself up so my family wouldn't suffer any more, but one of my friends told me not to, so I stayed in hiding. I went into the jungle with the rebels, but I didn't feel safe there, and had to carry a weapon to protect myself. I lived with the pro-democracy groups for several years, working as a teacher. I taught the children of the rebels. They had schools, but the rebels had to keep moving, so the kids didn't have a chance to study. At first I thought the rebels were trouble, but after I learned that they didn't kill innocent people. After I understood that, I helped them as a teacher. I stayed in the jungle from 1992 to 1999.

When we met Tun, he spoke very good English. He said that he had learned it when he was in hiding with the rebels, from the BBC News and the Voice of America.

I think it was essential to learn it. I also went to a school in the jungle for a couple of months. It was an intensive school [in English] funded by an NGO through the Dutch government. The pro-democracy movement received a lot of support from Western countries, especially the Scandinavian countries.

In 1999, I moved to the Karenni ethnic area, where I also worked as a teacher. There I trained people in nonviolent activities. These activities were organized by the NGOs. I was still living underground at this time. We didn't go into public places, we lived in hideouts, built small schools, hospitals, and health clinics. We helped a lot of people who got sick, with malaria. We trained villagers. They used to be animists, who used witchcraft. We educated them to use Western medicine. After a ceasefire, the Karenni organization was forced not to allow any pro-democracy activists, so I and my colleagues were asked to leave.

So we were forced to leave for Thailand. We crossed the border, we took risks, taking the bus. Some of my friends got arrested on the bus to Thailand. We eventually went to Chiang Mai. We had to negotiate with the police and also the intelligence officers. I say we, but I really mean I, so I can feel I am not alone. Without "we," we cannot do anything. In 2001, the Thai police arrested 31 Burmese pro-democracy activists (mostly DPNS members).

While I was in exile, I did political work for the pro-democracy party based in Thailand. I was a member of the

Foreign Affairs Committee of the DPNS. In January 2002, I was elected as a central committee member of the DPNS. I established contacts with foreigners, especially those who worked for NGOs, so they could launch human rights campaigns and to win political and financial support. I was briefly arrested twice by Thai immigration police. After the arrests, the Thai government asked the pro-democracy organizations to shut down their offices in the cities of Thailand.

I spent a month in Copenhagen, Denmark, as an intern with the International Labor Movement Forum in 1999 and, in 2001, I took a six-month course, titled "International Conflict Studies" in Sweden. The first time I came to the US was in July 2001, to attend the Conflict Transformation Across Cultures (CONTACT) Summer Institute at the School for International Training (SIT) in Brattleboro, Vermont. After, I went back to Thailand, and took a distance-learning course with SIT. Then I was given a chance to study for a Master's in Conflicts Transformation at SIT in Vermont, in 2002.

After a few months in the US, I decided to apply for asylum, because Thai government policy toward the pro-democracy group changed, so they started arresting members. They wanted economic ties with the Burmese regime, so they wanted to show that they didn't support the pro-democracy movement. They released statements which made clear their change of policy toward the pro-democracy movement. So it would have been too dangerous for me to go back to Thailand or Burma.

Just before I came to the US, I got married, to Chan, a Burmese teacher. We had met in the jungle. We had a traditional ceremony in Chiang Mai, Thailand, and we were remarried in a civil ceremony in Vermont. Chan had also learnt English in the jungle. She was also an activist and so she is afraid to go back to Burma. She joined organizations working for democracy, one of which is a subdivision of the

National League of Democracy (NLD) for members exiled from Burma. NLD, the largest political party in Burma, is led by 1991 Nobel Peace Laureate Daw Aung San Suu Kyi. The NLD-LA, a branch of the NLD for those in exile, has been labeled an enemy of the state. Chan also worked as a correspondent for the Irrawaddy Publishing Group (IPG). She contributed several articles to the IPG about the Burmese military regime's human rights violations. Her father was also politically involved in the NLD-LA, as was her brother. They have both been arrested and tortured by Burmese authorities.

Chan got a chance to study at the Community College of Vermont. She spent some time living in Burlington but eventually left because she was unable to find a place to live there. Both Tun and Chan had received scholarships to study from organizations for Burmese students, set up to help those whose studies were interrupted by the regime. Chan is now finishing her bachelor's degree at a prestigious college in the US northeast.

Tun continues his story:

My family (my mother, father, sister, and brother) is still in Rangoon, in Burma. I talk to them on the phone two or three times a year, but I don't mention my name so as not to cause more trouble for them. The Burmese authorities know where I live. I don't usually write because all letters are opened. I can't send a fax because the Burmese people are not permitted to use fax machines. One Burmese activist who worked for a Dutch company used their fax machine and as a result was tortured to death.

I have a fake passport from Burma in my name (I bought it; the Burmese can buy really good fake passports in Thailand). When I applied for a visa I met the consul both in Bangkok and Chiang Mai, I had to tell them the passport was fake. When Chan needed to leave, she couldn't get a passport from the Burmese government, so she contacted her friends in

> Burma and they paid Burmese immigration officials to issue her a Burmese passport. She used that passport to travel to the United States on a valid F-1 student visa.

Defining persecution

Individuals applying for asylum have to show that they have been persecuted. But how does the system determine what counts as persecution in different countries? How bad must it be? What are the different kinds of persecution, and how does persecution differ from one country to another? What is serious enough to qualify as persecution under the law, and (perhaps more importantly) by the asylum hearing officers? There is a body of law in the UK and the US about this question, both about how it should be decided, and about what kinds of persecution qualifies, but what is just as important, or more important, in practice, are the views of the officers themselves, who decide that a particular case is or is not persecution.

To reiterate the basis for a claim of asylum: it is granted to someone who is unwilling or unable to return to their home country because of past persecution or a well-founded fear of persecution on account of race, religion, nationality, membership in a particular social group, or political opinion. For the claim to be recognized, the person has to be credible, as we saw in the last chapter. Now we are going to look at the elements of the definition in practice. First we will unpack the first part of the definition – what amounts to persecution and whether the fear is "well-founded" – and then we will see what is meant by "on account of" the several categories listed in the definition.

When is a fear of persecution well-founded?

When the fear is real

For the fear to be well-founded, the asylum seeker has to be afraid that what has happened to them in the past could happen again, and that fear has also to be reasonable in the eyes of someone else, in this case the immigration authorities. The use of both a "subjective" and an "objective" component is typical in the law, which is only willing to acknowledge things that are seen as "realistic." In one case, Vitore, a young, attractive, Albanian woman said that she was afraid of being kidnapped and forced into prostitution if she had to return to Albania. While that fear is not unrealistic, it was not supported by enough objective evidence to constitute a well-founded fear (*Rresphja* v. *Gonzales*, 2005). Huang, a Chinese asylum seeker, claimed that he was afraid of being forcibly sterilized on his return to China. He had two children, born in the US. The court decided that his subjective fear was not supported by evidence because the policies were more lenient with children born abroad, if the first child was a daughter (which his was) and because the area he came from had a relatively lax policy (*Huang* v. *INS*, 2005).

Many of the cases we observed in London included fears of persecution by the government should the asylum seeker return to their country; these cases were opposed by the Home Office, which argued that the fear of government persecution was unrealistic. One Iranian man, who claimed he distributed anti-government leaflets and CDs to fellow students, was considered not to be "of interest" to the government, who, at the most would only fine him on his return.

For the fear to be real, the applicant has to show that no part of the country is safe for them. If it is possible for someone to relocate safely to another part of the country, asylum will not be granted. Like everything else, this is subject to different interpretations. In a number of the cases we observed in London, the Home Office claimed that a person could relocate to another part of the country, sometimes in circumstances that were unrealistic at best. Women from countries where they must live under the protection of a man cannot realistically be expected to move alone to a place where they have no family with whom to live and no man to protect them. For example, Hina, the Pakistani woman we met in Chapter 4, was quizzed at length about whether she had relatives in another part of the country with whom she could live, despite her claim that her husband would track her down and kill her if she returned to Pakistan.

When it is bad enough

Harassment or discrimination is not a sufficient basis for a successful claim of persecution. An individual might not be able to find work or might have been fired from a job. Jelena, whose case we observed in London, was a Serbian woman from Croatia. In denying Jelena's petition, the adjudicator accepted that Serbians suffered discrimination in Croatia, but said "there is nothing to suggest that they can't find accommodation, or a job," as she claimed.

Someone may have had difficulty with the police, but if it is not serious, it is not enough on which to base an asylum claim. For example, the UK authorities denied asylum to a Roma woman who claimed that the systematic discrimination she suffered in her own country left her unemployed, marginalized, and frightened to walk down the street. They said that the discrimination she suffered did not reach the level of persecution. This was a typical response to the Roma asylum claims in the UK, even before all claims were denied as they are now, because, as citizens of the expanded European Union, Roma cannot seek asylum in the UK.

Having one's house burgled or one's laundry stolen is not bad enough to be considered persecution, according to US case law, nor is rock throwing or damage to property. In one case, the Federal Court of Appeals reinforced the immigration judge's opinion that "the harm that Cadavid suffered did not rise to the level of past persecution. He received two threatening letters and phone calls instructing him to abandon his work for the Liberal Party" (*Jimenez* v. *US Attorney General*, 2005). This evidence of harassment has to be seen in context. In addition to the relatively low level of activities Cadavid Jiminez claimed as persecution, the court noted that his family was still in Colombia and had no problems, nor had the mayoral candidate he was supporting experienced problems with the paramilitary organization since relocating within Colombia. The court made it clear that a claim of persecution must "present evidence of more than a few isolated incidents of verbal harm or intimidation that is unaccompanied by physical punishment, infliction of harm, or significant deprivation of liberty" (*Jimenez* v. *US Attorney General*, 2005).

The problem with the examples we describe above is not the fact that they are "merely" harassment, but that there is nothing more in the complaint serious enough to rise to the level of persecution. In another case, the US Court of Appeals granted asylum to an Armenian who was persecuted because of his wife's Azeri ethnicity. The persecution included death threats, life-threatening attacks, as well as harassment and systematic discrimination. Harassment was a part of the package of persecution, not the whole package (*Khodaverdyan* v. *Ashcroft*, 2004).

For persecution to be bad enough, it has to be relatively recent. If a person waits too long after suffering persecution and doesn't come to any harm in the meantime, they will not be granted asylum. In the US we have seen many Mauritanian clients who were persecuted in the late 1980s, when the country was in a very unstable state. Some of them stayed in Mauritania, or spent a number of years in Senegal, waiting for the situation to improve enough for them to return home, or for the opportunity to leave the continent. By the time we saw them in the US, the situation in Mauritania was more stable, so the persecution they suffered more than a decade earlier just wasn't enough for a successful asylum case. Allassane's case is typical. In the 1980s he was subject to persecution because he was an educated Fulani, an ethnic group which suffered persecution at the hands of those of Arab descent in Mauritania. He was targeted by the government because he was a member of FLAM, a political organization of Fulanis trying to obtain equal rights. He was arrested in 1982 and 1983. He fled to Morocco in 1984, where he lived while waiting for conditions to improve in his homeland. In 1989, the situation deteriorated into ethnic cleansing of the Moors (the black Mauritanians), so Allassane could not go home. Instead he looked for somewhere else to go, and finally found a smuggler to take him to the US in 2001. By then, his claim looked really out of date and, like many of his countrymen, he couldn't show that he was still at risk if he returned.

When it is persecution not prosecution

An asylum seeker must make it clear that the claim is not just a complaint about the legitimate actions of the government. It makes sense that someone will not be granted asylum because they want to avoid prosecution for criminal behavior. Like everything else in this area, however, it can get quite complicated. When is an action of the government a legitimate prosecution and when is it persecution? It depends in part on whether we think it is acceptable to prosecute people for the actions in question. In Chapter 4, we saw what happened to Fatima, the Iranian woman who fell in love with a Pakistani journalist and got pregnant. She was threatened with death by stoning by her brother and her father. To back up her claim, an Imam (a Muslim legal authority) stated that it was legal to kill an unmarried woman who got pregnant. The US authorities ultimately decided that this was persecution, even though it was legal in Iran. Similarly, the UK granted asylum to an Iranian woman who feared prosecution for adultery after leaving her violent husband (McDonald and Webber, 2005: 735). The Australian courts have decided that the fear of prosecution by someone defying the one-child policy in China was not persecution because it resulted from behavior which was illegal, though as we shall see later in this chapter, that is no longer the case in the US (*A* v. *MIEA*, 1997). Some authorities in the UK also claim that homosexuals are legitimately prosecuted rather than persecuted as the government has the right to regulate sexuality in accordance with their society's sense of morality (ICAR, 2005). The legal principle is that, if something is a violation of human rights, or if it is carried out in a discriminatory or excessive fashion, then it is considered persecution. It is, however, difficult to determine whether a prosecution is genuine or whether it is trumped up as a way of persecuting someone. Benjamin Paradza, a Zimbabwean judge, was charged with corruption and perverting the course of justice because he ordered the release of a city mayor arrested for holding a political rally. He fled the country and went to South Africa, and then claimed asylum in the UK. He was turned down and was granted asylum in New Zealand at the request of the UNHCR (Mulrooney, 2006). Clearly the UK and the UNHCR (and New Zealand) felt differently about the legitimacy of Paradza's prosecution.

One particularly problematic area is that of conscription laws. In general, we don't grant asylum to people who want to avoid serving in the military. Yohannes Habtemicael, an Eritrean, was hired by an Ethiopian NGO to supervise UN supported children's feeding centers. He was sent to Barentu, a small town in Ethiopia, where the EPLF (Eritrean People's Liberation Front) attacked the town and defeated the Ethiopian forces. Habtemicael was forced by the EPLF to help with its wounded, bury the dead, and to undergo political "reeducation." He was also pressed into military service to replace soldiers who had died. He was told that any sign of opposition to the EPLF would lead to severe torture, and that any effort to escape with a weapon could lead to summary execution. Nevertheless, Habtemicael managed to escape with his rifle, after a gun battle in which two EPLF soldiers were killed. He fled with two others who had also escaped, to Sudan and then Saudi Arabia. After six years in Saudi Arabia, he was told that he would be deported unless he converted from Christianity to Islam. So he obtained a tourist visa to the US and, after his arrival, a student visa. Habtemicael argued that he had been the victim of political persecution by the EPLF and that he feared further persecution based on his political beliefs should he return to Eritrea, now controlled by the EPLF. The court, however, decided that any action taken against him by the Eritrean government would be on account of his desertion from the EPLF and the deaths of its soldiers, and not on account of his political beliefs. If he were conscripted on his return, it would be because he had not completed his military service requirement, which is not a basis for asylum (*Habtemicael* v. *Ashcroft*, 2004). The legitimacy of the activities of the EPLF at the time Habtemicael was impressed into their forces didn't seem to matter to the court; the rebels are now the government, and Habtemicael is the loser.

In one case we observed in London, the UK AIT denied asylum to an Iraqi, about whom the Home Office representative said at the hearing:

The appellant has stated that he was selling guns openly, when the KDP said it was illegal. This was very foolish. Secondly, he said the PKK persuaded him to do business that way, it was foolish, as the PKK was buying arms illegally in Northern Iraq. The KDP banned that organization – it would be in everybody's interest to conduct these dealings with the highest amount of secrecy possible. Whether you find the appellant credible or not, the appellant himself admits essentially he is on the run from the law. The appellant knowingly and illegally sold arms for an organization banned in the region, considered a terrorist organization.

> If the appellant did that in any country he'd be prosecuted. The appellant states he doesn't want to return to Iraq because he would be imprisoned, but he'd be imprisoned anywhere.

The Home Office is making a political decision about the relative merits of the activities of the various political groups in Iraq at the time, again to the detriment of the asylum seeker's claim.

The cultural perspective is essential here. For Westerners, the idea of killing someone for getting pregnant while unmarried is repugnant, whereas prosecuting someone for selling guns illegally, but for a political cause, is not. Thus the former is considered persecution, while the latter is classified as prosecution. Here again, we give asylum to those who behave like we would, but deny it to those who do things we regard as poor choices, wrong, unreasonable, or unlikely to lead to political change.

The distinction between prosecution and persecution seems to have been misused by the UK authorities as another way of denying claims. We are told in the Asylum Aid report (1999), for example, that:

> The "prosecution not persecution" argument is used a good deal in refusing Turkish Kurds. SM had been harassed on account of her husband's involvement with the PKK (Kurdish Workers Party). The Home Office told her: *"Those who involved themselves in the activities of such groups, at whatever level, cannot expect to be exempt from suspicion, investigation and ultimately prosecution."* This assumes all PKK sympathisers have taken part in the violence; in fact, the Turkish government's rationale in banning the PKK is the suspected violence of its members. By accepting this blanket indictment of all PKK sympathisers, the UK authorities not only assume the guilt of members of the group but also pretend that the "culprit" will be brought to trial – as we have seen, detention without trial is more the norm. And it assumes a fair trial, for which the behaviour of the Turkish authorities towards the Kurdish resistance does not provide a shred of evidence. (In any event, even if a prosecution has been brought, it is more than likely that the defendant will have been tortured, which would be a strong argument against return – provided the asylum-seeker concerned

has a lawyer who is up to arguing the point.) One of the ways repressive states try to quell dissent is by outlawing it. The Convention is there to protect individuals whose political activities are banned, not to collude in their criminalisation.

(Asylum Aid, 1999: 44–5)

This says it all: protecting people who engage in political activity, especially that which is banned by the government, is exactly what asylum is all about. It is not, however, what the asylum authorities are all about.

The US authorities can also show excessive respect for the laws of other countries when many would agree they are a violation of human rights. In a recent case which came to public attention and merited an editorial in the *New York Times*, Xiaodong Li, a Chinese Christian, was arrested and tortured for organizing an underground church. Before his case came to trial, he fled to the US. At his hearing before an immigration judge, he was granted asylum, but the Bush administration had the decision overturned. At the trial in the Federal Court, the government argued that Mr. Li was simply being persecuted for breaking China's laws against unregulated churches. After a public outcry, including from the government's own Commission on International Religious Freedom, the decision was reversed (*New York Times*, 2005). Outlawing "underground" churches is a clear violation of human rights in the US.

Past persecution vs. future fear

Evidence of past persecution of others, as well as oneself, is used to show a "well-founded fear of persecution." The US statute actually says "because of persecution *or* [italics ours] a well-founded fear of persecution." It is therefore possible to obtain asylum based only on a fear of persecution, rather than past persecution or only on past persecution, though this happens rarely. Usually the applicant describes both persecution they have experienced in the past and fear of future persecution. Someone who has suffered persecution in the past generally has a legitimate reason to fear it in the future. The UNHCR *Handbook* makes this clear for current applications: "It may be assumed that a person has well-founded fear of being persecuted if he has already been the victim of persecution for one of the reasons enumerated in the 1951 Convention" (UNHCR, 1992: para. 45). In US law, evidence of past persecution raises what is known as a "rebuttable presumption" of future persecution. To rebut this presumption the authorities must show that it is not reasonable to fear future persecution, usually through evidence that conditions have changed since the applicant was persecuted.

It is legally possible, though rare in the current climate, for a person to get asylum based only on severe persecution in the past, where future persecution will not happen. Victims of Nazi persecution could have gone back to Germany after World War II, but were granted asylum on the basis of past persecution. More recently, an applicant has occasionally been granted asylum based on past persecution alone, because the harm was so terrible that they are still suffering from it, or because it would be inhumane to expect them to return to their country. For example, Margaret, from Zimbabwe, was raped by the military, but stayed there for a few years after it happened. Staying put after a trauma such as this is often interpreted by the authorities as evidence that it can't have been so bad. In this case, however, Margaret came to the US as a bone marrow donor for her sister, who had leukemia. When she was tested, she found out that she was HIV positive, which could only have been the result of the earlier rape. The authorities decided that, in these circumstances, past persecution was enough for them to grant asylum, as she would undoubtedly continue to suffer from the persecution. So the amount and duration of her suffering was the measure by which the authorities evaluated the case, rather than the nature of the persecution. The case of Agron Neli, an Albanian, details persecution which included execution, murder, and lifetime imprisonment of various members of the family, multiple arrests and sometimes severe beatings of Agron, and repeated threats of bodily injury or death to Agron, his wife Ariana, and his children. In cases of such atrocious torture the court decided it didn't matter whether things had improved since Agron and his wife had fled Albania (*Neli* v. *Ashcroft*, 2003). Cases in which someone claims asylum based on already having been subjected to FGM or forced sterilization as part of coercive population policies present legal difficulties, since there would be nothing to fear in the future, though courts have recognized that eligibility can be based on past persecution alone (*Singh* v. *Ilchert*, 1995). The argument is that FGM or forced sterilization has a continuing effect on the person for the rest of their life. In most cases, however, applicants present additional evidence which contributes to a future fear, so the problem does not arise.

The UK authorities sometimes take a different approach, despite the UNHCR guidelines. They often blithely assume that a person who has been tortured in the past will not be tortured again should they return to their home country. The Asylum Aid report says:

> A Home Office condition that defies both common sense and international human rights law is that the asylum-seeker – whose past torture is not disputed – should demonstrate, if returned to the country of origin, that there is "a reasonable likelihood that you would suffer such treatment again for a Convention reason." This not only falls foul of the ECHR [European Court of Human Rights], but also conflicts with the lower standard of proof established in asylum cases in the UK. The demonstration of "a reasonable degree of likelihood" in the future is bound to depend heavily on what happened in the past. Torture before leaving – itself difficult enough to prove – is as much demonstration any asylum-seeker is likely to have of a reasonable degree of likelihood of torture in the future. The law concurs with common sense in accepting that past torture is adequate in establishing danger in the future in the absence of a change of circumstances. But the Home Office seems not to be deterred by either the law or reason.
>
> (1999: 22)

Imputed persecution

Some people are persecuted because they are related to someone wanted by the authorities for his activities. The classic story is one in which the military are looking for an activist who is in hiding, and when they come to his house, they find his wife, whom they beat and rape. The wife, if she escapes, can seek asylum based on the persecution she suffered because of her relationship to her politically active husband. As we shall see in Chapter 6, this is a particularly common story for women, but happens to male relatives as well, as we can see from the story told by one lawyer we interviewed:

> I've had lots of cases of people who were associated with people. One example was a Burmese case. In 1988 there was a big national uprising, people were protesting all over the country, this guy was a police officer. He gave a little speech, everyone was doing it. They [the activists] were very keen to get police officers to show how widespread it was. He spoke for a couple of minutes before a very large crowd. His main problem was that his brother was a member of a student organization, he helped his brother who was arrested after some people protested and was beaten badly. They [the authorities] came to the client's home; the client used his police authority to help his brother escape to Thailand; they were looking for his brother after that. He has a claim of his own. In another case, a client from Cameroon, who had been the sister of an SDF member in Cameroon – the military came to look for her sister, she was beaten and raped because of it, as a result she got AIDS, came here, [and sought asylum].
>
> (McHaffey, 2005)

Many people are persecuted simply because they are members of the family of a political activist, either because it is assumed that they, too, hold the same views, or to harm the activist indirectly. Nana, a Liberian, was an example of this. Here is her story as she wrote it:

> When the rebels of Charles Taylor's National Patriotic Party of Liberia invaded Monrovia and captured our area, they began searching for <u>Prominent Personalities</u> in the community. A number of these personalities, including my <u>father</u> was <u>arrested</u> and accused of <u>embezzling government funds</u> and misuse of public office, some of the relatives, including <u>myself</u>, of these officials were <u>tortured and raped</u>. My parents, two brothers and I were tied together and kept in the sun for about six hours before the rebels decided to kill my father and brothers. Consequently they were slaughtered in my presence, and I was given my father's head to

bury. While we were still being kept in the sun, another group of rebels belonging to Prince Johnson attacked our captors and heavy fighting broke up between the two groups. As the fighting intensified, our captors were forced to flee, the rebels leaving us in the hands of another rebel group. They, too tortured and forced me to show the whereabouts of my husband so that he could be recruited into their group. But by then my husband had gone to another part of the city in search of food and because of the worsening security situation he could not return . . . In view of losing my father and brothers left me with no choice but to run safety . . . I pick up my kids and headed east out of Liberia to our neighbouring state Sierra Leone.

As Nana's story makes clear, she was persecuted because she was related to someone who was selected for persecution by a group of rebels, not because of anything she herself was supposed to have done. She was simply caught in the middle of a terrible war and suffered because of who she was, not what she had done.

These claims are based on the persecution asylum seekers personally suffered as a result of their relationship to political activists. Julia is another person whose asylum claim is based on what happened to her family as well as to herself as a result of her husband's activities. She fled from Liberia after Charles Taylor's soldiers came to her house and demanded that her husband, James, come outside. Julia and her husband did not respond, so the soldiers broke down the door, tied up her husband and dragged him outside where they shot him. Then they came back into the house and gang raped Julia in front of her mother, who was so traumatized that she had a heart attack and died that night. Later, Julia went outside to look for her husband and found him, decapitated. James, Julia's husband, had been a medic in the military during Samuel Doe's presidency, and was therefore an enemy of the current leader, Charles Taylor. The soldiers were part of the security forces of Charles Taylor, and they continued the killings. Julia was terrified that they would come back and kill her and her children, so she escaped to the US.

When it is public, political, and personal

Asylum is defined in terms of politically motivated, rather than personal, persecution, and although many asylum seekers are victims of politically motivated aggression or threats, often they do not understand or know how to represent their traumatic experiences in political terms. An applicant's understanding of a personal story may not necessarily include information about others in the political group who had similar experiences. Each cultural group has its own genres for reporting on personal experience; for example, some report events that extend far beyond the person, and others restrict information to what an individual has actually witnessed (Shuman, 2005). However, the authorities require that the story be framed in terms of the applicant personally suffering persecution as a result of something broader.

Sheila, whom we met in Chapter 1, is a Tamil from Sri Lanka. She had come to the US for medical treatment and was afraid to go back to Sri Lanka because the situation was so dangerous. She was surrounded by violence, but none of it was directed at her in particular so it is not considered persecution within in the meaning of the definition. Similarly, in a US Court of Appeals case, the court decided that the asylum seeker, Rubina Begum Ahmed, a Muslim from India, had not shown that she had personally suffered persecution because of her religion. Nor had she shown that the Indian government systematically persecutes all Muslims, though she had included information about violence targeted at Muslims in India generally. This general violence was not directed at her in particular, so she lost her claim (*Shaikh* v. *Ashcroft*, 2004).

The need to prove personal persecution is central in asylum law. Without it, states fear that whenever a country is undergoing civil unrest and violence, they would be required to receive millions who are displaced by the violence, or even those, like Sheila, who find it frightening to live under such conditions and who are able to make it to a country offering asylum. After all, the officials reason, any sensible person who had the opportunity would leave the scene of violence; tragically, it is not possible for the millions around the world who live amidst civil unrest to find safe haven. The one situation where personal persecution is not necessary is for refugees, as we saw in Chapter 1.

Proving that the persecution is personal can be very complicated. If the group to which the asylum seeker belongs is very likely to be selected for persecution, it may not be necessary to show that one has been personally targeted. Jopie Eduard and his wife were Christian Indonesians who had fled to the US and were afraid to go back because they believed they would be persecuted because of their religion. The court acknowledged that Indonesia was "rife with civil uprisings" not specifically directed toward Christians, but they also recognized that there was a pattern of persecution directed towards Christians, including physical acts of violence, pressure to convert to Islam, and the routine burning of churches (*Eduard* v. *Ashcroft*, 2004).

By the government

For a claim to succeed, an applicant must show that the government was involved in the persecution, either directly or indirectly. An asylum seeker can claim persecution by an individual or a nongovernmental entity only if the persecution can be connected to the government, by showing that the government couldn't or wouldn't prevent it. For example, Diana Younis and her family, Israelis, unsuccessfully claimed asylum in the US because of actions toward them by the Muslim family of a young woman with whom their son was having a relationship. The court had no difficulty dismissing the claim because the hostile acts which the family suffered at the hands of the Muslim family were personal retribution for the unacceptable premarital relationship, not by the government and therefore not persecution (*Younis et al.* v. *Gonzales*, 2005).

Emmett, from Liberia, was a Jehovah's Witness who came to CRIS seeking asylum. When we asked him to describe the problems he had, he told us about someone in the construction business who had made his life very difficult. The person had been stealing supplies from the company and started harassing Emmett when he objected, using his religion as the basis for the harassment. Emmett had not gone to the authorities, so we couldn't argue that they had not protected him, nor was there any good evidence that it would have been useless for him to seek help from the police. So Emmett didn't have a claim for asylum.

It is often hard to define "the government" in countries undergoing civil unrest, or to be clear who, exactly is doing the persecuting, and on whose behalf. As the Asylum Aid report makes clear: "Civilians today are as likely to face persecution from armies, insurgents, militias and mafias as from governments" (1999: 14). Often, it is possible to prove that the government implicitly condones the behavior. In situations where there is civil war, this is pretty easy to prove. In some cases, as Tony Waters observes in the case of Rwanda, fleeing refugees are the first indication to the outside world of the existence of persecution (Waters, 2001: 199).

When the killing is done by rebel forces, as in the case of Julia in Liberia and Mustapha in Sierra Leone, it is clear that the government can't control the violence. When it is done by private citizens, like the Muslim extremists in Bangladesh in Grace's case, the applicant has to provide evidence that the government knew about it and didn't do anything about it. Grace was persecuted because she was an active Southern Baptist in Bangladesh. After 9/11, she was attacked on the street by Muslim extremists. Later, a group of men broke into her home while she was praying with her family. When the men attacked Grace's husband and destroyed the family home, the police refused to do anything. The extremists argued that the family was on the side of the US (the enemy) and that they would kill them if they did not stop worshipping their "American" religion.

As we shall discuss in Chapter 6, claims based on government lack of control over gender persecution are often the most difficult ones to argue. We see this especially in some cases where domestic violence is the basis for an asylum claim. Recently, some asylum claims have been successful because the applicant was able to prove, either that she went to the police and received no protection, or that there was good evidence that she would not get any protection even if she had gone to the police for help.

In the classic domestic violence asylum claim, a woman says she was battered by (usually) her husband, and tried, and failed, to get help from the police. In one decision, which has received a great deal of publicity in the media, the Board of Immigration Appeals denied an application (*In the Matter of R.A.*) by a Guatemalan woman who had been brutally beaten by her husband, an officer in the army. Rodi Alvarado married a Guatemalan army officer at the age of 16; from then on, she was subject to serious abuse, and her efforts to get help from the authorities were unsuccessful. Her husband raped her frequently, kicked her in the spine when she was pregnant, dislocated her jaw, tried to cut off her hands with a machete, kicked her in the vagina, and used her head to break windows. He bragged to her about his power to kill civilians with impunity. He also told her, "You are my woman, you do what I say." Many of the attacks took place in public, but the police did not help her at all. She made a complaint but her husband ignored three citations without legal consequence. In fact, the police once called her husband to come and get her from the police station. The case has since had a complicated history, with Janet Reno, then Attorney General, vacating the decision just before she left office. Regulations to clarify how these cases should be decided were issued but have never been made final. John Ashcroft then sat on the case and the regulations for several years, until 2004, when the Department of Homeland Security filed a brief in support of Rodi Alvarado. Then in January 2005, Ashcroft remanded the case back to the BIA where it currently sits.

The question of whether the immigration authorities believe that the government can protect someone is an issue that is often connected to politics. When someone comes from a country that is a close ally of the asylum-granting country, or that shares cultural and religious practices and forms of government, the claim that their government would not protect them is less likely to be believed. For example, Jamaica, as a former British colony and current member of the Commonwealth, is on the list of "safe" countries to which the UK authorities can quickly return an asylum seeker. One Home Office refusal letter stated:

> In the light of ongoing initiatives by the Jamaican Government to fight crime and gang violence with the co-operation of both the police (JCF) and the military (JDF), there is a general sufficiency of protection for victims of criminal violence in Jamaica.

The Amnesty International report vigorously disputes this claim, and therefore the use of it as a basis for denying a Jamaican applicants asylum (Amnesty International, 2004: 13–14).

The UK authorities often use the fact that a country has signed a treaty protecting human rights as evidence that they would protect an asylum seeker, when the reality is that the signature on a treaty bears no relationship to what actually happens in the country. For example, the Asylum Aid report states:

> The Czech government has signed the Framework Convention for the Protection of National Minorities. For all officially recognized minorities, including Romanies, the Czech legal system guarantees equal rights and duties. No mention is made of *how* the Czech legal system is able to guarantee equal rights and duties to minorities, nor of what safeguards and sanctions are provided.
>
> (1999: 42)

The authorities are more likely to believe that the Czechs are adhering to their treaties, as the Czech Republic is considered a "civilized" country, like us, and therefore we are reluctant to allege that they do not stick to their promises. Now that the Czech Republic is a member of the European Union, there is no chance of asylum for Czech Roma who claim that they have been persecuted.

The Asylum Aid report also looks at what happens in less developed countries. Here, too, there is a strong reliance on formal documents over actual practice.

> A number of sub-Saharan African governments are credited with good behaviour because of amnesties for political opponents which, though on the statute book, are often not observed. Asylum-seekers from Ghana, Uganda, and the Ivory Coast have good reason to know that such protection on paper counts for little in practice.
>
> (1999: 42)

The authorities seem also to take the word of the country and thus deny the applicants' claims which are at odds with the country's expressed policy. The Amnesty International UK report says:

> The Secretary of State further notes that the Algerian Government does not condone such violations. [However] Amnesty

International's research indicates that torture in Algeria remains prevalent and systematic in nearly all cases involving alleged links to what the government describes as "acts of terrorism or subversion." However, torture is not confined to cases of this kind. The security forces have also repeatedly tortured political activists arrested during or after demonstrations protesting against government policies or measures. Amnesty International does not accept the Algerian government's refusal to acknowledge that secret detention and torture are a problem in Algeria.

(2004: 11)

Persecuted, not persecutor

Both US and UK asylum law require that the applicant is a true victim of persecution, and not someone who was also involved in persecuting others. The UK relies directly on the 1951 Refugee Convention, which specifically states that someone who has committed a "crime against peace, a war crime or a crime against humanity" cannot be granted asylum (Art. 1F). US law bars from asylum anyone who "ordered, incited, assisted, or otherwise participated in the persecution of any person on account of" the five categories (Immigration and Nationality Act, s. 208(b)(2)(A)(i) and 241(b)(3)(B)(i)). The cases on this issue generally deal with serious situations, such as someone who was a member of the Maoists in Nepal (Country Guideline and Starred case of IG (Nepal), 2002), or a Peruvian who was a member of the civil guard who was a translator in interrogations of Shining Path members (*Miranda Alvarado* v. *Gonzales*, 2006), or an operative of military intelligence in the Philippines under Marcos (*Higuit* v. *Gonzales*, 2006). The problem arises for those who are members of anti-government organizations which support terrorism, even though the asylum seeker herself has not participated in violence. In the case of the pro-democracy Burmese (such as Tun and Chan), the immigration authorities have allowed a blanket exception to this barrier, on the assumption that many members of the group do not themselves participate in the violence of the few.

Since 9/11, there have been reports of problems in the asylum claims of people who have allegedly offered "material support" to terrorists.

In one case, a Sierra Leonean woman was raped (as was her daughter) and cut by guerrillas and kept captive in her house for four days (*International Herald Tribune*, 2006). Her application for asylum was refused because the authorities claimed that she had given shelter to the guerrillas! A Nepali health professional who was kidnapped by Maoist rebels and forced to provide medical treatment to injured rebels was told that the medical treatment constituted material support to a terrorist organization. This case is pending before the Board of Immigration Appeals (Human Rights First, 2007). There are several thousand such cases, which are not denied but instead put on indefinite hold, leaving the asylum seekers in permanent limbo. In January 2007, the administration announced that it would exempt certain groups of refugees from these "material support" rules, which could make the situation easier for those who have been caught by this policy (Human Rights First, 2007).

Henri is one of the cases put on hold for a long period. We received no response for three years after his hearing; then Henri got impatient and (without consulting us) filed a false claim for a green card with an "attorney." When the authorities connected the two claims, they denied Henri's asylum claim on the grounds that he assisted in the persecution of others by "directly and indirectly supplied RDC soldiers with every-thing from money to food to weapons and ammunition, and admitted to participating in three coups d'etat which resulted in multiple civilian deaths and the execution of political opponents by RDC soldiers" (Referral Notice, 2006). Henri denies these charges, and his case will ultimately be heard by the Immigration Court.

On account of

For an asylum claim to be successful, it has to fit into one of the legal categories set out in the 1951 Convention, which we listed earlier in the chapter.[1] An asylum seeker also has to show that the persecution was actually "because of" the category. It is not enough to show persecution just by proving the circumstances we have described above. This can be a complicated legal issue, but for our purposes it is enough to say that, somehow or other, the authorities have to be convinced that the persecution was because of the legal category. In many of the cases we have seen this is not a problem. For example, it is perfectly obvious that the government was after Tun because of his pro-democracy activities.

Proving the intent of one's persecutors can seem an impossible task. The classic US case on the subject is an appeal to the US Supreme Court by a Guatemalan asylum seeker who argued that he was afraid to return because he would be persecuted on account of his political opinion. Guerrillas tried to conscript Elias-Zacarias into their movement. The court held that a guerrilla organization's attempt to coerce a person into performing military service does not necessarily constitute "persecution on account of . . . political opinion." It said: "Elias-Zacarias objects that he cannot be expected to provide direct proof of his persecutors' motives. We do not require that. But since the statute makes motive critical, he must provide some evidence of it, direct or circumstantial" (*INS* v. *Elias-Zacarias*, 1992: 483). Other countries do not require proof of the motives of the persecutors. In an Australian case concerning an applicant who fled China after violating the one-child policy, the court refused to require that the applicant prove personal enmity in the punishment for his behavior. It also pointed out the difficulty, or even impossibility, of an inquiry into the motives and feelings of persecutors in a foreign country (*Chen Shi Hai* v. *Minister for Immigration and Multicultural Affairs*, 2000).

Each of the asylum categories (race, religion, nationality, membership in a particular social group, or political opinion) presents different problems for determining what counts as persecution. First, these categories are culturally specific, and they do not mean the same thing across the globe. Second, in some cases, identification with a category emerges in a politically fraught situation; in other words, the categories are not fixed and stable. The instability of the categories themselves creates problems in the asylum process.

Race/nationality/ethnicity

Many asylum applicants describe themselves as targets of either racial or ethnic/national persecution. Generally, the law does not recognize the reality that group identity and membership is not a fixed biological fact but rather can change in response to circumstances. We described in Chapter 3 the case of Colette, the young Rwandan woman who grew up as a Hutu until it was discovered, during the genocide, that her grandfather had been Tutsi. As a result she became identified as a Tutsi, an identity which was itself suspect because of having benefited in the past from the status of Hutu (Longman, 2001). Some groups would not have identified themselves as such were it not for their shared experience of discrimination. Some Gypsy/Romany people identify with the larger category for strategic reasons, even if culturally they experience no alliance. Becoming a refugee creates new coalitions (Moorehead, 2005). Ethnicity scholars describe a distinction between self-ascribed and other-ascribed, or achieved and ascribed identities to account for some of the different ways that groups identify themselves and are identified (Barth, 1969). Other-ascribed group identification, that is, how outsiders define a group, sometimes includes stereotyping, if not discrimination. Persecution on ethnic, racial, or national grounds often begins with structural inequalities in a society. Civil wars and changing regimes of power alter relations among members of a society, creating new alliances and new targets of persecution.

Asylum case law has allowed persecution on the basis of ethnicity, though it is not in the original definition; it is a category that is deemed to fall in between race and nationality. Dev, whom we met earlier, was an ethnic Nepali in Bhutan and part of the group which were persecuted because of that ethnicity. The label "ethnic" does not mean the same things in different parts of the world. In some cases, "ethnic" refers to a group, such as Ethnic Basques, that has lived in a particular place with a shared language and culture for generations. In contrast, ethnicity in the United States refers to immigrant groups. The "ethnic" category can refer to indigenous or displaced peoples, to minority or majority populations. Ethnicity can overlap with, or be separate from, racial and religious categories. For example, in the former Soviet Union, the category "Jewish" was a legal category, rather than a religious one; many of those who left the Soviet Union were unfamiliar with Jewish religious practice.

Asylum authorities may have a different view of the connection between race and ethnicity than the applicants and their societies. The Amnesty International report includes a long section about the implications of enforced return to Eritrea and Ethiopia of asylum applicants of mixed national origin, who are likely to face persecution on return to either of these countries. The report quotes from a refusal letter:

> The Secretary of State is aware that about 75,000 persons have been deported to Eritrea from Ethiopia during the past three years including those of mixed parentage, most have apparently been accepted in Eritrea as citizens despite the fact the [sic] only one fourth of them considers themselves to be Eritrean. Nevertheless the Eritrean government has offered considerable assistance to these people. He does not therefore consider that having one Ethiopian parent would have caused you to have suffered discrimination in Eritrea and this damaged your overall claim's credibility [sic].
>
> (quoted in Amnesty International, 2004: 23)

The report disagrees with this assessment:

> At the time of liberation and independence from Ethiopia in 1991, hardly any non-Eritrean Ethiopians were granted Eritrean citizenship, and dual Ethiopian and Eritrean nationality was not accepted. Ethiopians still reside in Eritrea as aliens (mostly migrant manual workers) but Eritrea does not accept back for permanent residence or naturalisation anyone of full or part Ethiopian origin. Eritrea will not give citizenship or a passport to anyone of part Ethiopian origin and indeed requires Eritreans, for the purpose of passports and travel to Eritrea, that they fully prove their Eritrean origin and confirm payment of obligatory development tax . . . Owing to the extensive activities of government security agents and informers, Ethiopian origin cannot be hidden.
>
> (2004: 23)

The report also says: "the term 'Ethiopians of Eritrean origin' is problematic. All those of full or part Eritrean origin who were previously considered, or considered themselves to be, Ethiopian citizens, were stripped of their Ethiopian citizenship arbitrarily and without any legal recourse" (2004: 23). The Home Office describes some asylum seekers as of mixed race and not at risk should they be returned because others can't tell. The report points out:

> . . . the term "race" is misleading and inappropriate. Those of full or part Eritrean origin who were born, or were long-term residents, in Ethiopia mostly speak Amharic and not all speak Tigrinya (the national language of Eritrea). Yet many are physically identifiable as being of Eritrean origin, through the greater Middle Eastern historical influences and contacts further north. They may be identifiable by their speech or cultural signifiers. In addition, they are identifiable by the local urban neighbourhood association (Kebelle) authorities and neighbours' or citizens' knowledge of their identity, as well as other government and police records. Kebelles are the local administrative units which closely control the status and activities of residents, with particular reference to political issues. This would include control of resident Eritreans, when their redefined legal status [creates] suspicions that they are agents of the Eritrean government.
>
> (2004: 23)

This is an example of the complexities occurring as a result of other-ascribed ethnicity. How Eritreans describe themselves and how others describe them are easily at odds, and it is difficult for asylum officials to evaluate the vulnerability of often shifting identities. Our discussion has only scratched the surface of what is a very complicated set of categories, which differ among different groups at different times and places. Like so much else in this area, however, these complexities are usually disregarded by the immigration authorities in their quest for clear categories. As a result they are applied in an arbitrary way which does not represent the way they are used by the asylum applicants themselves or their persecutors.

Religion

Religious persecution is another category frequently used in asylum claims. In the last chapter, we met Wei, a Chinese woman who practiced Falun Gong. Wei's husband had been practicing Falun Gong for several years because of the health benefits it gave him; he was arrested, tortured, and imprisoned for five years for doing so. Wei herself began practicing more recently, and was also involved in distributing leaflets and DVDs about the practice. She went into hiding after the police raided her house for Falun Gong materials, and then fled the country and sought asylum in the UK when her father told her that a wanted poster for her arrest was displayed in the street.

Grace, whose case we mentioned above, was persecuted because she was an active Southern Baptist in Muslim Bangladesh. She and her family escaped to the US; they have been attacked several times since their arrival, she believes by Muslim extremists.

People persecuted because they are Christian seem to have better luck gaining asylum in the US than those persecuted because they are, for example, Muslim; this may be another example of the arbitrary implementation of the "neutral" law, or evidence that Christians are more often persecuted in non-Christian countries than Muslims in non-Muslim countries. One lawyer had this to say on the issue:

> I'm going to have more time with a claim of Christian or Jew than Moslem, but I just don't know if I have a sound basis for this thought. We have had pro bonos handle cases of Christians and Jews fleeing persecution on account of their religion – I remember in the last year we won a case of young Jewish woman from Russia that I thought was quite weak, but was granted.
>
> (London, 2006)

She also described "outrageous denial to Moslem clients" but pointed out that these were on political claims, providing another example of the extent to which religion is not always an isolated, separate category but is connected to ethnicity and political affiliation.

People who convert to religions which are not the state religion may face persecution, especially in those Muslim countries where it is against the law (see Perlez, 2006). Mohamed, the Sudanese we met in Chapter 2, is a Muslim who went to the United Arab Emirates (UAE). He converted to Catholicism. He first went to Romania where he trained to be a pharmacist. While there, he had lots of problems with what he described as "fanatical" Muslims; he didn't hide the fact that he didn't go to the mosque. He moved back to the Sudan from Romania, where he spent five years before going to the UAE. His wife is Catholic, from the Philippines. They met in UAE, where she was working. They had a daughter whom they named Sylvana, which is clearly not a Muslim name. Mohamed's manager said to him when he heard the name: "Are you crazy?" "I said it's my wife's decision; she had the child for nine months so she decided its name." Josielou, Mohamed's wife, came to the US in 1996 to have their daughter. The people in UAE disapproved of the daughter being an American. Even after receiving asylum in the US, Mohamed is afraid to tell his family that he converted to Catholicism out of fear that the more people know of his conversion, the more likely it is that he will be persecuted by Islamic fundamentalists.

Religious persecution is at the center of asylum policy, both because it is a founding principle of the United States, and also because, as we saw earlier, international asylum policy was created in large part as a response to Nazi persecution of Jews and other groups during the Holocaust. As long as the religious persecution is recognized and documented, applicants must only prove themselves to be members of the targeted group and to have personally experienced persecution or threats, as we saw in the case of the Indonesian Christians (*Eduard* v. *Ashcroft*, 2004). But, as we saw earlier, discrimination without more serious persecution is not enough. The UK authorities seem to be less deferential to religious claims than their US counterparts. A London barrister told us that he often had cases of religious persecution which were denied because they were considered to be only discrimination (Ahluwalia, 2005b).

Social group

The most complicated category on which asylum claims are based is that of "membership in a particular social group." This category has been defined by the courts as persecution directed toward an individual who is a member of a group who share a common immutable characteristic which either can't be changed, or is something that a person should not be expected to change. Shared characteristics can be something innate, like sex, color, or kinship ties, or a shared past experience, such as former military leadership or landownership. The characteristic that is shared must also be perceived in a way as to result in persecution, and the persecution itself must be because of the shared characteristic. For example, the Australian courts have decided that parents who defy the one-child policy in China are persecuted not because they are members in a social group, but because of their behavior (*A* v. *MIEA*, 1997). This is all pretty complicated, and, like the other bases for asylum depends a lot on the actual facts of the case. It may be easier, if there are other possible bases for a claim (which there often are), to make the claim on the other grounds, as for instance an asylum seeker who is politically active for the group of which he is a member, who can claim on the ground of political affiliation.

Michelle Thomas, a white South African, claimed asylum, with her husband and children, based on her membership in what has been described as the social group "*par excellence*," a family (McDonald and Webber, 2005: 739). Her father-in-law "Boss Ronnie" was a foreman at Strongshore Construction in Durban, South Africa. "Boss Ronnie" was a notorious racist with a long history of abusing his black workers, both physically and verbally. Because of this family relationship, Michelle and her family were harassed a number of times; the family dog was poisoned, the car vandalized and the tires slashed. At one point, human feces were thrown at the car, and at another, four black men approached Michelle and tried to take her daughter from her arms. Their asylum claim was supported by the fact that her brother-in-law had also suffered similar problems, including having his car vandalized and receiving threats. Michelle speculated that "Boss Ronnie" was himself not the subject of threats and harassment because his house was essentially a fortress, so his unhappy employees went after his family. The court said that Michelle and her family were "persecuted by Black individuals precisely because of their familial relationship with their racist, white father-in-law" (*Thomas* v. *Ashcroft*, 2004).

The category of social group is a place where the law can be expanded to take in "new" forms of persecution, or, more accurately, old forms that we are now willing to recognize as an appropriate basis for asylum. This is particularly true in the recent willingness to recognize gender persecution, a subject that we will discuss in detail in Chapter 6. Fauziya Kassindja provides a good example of the expansion process. As we saw in Chapter 4, her claim was based on her fear that if she stayed in Togo, she would be forced to undergo FGM. The problem with the "social group" category is that, depending on how you define the group, it can include vast numbers of people or relatively few. The asylum authorities are, of course, concerned that groups be defined narrowly, because otherwise the category could be used to open the floodgates to let in the hordes they fear so much. As a result, the social groups are sometimes strangely defined. For example, the court deciding Fauziya's case defined the group as "women of the Tchamb-Kuntsuntu Tribe of Northern Togo, who oppose the practice of FGM." They did not define a category that would include all women at risk for FGM (some estimates for this category would include 125 million women!) or even all women from Togo at risk. This problem of identifying the group narrowly seems particularly acute in gender-based asylum claims. In the case of Rodi Alvarado, whom we mentioned earlier, the Board of Immigration Appeals agreed that the treatment she received from her husband was sufficient to be considered persecution, but denied her claim because she was unable to show how the battering was "on account of" one of the protected categories. The social group Rodi tried to use as the basis for her claim was "Guatemalan women who have been involved intimately with Guatemalan male companions who believe that women are to live under male domination," a truly convoluted category.

Trying to fit domestic violence into a social group runs into the problem that it is broad enough to go beyond specific cases of women who share distinguishing and identifiable characteristics. Scholars have tried to define domestic violence in terms of membership in a social group, as "battered women who express their opposition to their constant subordinate position, and who because of their gender, lack the benefits and assistance of government agencies and of society in general" (Aliaskari, 2000: 249). But we should note that a political dimension is added here in the "expression of opposition to their constant subordinate position." One could argue that anyone who manages to get to the West to make an asylum claim has, almost by definition, expressed a "political" position on her treatment at the hands of her batterer.

Political opinion

Most frequently, applicants claim that their political opinions made them targets of persecution. Tun, whose story began this chapter, is an example of someone who was persecuted because of his political opinion, as was his wife, Chan, who also worked in the pro-democracy movement. Chheung, who was from Cambodia, got into trouble when he wanted to leave the Cambodian People's Party. He had been a member since 1979, and decided to leave in 2000. After he told the Party that he wanted to leave, they investigated him, spied on him, and harassed him. Three of his close friends, who also left the Party, disappeared. Another person he knew was imprisoned for trying to leave the Party. Chheung had been a manager for the government, but after he left the Party, people stopped trusting him, so he had to leave his job. After he fled Cambodia for the US, his wife (who was still there) wrote to him asking him to stop telephoning home to ask about his family and to stop writing letters home. Since his departure, his house has been under surveillance, and people have been asking his children where he went.

Political opinion is a broad category that can encompass a range of activities with opposition parties, or membership and activity in a group of which the government does not approve, or, as in the case of Chheung, reluctance to participate in a political party. For example, those who protest blasphemy laws in Pakistan, or who work for women's rights, or who protest the one-child policy in China, can all claim that their persecution was on account of their political opinion. In fact the US law, which expressly makes objection to coercive population control a basis for asylum (like the one-child policy in China), counts this as persecution based on political opinion.

The case of Yun Jun Cao, a pediatrician from China, shows the complicated connections between population policies and political activism. Cao successfully claimed asylum based on her activities after she discovered that her hospital was killing live newborn babies born in violation of China's population control policies. She was, of course, aware of the policies, including the fact that officials often forced women to have late-term abortions, but she only learned of the infanticide after she noticed a woman crying in the obstetrics ward and was told that the child had died suddenly after she had given birth. She began noticing a pattern of women crying in similar circumstances, and confronted a colleague who told her the hospital injected the newborns with alcohol to cause death. Cao was horrified to learn this and, a few months later, told a visiting journalist from Hong Kong what she had discovered and agreed to send material to him so he could write an article about it. Her letter was intercepted by the authorities and as a result she was arrested; she claimed that she was detained, interrogated, and beaten. She was not charged with any crime but was told that she could be charged with sedition and sentenced to ten years' imprisonment. She managed to flee and came to the US on a visitor's visa (*Yun Jun Cao* v. *Attorney General*, 2005).

The political opinion may be imputed rather than direct. Many activities, in particular contexts and at particular times in history, are seen as political. For example, in the film, *Chasing Freedom*, Mina, the woman from Afghanistan whose case is followed in the film, was persecuted for teaching Afghani girls (Court TV, 2004). It is hard to remember, but there was a time when such behavior was punished in the US – before the Civil War, where, in many states, teaching slaves to read and write was regarded as a crime. After the war in Afghanistan in 2002, girls had some opportunity to learn. It is unclear whether this is still true, now that the Taliban is more powerful again. A recent case, in which an Afghan headmaster who taught girls was beheaded by Taliban militants, indicates that teaching girls is still very risky (Khan, 2006).

The political activity used as a basis for an asylum claim has to be extensive enough to be likely to result in persecution. This is particularly true in the UK, where the Home Office frequently decides the activity is not serious enough to warrant protection. The Amnesty International (UK) report describes a case in which the Secretary of State did not find it credible that an Iranian woman "*would be of interest to the authorities for carrying out the low-level political activities you describe.*" The same refusal admits, however, that the Iranian authorities have a "*general intolerance*" to all opposition to the regime (Amnesty International, 2004: 41). The Home Office also argues that a member of the FIS (Front Islamique de Salut, the banned Islamic fundamentalist party in Algeria) can only be the subject of persecution if they participated "*at a high level or involved in terrorist activities were likely to be of genuine interest to the Algerian authorities*" (2004: 41). This assertion is without any supporting evidence and seems to be another way of limiting the number of people who can get asylum. Likewise, in one of the asylum appeal cases we observed in London, an asylum seeker was rejected because he only provided food and clothing through intermediaries to the PKK.

More than one reason

Many of the examples we have used in the sections above have, in fact, been a combination of more than one basis for persecution. This is particularly true for "race," "nationality," and "membership in a particular social group," which often merge with political opinion. Being able to make a claim based on more than one factor often strengthens the asylum seeker's case, and suffering persecution for more than one reason is quite common.

The question of whether something is political or based on another factor is very difficult to separate out. So often, people get into trouble with their governments for pressing for rights which the government does not want to give. These may be rights for minority group members, religious minorities, or for women. The agitators are usually members of the groups for which they claim rights, thereby giving them two bites at the asylum apple.

We saw, for example, that Dev's activism was on behalf of ethnic Nepalis in Bhutan. The government discriminated against ethnic Nepalis on the basis of their ethnicity as well as their religion. Everyone, including ethnic Nepalis, who had their own traditional dress, was required to wear the national dress of the majority group (the Drupka). The majority group in Bhutan are Buddhist, while the ethnic Nepalis are Hindu. The government required that the Hindus get permission to build temples (which was not granted), though it subsidized the building of monasteries and shrines for the Buddhists. The property of ethnic Nepalis was seized and their religious worship impeded. Dev was an activist in an opposition party to try to obtain rights for his group. As a result he was imprisoned and tortured. So Dev's asylum claim is based on religion, ethnic group, *and* political opinion.

Diallo, whom we met in Chapter 1, was persecuted because he is a "black Moor," a member of a minority group in Mauritania which has suffered long-standing persecution by the Muslim leadership that has held power since a coup in 1984. Diallo is one of many Mauritanians we have met who claim persecution based on ethnicity (or race, depending on how you define it). Diallo was also active in a political party that was concerned about the rights of members of his ethnic group, so he can also claim persecution based on political opinion.

Sam, an evangelical preacher in Ghana, is an example of someone whose political activism is connected to his religion. At times he was critical of the government, mainly because it did not allow freedom of worship. He was arrested and detained for a month, during which time he was beaten and tortured. As a result of his brutal treatment in detention, he was hospitalized for several months. Some time later, he returned to public preaching. When three members of the ruling party stopped him and said he would not be allowed to preach, he began to fear for his safety and arranged to get a passport. When he received information that he was about to be arrested, he fled to the UK (Asylum Aid, 1999: 83).

Like those whose claims are both political and based on nationality, many of those who claim asylum based on religion also have other grounds, such as political opinion or nationality. The Soviet Jews whom we mentioned earlier were granted refugee status both on the grounds of religion and because being Jewish in the Soviet Union was a defined nationality.

James is an example of a case in which there are two bases: religion and political opinion. He was a Roman Catholic in Pakistan, who was active in a Christian Youth Organization. He worked to help women who faced discrimination in the workplace. He was also involved in protesting against the blasphemy laws instituted in Pakistan, as well as the burning of churches and Bibles, and the desecration of cemeteries. His claim is based both on persecution because he is a Roman Catholic in a Muslim country, and because he engaged in political activity against the government and against activities that the government condoned (or at least ignored).

Mahomed, the convert from Islam to Catholicism, who was granted asylum in the US, also had some political basis for his claim. Before he left Sudan, he had political problems. "Since I was young, I was always anti-fanatic Muslim. I used to get into trouble and they came to my brother to tell him . . . He was very politically active. He also has asylum here and lives nearby."

As we have seen, membership in a social group also overlaps with the category of political opinion. For example, Irina, a Russian lesbian (classified as a social group) was granted asylum after she was persecuted because she championed the cause of gay rights (expression of a political opinion). As one lawyer we interviewed said:

> The gender cases – there is always an element of gender in other cases. I try to make as many arguments as I can, something can be closer on one group, or might make it on another. For example, a Cameroonian woman, it was a sort of a DV [domestic violence] case, had some political overtones – I was trying to stick to that as much as possible. Her husband abused her pretty badly, he was an area organizer for the ruling party. They didn't get along – one of the problems in the relationship was that she voted for the opposition party – he found out and he beat her mercilessly. There were other issues – she did things to avoid being pregnant because he wanted a baby every year and she wanted to go to school – we made a political feminist argument, she believed in education.
>
> (McHaffey, 2005)

Whether something is called persecution based on one ground or another, or a combination, is often a matter of which category is most acceptable to the decision maker and which is easier to prove. As we have seen, in the cases where one of the possible bases is membership in a social group, it is often easier to find another, clearer ground on which to base the claim. An example of this is the case in which the BIA granted asylum to Damia, a young Moroccan woman, because she had suffered persecution by her father on account of her religious beliefs. Her father beat her regularly for acting inappropriately according to her family's fundamentalist Muslim beliefs. The BIA contrasted the father's orthodox Muslim beliefs and the applicant's liberal Muslim beliefs. Thus this case seems to have been based on religious persecution, even though it was clearly closely connected to gender persecution (her brothers were not beaten).

Conclusion

What counts as persecution is not easily answered and is not a matter of universal agreement. As scholars of human rights policy have observed, even basic human rights do not have universal agreement (see e.g. Jones, 1989). Even the category of torture is disputed, as the recent debate about its acceptability in the "war on terror" demonstrates (Weschler, 1990). For the most part, the US, UK, and other Western countries are more likely to grant asylum when individuals have experienced something that Western culture understands as abhorrent. As we have seen, one culture or nation may accept a form of punishment (stoning) for an act that another does not regard as deserving punishment at all (becoming pregnant before marriage or with a person from another faith). Our research suggests that more exotic, abhorrent acts of persecution are both more recognized as persecution and more susceptible to the suspicion discussed in Chapter 4, as to whether or not such an act could have actually occurred.

Note

1. Since the passage of the Real ID Act in May 2005, applicants for asylum have to prove that their race, religion, national origin, political opinion, or membership in a particular social group constituted "at least one central reason" for their persecution. Current law requires applicants show that their persecution was based "at least in part" on one of these factors It is not clear that this change will make much of a difference to asylum seekers.

6   The personal is political

Taking gender into account

Mende's story

We introduced Mende in Chapter 1. She was the person who finally was given asylum in Britain because of a lot of publicity about her case. Here is her story:

> I come from the Nuba tribe, in the Nuba Mountains of Sudan, one of the remotest places on earth. I lived in a village of mud huts with grass-thatched roofs, nestled in a fold of the big hills.
>
> (Nazer and Lewis, 2003: 1)

One night, when Mende was about 12, she and her family were woken from sleep by a fire in the village. It soon became clear that it was part of a raid by the mujahedin, Arab raiders. Mende, her mother, and her father ran to escape.

> We ran through scenes from your worst nightmare – my father leading, me following clutching his hand tightly, and my mother right behind us. I still held Uran [her cat] in one arm ... Women and children were running in all directions, crying and screaming in confusion and terror. I saw the raiders cutting people's throats, their curved daggers glinting in the firelight. I saw them grabbing hold of children, and pulling them out of their parents' arms
>
> (2003: 3)

In the chaos, Mende was separated from her father by a herd of cattle fleeing the fire. While she was frantically trying to find her father, she was grabbed from behind by a man who pinned her to the ground.

> I kept trying to shout for him [her father]. But the man clamped his grubby hand over my mouth. "Shut up," he hissed, in Arabic. "Shut up and lie still. If you keep shouting, the other men will find you and they will kill you."
>
> (2003: 4)

Mende was taken away to the forests amidst the sight of women being attacked, and the "stench of burning, of blood and of terror" (2003: 5). "I had no idea if any of my family had escaped, or if they had all been killed in the raid. I had no idea what would happen to me now" (2003: 5).

What happened was that Mende became a slave. The raider took her on a perilous journey to Khartoum, the capital of Sudan. During the trip, she was raped by one of her captors. She suffered excruciating pain as a result, because she had undergone FGM of the most extensive type, infibulation, a couple of years earlier. Her rapist ripped open the scar that had been left after the FGM. After they arrived in Khartoum, Mende and several other girls, who were also kidnapped, were put to work in the house of the person who sold her into slavery, though she didn't realize what had happened at the time. In fact, she knew nothing about what was happening to her. She worked in a basement with the other girls, preparing food for a Muslim festival. They were told what to do by another Nuba slave, Asha, who told them they would soon be leaving the house separately for their ultimate destination, the homes of their new owners. Asha advised the girls that they must always obey their master, otherwise they would be beaten. Soon after, they were visited in the basement by a group of people who looked the girls over to decide which one to buy.

The following day, Mende was taken to the house of the family to whom she had been sold: Rahab, and her husband, Mustapha. The first night she was locked into a small, dirty, messy room away from the house. This room was her home for the six years she spent as a slave in that household. The following morning, Rahab told Mende what her future held.

> "You are going to live here and work for me. You will stay for the rest of your life . . . I have two little girls that you have to look after. You must treat them very well. You have to clean the house and keep it very, very neat and tidy. You have to clean the yard and the patio, at the front of the house." She told me that I had to wash the clothes, and "iron them." I didn't even know what an iron was. But I remembered what Asha had told me. So I just nodded and said. "Yes, master," to everything.
>
> (Nazer and Lewis, 2003: 141)

Mende worked from early morning until late at night. She ate the family's leftovers, on her own plate, alone, as they believed she was diseased and dirty. "And so it went on-day after day, the same drudgery, the same constant abuse. One day merged into the next, almost without my noticing" (2003: 148).

> It was hardly surprising that soon something went seriously wrong. I was using a duster to swipe cobwebs out of a corner, as Rahab had shown me to do. But the duster caught the lip of a vase and it went crashing to the floor.

Rahab was furious.

> "Do you know how much this cost me? This one vase is worth more than your whole filthy tribe!" My head jerked back as she grabbed me by the hair and I felt a stinging slap against my cheek . . . "I'm sorry . . . Please don't hit me." But she did, again, and again and again.
>
> (2003: 149)

Rahab, never bothered to learn her real name. She was called *yebit*, "an Arabic insult, which literally means 'girl worthy of no name' " (2003: 139). For the first three years of her enslavement, Mende was not allowed out of the house. She was beaten frequently, sometimes in front of others. On one occasion, one of the guests goaded Rahab on. " 'Yes! Go on! Beat her!' she cried. 'It's the only way! Then she'll remember not to do it again, won't she?' " (2003: 167). Once Mende was seriously enough injured that she had to be taken to the hospital where she spent a couple of weeks, her first time out of the house. She was told to say that her injury was the result of an accident. Rahab also told a nurse in the hospital that Mende was her servant, apparently not wanting it publicly known that she kept a slave (2003: 185). This nurse, whose name was Nunga, treated Mende with great kindness.

> I wanted to tell Nunga the truth about everything. But I was afraid that if I did, Rahab would kill me. I had spent three long years completely under Rahab's control. She had beaten me, abused me and killed any sense I once had of my own worth. I believed that I was her slave and that she was my master. I believed that she was in absolute control and that she held the power of life and death over me.
>
> (2003: 187)

Mende grew into an attractive young woman. She began to have problems with men who visited the house, who thought she was fair game for their forced sexual attention. Fortunately, Rahab's husband, Mustapha, never assaulted her because, according to Mende's story, he was so much under his wife's thumb that he didn't dare. Mende believes that he set up, or at least was complicit in, the attempted rape by a visitor to his house on a day when Rahab wasn't home.

After Mende had been with Rahab for about six years, Rahab told her that she would be sent to London to be with Rahab's sister Hanan, who was married to a Sudanese diplomat. Hanan had recently had twins, so she needed extra help. Mende didn't even know where London was, and couldn't imagine how she would get there or what it would be like.

> I was very worried. Over the last six years, I'd learned how to survive as a slave in Rahab's house in Khartoum. I'd learned how to behave to avoid getting beaten. I'd learned how to stop the worst verbal abuse. I'd learned how to evade sexual assaults. I'd learned how to safeguard my few joys in life. In short, I knew the rules. Now all that was about to change.
>
> (2003: 212)

Mende had never found out what had happened to her family. It was too painful to think about them much. Around the time she was told she was going to London, Mende realized "that I had given up my real family for dead. I had become used to not thinking about them" (2003: 212). Luckily, soon after, Mende met another girl, Kumal, from her village, who had also been sold into slavery. Kumal told Mende that she had met a Nuba man who had told her that Mende's family had survived the raid. "He told me this, just in case I ever saw you. He said your mother and father and everyone are fine" (2003: 216). This knowledge gave Mende new strength.

For several months, there was no further talk of Mende going to London. "I was happy that the idea just seemed to be forgotten" (2003: 219). But it had not. It was becoming clear that a grown-up, attractive Mende was a threat to Rahab, which was partly why she decided to ship Mende abroad. Getting a visa was a bit of a problem because, although Mende had been told what to say to the Consul, she couldn't answer all the questions she was asked. She had been told to say she was going to work in the house of someone called Ali Bashir Gadalla, although in fact Rahab's sister was married to someone called Al Koronky. Mende found out much later that this particular deception was because Al Koronky had previously had a slave working for him in London who had escaped and sought asylum. Not surprisingly in the circumstances, his earlier application for a visa for Mende was turned down.

Mende was replaced in the household by another young Nuba slave girl whose story was very similar to hers, also including a rape and the resulting terrible pain because of an earlier circumcision. Mende arrived in London in May 2000, and went immediately to her new household. Hanan told her that she would be doing what she had done for Rahab, but that it was much easier in London because of all the household appliances. For Mende, this was more unfamiliar, frightening territory, as she had never before seen a washing machine and was terrified by the vacuum cleaner. In general, she was better treated by Hanan than she had been by her sister. She was not beaten or verbally abused. Hanan used Mende's actual name, rather than calling her *yebit*, and she was allowed her own food, and her own prayer rug, which, as a devout Muslim, was very important to her.

So it went on, until the day when Mende asked how she might telephone a number which she had been given in Khartoum by the Nubian friend who had told her about her family. After that her relationship with Hanan went downhill.

> She was no longer the kind woman who had hugged me when I first arrived in her house. She began to shout at me for no reason at all. She began calling me names. And she began watching me very closely, checking on me wherever I was in the house. Ever since I'd arrived, the only time that I was allowed outside on my own was when I took the rubbish to the bins on the driveway. Now, I noticed that Hanan was keeping an eye on me from an upstairs window. The incident with the phone number must have made her worried that I would try to escape.
>
> (2003: 271)

Escape is what Mende eventually did. When Hanan and the children went back to Sudan, the family was planning to leave her alone with Al Koronky, to which Mende objected strongly because it was a violation of Muslim law for a single woman to be alone in the house with a man. In the end, she had to stay with him for a week, but when he joined his family in Sudan, she was sent to stay with another Sudanese couple, Omer and Medina, who didn't know that she was a slave. They treated her with great kindness, which had the effect of making her aware of how miserable her life was. On one occasion, when Omer was driving Mende to her master's house so she could do the required weekly cleaning, he asked why she had been crying the previous evening. He started asking her about her situation with the Koronky family and was shocked when she admitted that she had no set hours, never got time off, and wasn't paid at all. He told her "no one works in London without being paid. That's the law here" (2003: 295).

Mende considered telling the whole story to Omer, but decided against it because he worked with Al Koronky, so it would put him at risk. Talking about her situation with Omer did give her the impetus to find someone else to help her. One day, when she was out doing the shopping for Medina (with them she was allowed out by herself), she saw a man she thought might have been Sudanese and told him her story. He had a Nubian friend, Babo, who spoke to Mende and they promised they would help her escape. She waited until Hanan came back from Sudan and returned to their house, so she wouldn't implicate Omer and Medina, who had been so kind to her. On the appointed day, she went outside to the trash cans and ran down the driveway to Babo, who was waiting for her. "These were my people, Nuba people, and I knew I could trust them . . . So, maybe my years as a slave were finally, finally over" (2003: 308).

Mende's ordeal continued for another two years, however, the time it took for her to win asylum. As soon as she was free, her protectors took her to a lawyer to start the asylum process. She had a great deal to learn about being free and being an adult in a big city. Over time, she learned English and wrote a book, together with a journalist with experience of slavery in Sudan who had taken her under his wing. By then, lots of other people had become involved in her case – journalists, politicians, supporters in England and other countries. Her application was initially declined, much to the horror of all those working with her. Damien Lewis, her journalist coauthor and friend, told her what the refusal letter said:

> Firstly, it says that slavery is not persecution . . . They say that
> although there is slavery in Sudan, the Sudanese government
> is not involved . . . They say that Sudan is such a large country,
> that the Sudanese government would not notice if you were
> sent back . . . and it says that although the Nuba have suffered
> in the war because the government forces have attacked
> them, there's a cease-fire now in the Nuba Mountains, so it's
> safe for you to go home.
>
> (2003: 321–2)

All that was contrary to the truth. Clearly the Sudanese government
was involved, because Mende was working for a Sudanese diplomat.
In the war, there had been many ceasefires, all of which had been
broken before. In a statement Mende made for the press after the
denial, she said:

> The British Government says that my asylum claim is not
> based upon suffering due to my race, religion or nationality.
> How can they possibly say this, when I was enslaved and
> oppressed by Arabs because I am a black, Nuba person?
> . . . I am one of the few Sudanese who have stood up and
> exposed the government's role in war-driven slavery in Sudan.
> How can they possibly say my life would not be in danger if
> I were sent back?
>
> (2003: 323–4)

In the end, it was this last argument which was the basis for the
reversal of the initial decision. The media had a field day with the
decision, and one well-known politician promised to go on a hunger
strike to make the government change its mind. Before that became
necessary:

> [T]he Home Office Minister wrote "I have read Ms Nazer's
> account of her experiences in Sudan. In view of the wide-
> spread publication of her book and the high profile given to

> her claims both in Sudan and elsewhere, I am satisfied that Ms
> Nazer would face difficulties which would bring her within
> the scope of the 1951 [refugee] convention were she to
> return to Sudan."
>
> (2003: 331)
>
> So Mende is now free and living in London, speaking frequently about
> slavery. She is in touch with her parents, though she hasn't yet been
> able to see them.

Gender in the asylum process

The private is the public for those for whom the personal is the
political.

(MacKinnon, 1987:100)

We have seen in previous chapters several ways in which women are
treated differently from men in asylum claims. In Chapter 4 we saw
that their credibility was evaluated differently than men's. We also saw
in Chapter 5 how some of the claims based on membership in a social
group were essentially gender-based claims carved out of this category.
In this chapter we look at the whole issue of gender, to see how it plays
out in the asylum process. In particular, we examine cases in which
persecution of women is considered private, rather than public and
political, and thus warranting asylum. We will show that, despite the
fact that women's claims are often treated less seriously than men's,
gender itself is the one area where there has been expansion rather than
contraction in asylum policy (Copeland, 2003). In fact, some lawyers
have told us that it is now easier to get asylum using a gender-based
ground than other grounds. In particular, as we discuss in greater detail
below, women escaping from practices that asylum officials in the West
regard as "barbaric" elements of traditional culture are sometimes
recognized as good candidates for asylum. This is a tricky area, because
countries do not want to interfere in the sovereignty of other nations,

including their right to practice their own traditions. At the same time, resisting such practices can be recognized as political activism and a ground for asylum. One author who interviewed a number of women asylum applicants in the US actually argues that women are strongly encouraged (or bullied, as she implied) into making their claims on gender grounds, even when those grounds were not the actual reason they fled their homelands (Oxford, 2005).

Increasing recognition of gender-based claims can be seen in official guidelines published in the last decade or so. These guidelines, in a number of countries, including the US (US Department of Justice, 1995) and the UK (UK Asylum Appellate Authority, 2000), follow the 1991 UNHCR gender guidelines. The most comprehensive guidelines were passed in Australia in 1996 (Crawley, 2001). The 1995 US guidelines, which were billed as "groundbreaking," were suspended when George W. Bush became President. These guidelines would have provided a framework for the adjudication of gender-based claims, and particularly allowed gender to be considered as a basis for "membership in a particular social group." Without the guidelines, the authorities in the US craft their own definitions of social group to include gender. As we saw in Chapter 5, cobbling together a social group can be convoluted and artificial.

Canada has been at the forefront of the development of gender-based asylum law and in 1993 passed guidelines (CIRB, 1993) allowing the authorities to grant asylum to women who demonstrate a well-founded fear of gender related persecution by state or non-state actors (Troper, 1995). The guidelines also included the fear based on failure to conform to gender-based religious or customary laws in their homeland. We have seen that many gender-based claims are closely connected to cultural and religious values; this guideline makes the connection an appropriate basis for an asylum claim.

In 2000, the UK also adopted gender guidelines designed to change the perception of the typical asylum applicant as male. These guidelines also made possible the granting of asylum to people persecuted by non-state actors, and included harm inflicted by a spouse or family member. If persecution was sufficient to rise to the level of "serious harm" if it occurred outside the family, it also amounted to serious harm if done by a family member. The UK guidelines enumerate the types of harm that would be considered, and included domestic violence, forced marriage, bride burnings, and honor killings. They also address a number of issues about the appropriate way to interview women applicants, and how to deal with claims that include sexual violence.

It should be noted that these are guidelines, not law or regulations, and therefore are not mandatory. As we have already seen, the UK authorities are very reluctant to grant asylum to anyone, and that seems to include those making gender-based claims, despite the existence of the guidelines. Reports by Asylum Aid and the UNHCR also describe many occasions where the guidelines about the appropriate treatment of women applicants have been disregarded, and a recent report by the Refugee Women's Resource Project specifically addresses these problems and makes suggestions for change (Refugee Women's Resource Project Asylum Aid, 2006). The lawyers we interviewed were also skeptical that they were being used properly. Crawley points out that the Home Office does not acknowledge any particular problems which women may experience in the asylum process (2001: 202).

The numbers

Unfortunately, we know very little about how many women apply for asylum compared to men – seemingly a simple statistic. This is especially true in the US, where the USCIS doesn't keep separate statistics on the gender of asylum claimants. The UNHCR puts out an annual overview of global refugee trends, in which they report that about half the world's refugees are women (49 percent), though, of course the proportion varies greatly depending on the area of the world and the nature of the refugee situation. (UNHCR, 2005: 5). Others put the proportion of women much higher (Bahl, 1997). However, the percentage of women who seek asylum (as distinct from being refugees) is much lower. In the UK, for example, data show that women make up about one-quarter of the applicants. In the US, it is not possible to find any data about the proportion of women asylum seekers, though informal evidence would put the proportion at between a quarter and a third of all applicants.

If we know little about how many women seek asylum compared to men, we know even less about why there are fewer women. Some scholars have speculated that it is harder for women to flee their homeland, as they are more likely to have to coordinate their flight with others, including husbands and children (Holzer *et al.*, 2000: 260). They contrast this situation with the typical asylum seeker, who is young, male and single, which makes him more mobile. It also, ironically, increases the likelihood that he will be refused asylum, because this is also the typical profile of an economic migrant rather than someone genuinely fleeing persecution. These differences seem to account for the fact that, as one source claims, females who apply for asylum are five times more likely to be granted it than males, and married asylum seekers are twice as likely to be granted asylum than single asylum seekers (Holzer *et al.*, 2000: 260). In the UK, the approval rates for men and women are closer. For 2003, women asylum applicants made up 28 percent of all applicants and had a higher success rate (9 percent compared to 5 percent). The percentage of those allowed to stay under the category Exceptional Leave to Remain were about the same (11 percent for women, 10 percent for men) (UNHCR, 2005).

A higher proportion of women are removed in expedited removal than are men, compared to regular immigration proceedings. We can only speculate about the reasons for this disturbing trend; perhaps women have a harder time pushing the authorities to hear their claim of asylum at the border, especially in cases where they would have to disclose gender-based reasons, which are acutely personal and known to be especially problematic for women (Musalo *et al.*, 2001: 50–1).

Women's asylum claims

Women's claims for asylum are often different from those of men. They share with men the fact that the highest proportion of their claims are based on political opinion. However, they are more likely than men to apply because of their association with political men, or because of family persecution, "imputed political opinion" rather than their own activities. One British report shows that 27 percent of their sample of women applicants claimed asylum on the ground of imputed political opinion, and 17 percent on (direct) political opinion (Refugee Women's Resource Project, Asylum Aid, 2003). Women's claims on other grounds may also be combined, at least in part, with claims based on gender. As we saw in Chapter 5, many are mixed claims, partly based on membership in a social group and partly on another basis, such as religion or race. The UK Refugee Women's Resource Project report says that, in their sample of 103 women asylum seekers, 37 applicants had more than one ground on which they claimed asylum, three had three grounds and three had four (2003: 49).

Comparable data are not available on the bases of women's claims in the US. In an effort to learn something about the types of women's claims, we collected data informally ourselves. We counted the bases of claims in an NGO which assigns cases to *pro bono* attorneys in a large city in the US. We selected client lists over a three-year period and found that only about a third of the claims by women were gender based, with a few mixed claims which included gender. The non-gender claims were, like those of the men, mostly based on political activity or religion.

These statistics show that, contrary to the assertions of some scholars, women's claims are not all gender based. There is, of course, a distinction between a gender-based claim and one in which gender is an issue. Spijkerboer argues that "gender and ethnicity are dominant in almost all cases of female asylum applicants" (2000: 193). He is not just describing the basis of the claim, but something more about the ways women are perceived in this process. One of the major issues about the treatment of women in asylum is how seriously their claims are taken.

Are women taken more or less seriously?

We have seen that, as far as we can tell with the limited statistics available, women are much less likely to claim asylum, but when they do, they have higher rates of success than men. In the absence of comprehensive research, it is hard to tell why this is so. Spijkerboer attributes it partly to the fact that women applicants disproportionately come from countries with high success rates (presumably because the persecution is more serious there) (2000: 194).

Women applicants seem to be taken both more seriously and less seriously. One can be taken seriously and still not be granted asylum and vice versa. Women are taken more seriously because they are less likely to be seen as "bogus asylum seekers" trying to beat the system to improve their economic position. This may be as much about cultural perceptions as about reality; we don't know how many of the women asylum seekers are using the system to improve their economic situation in exactly the way men are supposed to do. Whereas men who are denied asylum are often characterized as not credible, that is, not having experienced what they claim to have suffered, women who are denied asylum are more often characterized either as having experienced suffering in the private, rather than public and political, sphere, or as having no provable fear of return to further persecution (or both). Thus, while women may face less suspicion than men of fraudulently claiming asylum when their motives are economic, women face additional assessments of whether or not their persecution qualifies as public and political asylum.

Some of the reasons women are taken less seriously have been discussed in previous chapters. Their behavior is judged on the basis of cultural values about appropriate female behavior and, if their behavior does not fit, they are found not credible. In addition to cultural differences that can create misunderstandings between the applicant and the asylum officials, some factors are particular to women. For example, women may have more difficulty telling their stories, especially about sexual assault. Problems with interpreters are also connected to this reluctance; women are less willing to describe sexual persecution to a male interpreter, especially if they fear that he will reveal her secrets.

Cultural perceptions determine which story of persecution is most likely to be believed. Successful claims are those presented in a way with which those hearing the narratives can identify. This is true in law generally, though it is even clearer in asylum because cultural perceptions may differ significantly. Conley and O'Barr's work on courtroom narrative stresses the extent to which "reasoned," "unemotional," "objective" narratives are privileged over those with emotional content. They argue that, on the whole, it is easier for men than women to frame their testimony in culturally appropriate ways (Conley and O'Barr, 1998). We saw in Chapter 4 how important it was to present oneself in an acceptable way, showing the "right" amount of emotion. This seems to be more difficult for women, who are often caught between being labeled "hysterical" if they present themselves too emotionally, and "cold" or uncaring if they seem too unemotional. Spijkerboer observes:

> It may be that black women are expected to be more emotional than white women and that the display of emotion sufficient for a Bosnian woman is judged insufficient for a Zairian woman. Conversely, women from less developed parts of the world may be expected to grieve less about the loss of a child than other women because "they have more of them."
>
> (Spijkeboer, 2000: 65)

The content of a female applicant's story is judged, as well as its presentation. We also saw in Chapter 4 that judges were particularly inclined to make judgments about whether a mother's behavior toward her children seemed appropriate. In some cases they decided that the behavior of a woman was not credible because, in their view, a mother wouldn't act as she claimed, for example in leaving her children behind when she fled (see Spijkerboer, 2000: 55). This is one example of judges' cultural assumptions about appropriate maternal behavior.

Women's stories are taken less seriously in the evaluation of their political activities. Women in general are assumed not to have a political identity of their own, or to come to the attention of a government because of their political actions. Nor are they expected to have a fear of persecution independent of their spouse or other male relatives. While we have seen that women are more likely to file claims based on imputed political opinion, that doesn't mean they are *only* persecuted because of their relationship to a man. A significant percentage of women asylum seekers claim persecution based on their own political activities. But the authorities are less willing to acknowledge that these claims are valid than when men make such claims.

Because women's political activities sometimes blur social domains, for example using handicraft as a protest medium, they are not always regarded as participating in politics. The Refugee Women's Resource Project report described several cases that were rejected by the Home Office because they didn't fit the traditional idea of political behavior:

> ... one reported speaking against the government but in the
> context of women's groups in a country where social norms are
> repressive towards women; one knitted clothes for an opposi-
> tion group; another passed on sensitive information about the
> government.
>
> (2003: 98)

The report also describes a Ghanaian woman who attended rallies
and meetings, and subsequently supported an opposition party by
sewing flags and clothes for supporters. She was detained for her
actions and raped by police officers in detention. Despite this experience the adjudicator at her appeal dismissed her political participation
as "very low level." Similarly, a woman from Kenya who was arrested,
detained, and raped by police for her involvement with the Safina
opposition party, was refused asylum by the Home Office and told, "by
your own admission, you only attended four rallies and your political
activity was limited to making T shirts for Safina" (in 2003: 73).

In refusing gender-based claims, courts often argue that the violence
suffered by the applicant is private, usually perpetrated by a member
of the applicant's family and therefore not appropriate for asylum. As
we have seen, for persecution to be the basis of an asylum claim, it
has to be either performed by the state, or condoned by it, or the state
has to be shown to be unable or unwilling to prevent it. Much of the
violence against women takes place in domestic spaces, performed by
husbands, family members, or, in the case of FGM, women in the local
community. In many cases, the state provides little by way of protection
for such practices and often actively condones them. One scholar
observed "for most women, indirect subjugation to the state will almost
always be mediated through direct subjugation to individual men or
groups of men" (Wright, 1988–89: 249). The privacy of domestic space
is sometimes out of the purview of government surveillance or protection. Moreover, women's resistance to domestic violence is rarely
seen as a form of political resistance.

Spijkerboer, whose book about female asylum seekers is one of the
few empirical studies on this subject, talks about "normal" violence
and argues that such violence is not the stuff of which successful
asylum claims are made (2000: 94–100). He describes several cate-

gories of "normal" violence, including the domestic violence which is usually classified as private by the authorities; all of these kinds of violence serve to frame the claim as harm which is not specific to the applicant. One type of "normal" violence is random violence, which is seen as irrational but not directed at the applicant. It is constructed this way because the applicant is not asked about the possible causes of the violence. Spijkerboer then discusses "rational" violence, which is not persecution because it is seen as a normal sanction. The punishment suffered by women in the Middle East who refuse to adhere to the dress codes, or the forced abortions and sterilizations of Chinese women under China's one-child policy, are examples of this type of normal violence. Spijkerboer argues that these actions are framed as the predictable behavior of bureaucrats and therefore not persecution. We have seen that the willingness to accept these acts as persecution has increased since Spijkerboer's book was written, though the problematic distinction between prosecution and persecution remains (see Chapter 5). It is not clear that women are more susceptible to the framing of violence as random or rational; they are certainly more likely to be denied asylum on the ground that the violence is private.

Personal, not political

In the following discussion, we focus directly on the ways that women applicants' cases are vulnerable to the charge that the violence they suffered was personal, not political; that their political activities did not have a sufficiently public profile and therefore would not make them susceptible to further persecution should they return home; that what they experienced was criminal, not political; or that their motives for moving to the US or the UK are economic and personal rather than political.

Domestic violence

As we saw in Chapter 5, one of the most difficult bases on which to request asylum is domestic violence. In the US and the UK there has been an increasing willingness to recognize domestic violence as a crime; however, domestic violence as a basis for asylum can still be considered personal, rather than political, and an area in which the local authorities should protect the victim. We saw that if the applicant has evidence that the local authorities would not protect a victim of domestic violence, the case is stronger. The case of Rodi Alvarado, which we discussed in detail in Chapter 5, shows the possibilities and the problems of this approach. We saw how the authorities are reluctant to define a social group too widely for fear of being forced to grant asylum to all battered women.

FGM (female genital mutilation, also known as female circumcision, and female genital cutting)

This issue presents a similarly complex case. FGM, like domestic violence, can be characterized as personal, rather than political. Fauziya Kassindja, whose case we discussed in Chapter 4, has been described as the first woman to receive asylum based on resisting FGM. But, as we saw, her case was hard won and required the support of the media as well as NGOs. NGOs have politicized FGM; the question is whether an individual, personal experience of resisting FGM is "on account of" membership in a social group (remember the convoluted group the court set up to include Fauziya) is sufficient, or must one belong to a political group protesting FGM? Since the Kassindja case there have been a number of cases in which women have won asylum based on FGM. Courts now generally agree that FGM occurs on account of membership in a particular social group, so applicants do not necessarily require political activism for the claim to succeed (see *Mohammed* v. *Gonzales*, 2005). The *Mohammed* court was willing to consider Khadija, the applicant, as a member of a social group, either of Somali females (virtually all of whom were circumcised), or, more narrowly, as part of the group of young girls of the Benadiri clan. A number of recent cases have focused on the fears of adults about the risk that their daughters will suffer forced FGM should they have to go back to their homeland. By contrast, the British do not generally see FGM cases as connected to a social group, although – unlike the US – they do consider women a social group. As one British lawyer said: "The problem with FGM is that the social group is defined by the persecution; it is tautological" (Yeo, 2005).

Oxford stresses the role of FGM in her argument that women who come to the US are pressured into applying for asylum on gender-based grounds.

> None of the women I interviewed left the country because they were fleeing a forced circumcision or because they considered their own circumcision a form of persecution. Instead, they left because they were detained, tortured, and/or lived with the threats of detention or torture of a spouse. Upon their arrival in the United States, however, immigration attorneys and service providers instructed them that past persecution based on female circumcision would facilitate their ability to gain asylum.
>
> (Oxford, 2005: 29)

Our interviews with lawyers support her contention that FGM is seen as a good basis for an asylum application.

Rape

Rape is involved in a high percentage of cases in which women claim asylum, and also a few claims by men. It is usually part of the torture and beatings women asylum seekers undergo when they are imprisoned or being interrogated. It is also common that, when militias come to the house of a person being persecuted, they torture or kill the man and rape his wife (remember Julia, the Liberian described in Chapter 5). Rape is often used as a form of retribution against a man's wife, daughter, sister, mother, etc. She is punished for his political actions, a form of imputed political opinion that we have seen is a frequent basis for a claim of asylum by women.

The UK Refugee Women's Resource Project reports that nearly a third of their sample say they were raped, and about a quarter were raped by more than one person (2003: 51). One-third of the rapes were witnessed by family or friends, and about three-quarters of the rapes were perpetrated by agents of the state. When one adds sexual assault and threats of sexual assault or rape, the numbers are much higher. They may in reality be higher still because of the strong stigma attached to rape in many of the societies from which women asylum seekers come, which prevents women from talking about it.

Despite the changed perceptions of gender-based claims, the authorities in the UK often disregard claims based on rape, arguing that they are not serious enough to be torture, or that they haven't been proved, or that they are not "based on" one of the categories of persecution. The Refugee Women's Resource Project report quotes a QC who argued:

> If you don't recognise that rape can be part of deliberate persecution, then there is an inbuilt bias against the persecution that women face . . . After all, if a man was beaten unconscious during interrogation, it would be seen as part of the political persecution he suffered – but if a woman is raped, it is seen as a separate problem.
>
> (2003: 106–7)

This was also the case in the US until recently. It was not until the1995 gender guidelines that the INS made it clear that rape could be considered persecution. Prior to that, the BIA denied such claims because as they said in one case the military officials' rape and abuse were "strictly personal actions [which] do not constitute persecution within the meaning of the [statute]" (*Lazo-Majano* v. *INS*, 1987: 1434). In this case, the Court of Appeals overruled the decision of the BIA, but, as always, many such cases never made it to that stage.

Here again, we are in the midst of a reframing of the abuse. In the US, rape used to be considered a crime of passion, about sex; it has been quite successfully reframed as a crime of power and aggression. So, too, rape is now recognized as a tool of war and not a personal or private matter. The idea that rape is a political act, just as is torture, is one that is still not accepted by all those who hear cases, but more and more it is now seen as another form of persecution. It is easier for the authorities to accept this framing in those cases where the rape has taken place in public, not only because it is easier to corroborate, but also because it seems more "barbaric" and less "normal."

Unlike cases of torture, in which the motivation is assumed, applicants reporting rape are asked "What was the motivation?" Was the rape motivated by someone wanting to do harm to an individual woman, in which case it is not considered to be politically motivated?

Or was the motive to incite fear? Is one woman raped in order to terrify an entire group, of men as well as women? Rape is recognized as humiliating, but the question is, who is humiliated and by whom? What does it take to recognize it as an act by one group against another? The idea that rape is always political is not new (Brownmiller, 1975; Castel, 1992). This is not, however, always recognized by the asylum authorities.

All of the asylum process can be understood as a regulatory process, a means for regulating admission to citizenship. We will discuss this further in the conclusion, but in the context of gender and asylum, rape testimony provides a particularly good example of how the asylum process extends beyond determining credibility and the extent of persecution to make cultural assumptions about the divide between public and private. These assumptions have bearing on what can and cannot be said and how one should act. What can or cannot be said during a hearing is inseparable from what can or cannot be said in ordinary life. It is for this reason that women are caught in a bind during testimonies about rape. To say, simply, that rape is private is to ignore the social and public context in which it is always political.

Just the fact of testifying about trauma confuses the categories of public and private. Rape may begin as private, but insofar as it involves public humiliation, damage to a woman's reputation, or a change in her social status, it is public. Further, some women who testify about rape during asylum hearings are re-traumatized, thus returning a public discourse to a private one. The question for the asylum officials is not (necessarily) whether the trauma occurred but whether it falls into the category of political persecution. To answer this, asylum officials seek to ascertain whether the rape victim can or did seek protection from officials in her own country.

Honor killings, bride burning, and the clash between traditional cultural practices and Western values

The most obvious example of private persecution is that of domestic violence, but the category of domestic or private violence is also relevant in other cases of persecution, such as honor killings and abuse of women who protest or ignore dress codes or other gender-specific social regulations. Honor killings are acts of public retribution to preserve the public reputation of a family. The authorities have begun to accept the framing of these latter forms of persecution as political. For example, in the case of a Jordanian woman, the judge granted asylum based both on the ground that women who refuse to conform to the government's gender-specific laws and social norms constitute a visible and specific group that can be targeted for persecution, and (as the UNHCR Executive Committee [1985] recognizes) that a social group can include women who have faced harsh and inhumane treatment as a result of the social mores of their society. The judge concluded that the applicant believed in Western values and acted upon them. She expressed what her husband believed to be unacceptable Western values because of her attempts to gain her high school equivalency certificate. The applicant challenged the system and her husband responded by physically and mentally abusing her. She had tried without success to get a divorce in Jordan (*In the Matter of A and Z*, 1994).

Fatima, the Iranian woman we met in Chapter 4, fell in love with a Pakistani journalist and got pregnant. Her brother and her father threatened to kill her by stoning. As we saw, she was at risk of such a fate, had she stayed; death by stoning of unmarried women who got pregnant was legal in Iran. This punishment was perceived as political rather than private by the authorities in the US, doubtless in part for the reason we have seen in other contexts, that because stoning is regarded as "barbaric" in the West, the officials were willing to recognize it as political rather than private and thus grant her asylum.

The one-child policy in China

The tension between private choice and public control is very obvious in the case of the one-child policy in China. The history of the one-child policy as persecution is an interesting illustration of the cultural and political development of the acceptance of forced reproductive control as a basis for asylum. As we have seen in earlier chapters, we have moved from a general acceptance of that policy as China's legitimate concern for population control carried out through legal means, to one in which the persecutory nature of the means of achieving the objective is potentially the basis for asylum. The government of China claims that forced abortion and sterilization are strictly prohibited. In the US case of *Matter of Chang* (1989), the BIA accepted the assertions of the Chinese government that it used economic incentives and birth control measures, but forbade coercive measures. This is no longer the case; the asylum authorities are now willing to admit that the claims of asylum seekers tell the real story, in which force is used to implement the policy.

Spijkerboer describes at length a Dutch asylum case of the forced abortion and sterilization of a woman who was pregnant with her third child (2000: 70–3). The Dutch authorities denied her application on the ground that she knew she was breaking the law, a law which affected everyone. As we saw earlier, this framing was used in the US until the 1996 law was passed. The question of whether the state protects those who are at risk of forced abortion and sterilization carried out by overzealous officials enforcing China's population control policies is another issue. The US has become more willing to recognize that, in reality, the Chinese government is unwilling or unable to protect citizens from unauthorized forced procedures. In the US, section 601, included in the Illegal Immigration Reform and Immigrant Responsibility Act, 1996, declared that subjection to coercive methods of population control was to be considered past persecution or fear of future persecution on account of political opinion. The US authorities were willing to risk China's wrath at their inter-ference in its internal governance because, although the language could be applied to any country which had a coercive population policy, clearly China was the intended target.

Why did Congress, in a statute which was mostly about limiting the rights of immigrants and asylum seekers, add a category of asylum claimants? Part of the explanation may have to do with the fact that China is a communist country (remember how easy it was to get asylum from communist countries before the fall of communism); part to do with the power of the anti abortion lobby in the US; and part to do with our repugnance at the invasion of family privacy by the Chinese government. Stories of women being dragged from their homes and forcibly (without anesthetics) aborted or sterilized, shocked the conscience of Congress.

It was not always thus. As we saw in Chapter 1, in 1993, the *Golden Venture* brought about 300 Chinese to the US in a major smuggling operation (Westerman, 1996). One of the passengers, G, was arrested and was about to be deported. He appealed the deportation order, claiming persecution based on his fear of punishment because his wife had had a second child, contrary to the one-child policy. The court denied his application, arguing that mass application prevents a state policy from being grounds for asylum, even if it violates human rights. Between 1993 and the passage of the 1996 statute, other cases were denied asylum on this basis and many inconsistent government pro-nouncements on appropriate policy in this situation were announced, all illustrating ambivalence towards the state policy of another country.

Gender and trafficking

People fleeing persecution often have to rely upon covert if not private connections to escape, to acquire false passports, and to arrange for transport across borders. These connections are unofficial, though they sometimes involve government officials acting privately, or govern-ment officials acting as part of covert political groups. The connections also rely on alternative infrastructures, especially traffickers, who move people across borders for their own personal gain, rather than as part of a political action. Relying on these traffickers makes asylum seekers both vulnerable to further crimes against them and places them in association with illegal organizations. Are they, the officials ask, political asylum seekers or are they just illegal migrants? The people on the *Golden Venture*: provide a good illustration of the mix of reasons of those trafficked to the West. Some of them were asylum seekers, fleeing forced sterilization, while others were clearly economic migrants.

Women who are trafficked may fall into a separate category as they may be trafficked for sexual exploitation. In recognition of this, the Victims of Trafficking and Violence Protection Act was passed in 2000 in the US. It provided special visas to women who were able to help the government pursue traffickers of women. The trafficking of women and children for prostitution and as indentured servants has received much publicity recently. Congress passed this law to address public concern about the problem of such trafficking. The government needs those who have been the subject of trafficking to testify in prosecutions and, to be able to do so, the victims need to be allowed to stay in the country. While this legislation adds some protection for those women who have been trafficked, it may not help them much because they are too afraid of the repercussions to their family if they go to the police to expose their traffickers.

Aster is an example of this fear. She is an Eritrean who grew up in a refugee camp in the Sudan after her family fled the violence of Eritrea's liberation struggle from Ethiopia thirty years ago. She became a servant for a powerful Sudanese man, who was a member of the government. She was sent by him to the US to be a servant to a member of his family studying there, where she was treated as a slave. She escaped and was taken in by an American family. She is terrified to go to the police, for fear of what the man will do to her family, still in the refugee camp in Sudan. So her lawyer is engaged in an elaborate dance to enable her to take advantage of this visa. He is working with the local police chief to get him to say that she is cooperating with the authorities to bring her traffickers to justice without actually doing anything which might jeopardize her family. He is also filing an asylum application on her behalf.

This Act does not address the larger problem of the blurring of the categories of political asylum seeker and economic migrant in the case of women fleeing persecution and women sold as prostitutes (or men sold as laborers) as a means of escape. The power imbalance that produces the conditions in which people sell their bodies is, of course, never entirely economic. Despite evidence of violent assault, applicants are often denied asylum when economic and political transactions overlap.

Gender persecution of men

The claims of gender persecution that we discuss here include claims based on FGM, honor killings, rape, domestic violence, bride burnings, forced marriage, and violations of reproductive rights. These are behaviors which either by definition only happen to women, or which happen to women in vastly disproportionate numbers. However, there are some forms of persecution directed at men that can be defined as being gender-based. For example, men are sometimes raped as part of persecution on other grounds, such as political opinion or religion. Also, gender claims because of persecution for violations of reproductive rights can affect men. Persecution based on sexual orientation is directed both at men and women and will be dealt with in the next section.

When gender-based persecution is directed toward a man, he is even more likely to be judged by standards which fail to take into account the cultural implications of the persecution. For example, a man who is raped may feel even more shame than a woman. Yet the authorities often do not take this into account. The Amnesty International UK report describes how often men are not believed because they did not report their rape at the first interview. They quote a Home Office refusal letter:

> The Secretary of State notes that during interview you failed to mention rape. The Secretary of State also believes that it would be reasonable to expect that you would have mentioned this at the earliest opportunity. Furthermore the Secretary of State concludes that the fact that you did not undermines the veracity of your claim.

The report continues:

> Male rape is known to have been practised in Algeria. It is a taboo subject there, as it is in various other countries in North Africa and the Middle East. In practice, the shame associated with male rape means that very few individuals would feel able to talk about it openly afterwards
>
> (Amnesty International, 2004: 59)

Claims based on sexual orientation

Sexual orientation is a claim based on membership in a social group which includes both men and women. These claims risk not being accepted for asylum because the persecution is personal. Some asylum lawyers tell us that sexual orientation claims can be the hardest cases to prove, perhaps because we are ambivalent about whether it is acceptable to persecute people for being homosexual. One lawyer in California disagrees: "Gay sexual preference issues are the hot cutting edge part of asylum. Latin Americans – it's great, also Muslim countries are great for getting asylum" (Greenberger, 2002). It is possible that the treatment of these cases varies depending on whether the asylum seeker applied in a more or less tolerant part of the country, another example of the variation of a supposedly national standard. This seems to be less true in the UK, where the decisions do not vary depending on where they are made.

Persecution of homosexuals is considered normal in many countries. Proof that behavior we define as abnormal is accepted in the country of origin as normal can be an essential element of an asylum claim. Since the early 1990s, being a homosexual has been recognized by asylum law as membership in a social group, because it is an immutable characteristic. For example, Ulan is a young homosexual man from Mongolia who became involved with a much older man who promised to care for him. Soon the man began forcing Ulan to have sex with him. Ulan couldn't get any help from his friends or family because he had not told them that he was gay. When his friends eventually found out, they began harassing him, so he fled to the US and claimed asylum. In one recent case, the court granted asylum to a gay man with a female sexual identity, who was frequently harassed by the police for being seen publicly with other gay men. Giovanni was later assaulted and stabbed by a homophobic gang and subjected to "treatment" to "cure" his homosexuality. The court concluded that this was past persecution and that the man had a well-founded fear of persecution on the basis of his belonging to the social group of gay men in Mexico with female sexual identities (*Hernandez-Montiel* v. *INS*, 2000).

In the UK, in the past there was some debate about whether gay men constitute a particular social group, though now recognition is possible depending on the applicant's homeland (ICAR, 2005). "Homosexuals are a social group for a lot of countries, not *per se*. If they are identified by society as a separate group [then they can get asylum]" (Yeo, 2005). But such claims can be difficult. In one case, Zia Mehmet Binbasi, a Turkish Cypriot, claimed that he was afraid to return to Turkey because he would be persecuted as a practicing homosexual. The High Court reasoned that a group could not be a social group if its only common characteristic was concealed (Crawley, 2001: 169). Here, again, we have the problem of "private" behavior not being recognized as persecution.

Persecution of those who are HIV positive is also considered acceptable behavior in many countries. In the US, we have outlawed discrimination on the basis of HIV status, so that discrimination is at least officially defined as "abnormal." Often a person who seeks asylum on the basis of his homosexuality is also HIV positive. Jose, for example, is a Brazilian homosexual who has a long history of being beaten up and harassed, even as a schoolboy, before he came out. When he told his family about his homosexuality, they were horrified and told him that he had dishonored the family, and needed to be exorcised. Some thought he should sleep with a prostitute to cure him. He moved to a larger city in the hope that he would be safer there. Once, when leaving a gay club, the police started to beat him up, calling him garbage. They took him to jail, claiming it was illegal to be on the streets after 2am. He was kept overnight in jail with violent criminals who tried to rape him. In the morning he was released without any charges having been filed. He then moved to São Paolo where he hoped to be better off, but the prejudice there was overwhelming. He came to the US and has since contracted HIV. He fears that if he returned he would be persecuted both because of his homosexuality and HIV status.

We have seen that many claims, especially those on account of membership in a social group, can have more than one basis. This is also true of the homosexual cases. For example, Niccolai is a homosexual Roma, who comes from Romania where both homosexuals and ethnic Roma are subject to severe persecution. As a child he moved often with his family because of constant harassment by the police. His father was often detained on false charges, and beaten up frequently. When Niccolai was 21, he and his boyfriend were attacked and beaten up when they were walking in a park. Later he saw another gay man being attacked and, when he tried to intervene, he was also beaten severely. He tried to report the attack but was thrown out of the police station. He was also arrested after being seen in the park with his boyfriend. His father bribed the police to get him out of jail and helped him escape the country. Clearly, Niccolai's persecution stemmed both from his ethnicity and his homosexuality.

To prove persecution based on sexual orientation, applicants must present a case that describes the vulnerability they face as members of a social group in a particular society. Further, they need to describe how they are recognized as gay and whether the persecution is based on being openly gay or because someone "looks" gay. In one recent case, the Board of Immigration Appeals in the US decided it had to be the latter for asylum to be granted, as the High Court did in the Binbasi case; they denied a gay man's asylum application because he appeared too stereotypically heterosexual (*In re Soto Vega*, 2004). The problem with this view is that many gay men in countries where persecution is common of necessity try to look "straight." This interpretation also defines being gay in terms of behavior rather than an immutable characteristic, which is part of the definition of a social group. The UK authorities are also reluctant to give asylum to gays who are "discreet" (McDonald and Webber, 2005: 737). The High Court of Australia has pointed out, however, that it is often the fear of being persecuted itself that makes homosexuals behave in a way that is "more discreet than they would otherwise choose to behave within the limits of exercising their legitimate human rights" (*Appellant S.* v. *Minister for Immigration and Multicultural Affairs*, 2003). This focus on the public nature of one's homosexuality leads many of those hearing asylum claims to assume that, as long as an applicant doesn't flaunt his homosexual status, he can avoid harm. Here, as in other areas of gender persecution, public visibility is complex and involves secrecy, covert social networks, and a limited public profile. The argument that people are safe as long as they remain hidden is, of course, contradictory. The fact that they need to remain hidden is evidence that they are politically targeted for discrimination and persecution as a social group. The Refugee Status Appeals Authority in New Zealand recently recognized the role of acceptance by the community when they granted asylum to a gay Iranian who was too embarrassed at the time of his first asylum application even to mention his sexual orientation, but who had since evolved into a "confident – even flamboyant – man able to express his sexual orientation without inhibition" (Crewdson, 2007).

The paradigmatic claim of asylum is the male political activist targeted for his public activities, who then suffers persecution in a public place. In the gay male context, the parallel is a man who engages in public activities, such as attending a gay pride march or frequenting gay bars, who is then beaten up by the police in a public place. Both the targeted activity and the persecution are public. The further one gets from this paradigm, the harder it is to be successful in an asylum claim. Often, either the activity (e.g. using the internet to meet other gays), or the persecution (being beaten or disowned by one's family) takes place in private, making the claim more difficult to fit within the framework of asylum law. Sometimes it isn't easy to fit the claim into either the public or the private sphere. In *In re Toboso-Alfonso* (1990), the case that first determined that homosexuals could be a social group, it was not clear how Toboso-Alfonso's sexual orientation became known to the Cuban government. Nevertheless the BIA granted asylum because of the actions of the government, which included his being forced to register and to go to a government office every couple of months for a physical exam. He was also frequently detained by the police for several days without being charged, and was once sentenced to hard labor for sixty days.

When the activities of someone targeted for their sexual orientation are public, they merge into political activities, something we have addressed in Chapter 5. Gay pride parades are indistinguishable from other unacceptable parades in a country which persecutes its citizens for participating in public demonstrations in support of any cause that is anathema to the government. It is therefore not surprising that it is much easier to be granted asylum when the activity that triggered the harm looks like any other political activity.

Homosexual status can also affect women, though there seem to be far fewer cases of lesbians applying for asylum on this basis. This is similar to the situation of women asylum claimants in general, which we discussed earlier. Women may be unfamiliar with their eligibility to get asylum on the basis of their sexual orientation, and they may be reluctant to tell anyone about their lesbian status. As we have seen in the case of men, it is not proving that they are members of a social group that is the problem, but rather showing that the harm fits the definition of persecution. As with other sorts of gender-based persecution, the harm they suffer is much less likely to take place in public than for their male counterparts. Alla Pitcherskaia, a Russian lesbian, was under surveillance because her father was a political dissident (*Pitcherskaia* v. *INS*, 1997). She was first detained because she protested the beating of a gay friend, and was later arrested and imprisoned again for demonstrating for the release of a lesbian youth leader. She was added to a list of suspected lesbians after she was seen visiting an ex-girlfriend, though she denied that she was lesbian. Alla is unusual in that her activities were at least partly public, as was the harm she suffered.

Fara, by contrast, based her asylum claim on private activities as well as private potential harm. She is from a religious Jordanian family and married at 14. She and her husband later divorced. She came to the US and has since been involved in a long-term lesbian relationship. She fears that, if she is forced to return, she will be persecuted by her family and others for her nontraditional behavior. Marta's case is a combination of public and private activity. She is a Brazilian woman who was threatened by the authorities repeatedly because she was lesbian. She had been married to a man at the time. She fled to the US where she was granted asylum and is now married to a woman in Massachusetts (McHaffey, 2005).

In many societies, being a lesbian is abhorred by the social norms. If a woman's family finds out, she is very likely to be beaten, disowned, or forced into a marriage. In part because of the stigmatization of their status, and the general powerlessness of women in such a society, a lesbian is more likely than her male counterpart to be very closeted. Ironically, the greater her fear of the consequences of discovery, the less likely it is that there will be a public component to her asylum claim. If she knows that the police will support her family in their beatings of her, she is unlikely to go to seek their help, so she can produce no evidence of the lack of support, or of harm caused by the authorities, as is the case in some of the gay male claims. The belief of the asylum authorities that someone can avoid harm by not flaunting their sexual orientation is more likely to be a problem for lesbian asylum seekers because women are less likely to engage in targeted public activities.

The power of outrage

Even though some gender-based asylum claims have more often resulted in success recently, all gender-based claims are not equal. There is a body of scholarship which argues that those claims which are based on practices attributable to non-Western cultures, like FGM and honor killings, are much more often successful than those based on domestic violence, which is all too similar to behavior at home (see Sinha, 2001). So, we might argue that Fauziya Kassindja's case was successful because the persecution was attributable to the cultural "backwardness" of her homeland. She was able to cast herself as the cultural Other, as someone fleeing from a more "primitive culture." This interpretation arises from the present-day media depictions of the horrors of gender-related violence abroad, including such practices as bride burning in India, FGM in Africa, honor killing in the Middle East, and rape as a weapon of ethnic genocide in Bosnia, Rwanda, and Darfur. Here persecution is seen as both traditional and barbaric. The practices are framed in a colonial context: men steeped in a backward culture subjugating helpless women in ways that cannot even be grasped by the Western imagination. It draws on racialized concepts of the non-Western, and relies on the idea of a primitive collective pathology (manifesting itself in unimaginable stories of violence against women at the hands of barbaric men). The view that this is indeed "barbaric," and therefore persecution, was stated specifically in a recent decision by the US Court of Appeals. In that decision, the judge made it clear that he didn't want to use the abbreviation FGM but rather the words themselves. He said: "The use of initials, if it has any effect, serves only to dull the senses and minimizes the barbaric nature of the practice" (*Mohammed* v. *Gonzales*, 2005: 789).

Thus the outrage which makes such a claim successful is toward particular practices rather than about the overall problem of violence against women. The decision to grant asylum in the case of a "barbaric" cultural gender practice creates the illusion that the persecutory act is wholly unlike the violence that women in the West suffer. For this reason, "ordinary" domestic violence is much less likely to result in a successful asylum claim, even when it is accepted by the policy and/or practice of the homeland of the applicant, and sometimes even when the woman sought and failed to receive protection from the state. One of the cases in the film *Well-Founded Fear* features an Algerian woman whose rape and persecution is attributed to the horrible state of things in her homeland, rather than to political persecution targeted at her (Robertson and Camerini, 2000). The asylum official expresses compassion for her suffering but says that, nonetheless, her experiences don't fall into any of the asylum categories. Honor killings, FGM, and rape as a weapon of ethnic cleansing are seen as public violence, in contrast to domestic violence, which, in its corollary form in the US is seen as private but deserving public protection. Honor killings are intended as public events, to preserve the public reputation of a family. FGM is public in the sense that it is a culturally sanctioned practice. Rape as official policy is also public. But consider the case of the category "public romance" in India. Recently, the *New York Times* reported the police harassment of couples for "indecent public affection" in a public park in Meerut, India (Sengupta, 2006). The couples were arrested, beaten in some cases, and warned not to meet publicly. The couples and their parents responded with anger for the shame brought to their families for being publicly humiliated on television. Here again, the layers of public and private are complex, involving shame, probably best defined as a public defamation of character and reputation.

In countries where there is a merging of law and religion, as, for example those Islamic countries whose legal system is based on Sharia law, the definition of what is gender based, what is political, and what is religion becomes murky. Damia, the Moroccan woman whom we met in Chapter 5, suffered several beatings at the hands of her father, who punished her for acting inappropriately according to the family's fundamentalist Muslim beliefs. This case was framed as one of religious persecution, but could also be seen as a clash of different gender norms or political conflicts about male domination. Religion is a stand-in here for patriarchal norms (the brothers were not beaten) and social arrangements concerning the status of women. The religious beliefs are considered foreign and "barbaric" by Western judges, and therefore someone who objects to them is a good candidate for asylum. The violence Damia suffered at her father's hands could have been defined as private, but the "barbaric" nature of the behavior trumped the family privacy argument. The BIA contrasted the father's orthodox Muslim beliefs and the applicant's liberal Muslim beliefs, which framed the persecution as based on religion.

The ordinary and the catastrophic

When asylum officials reject a case, they are not necessarily saying that someone didn't suffer a trauma. They are not denying the fact of catastrophe. Instead, when, for example, they deny a case about rape or domestic violence because the rape or violence was not political and/or because the woman was not persecuted as a member of a targeted social group, they are saying that the catastrophe, the trauma, the violence was part of another realm, crime, ordinary everyday crime, rather than political persecution. But notice how these categories are differentiated: ordinary crime versus political persecution. Ordinary crime, like the "normal" violence discussed above by Spijkerboer, is part of ordinary life (2000: 94–100). Ordinary life is associated with the personal rather than the political. And women, as people seen to occupy ordinary, domestic life, rather than political (public) life, are more likely to be the victims of crime.

Catastrophic, traumatic events in places of political turmoil can become tragically ordinary. Over prolonged periods of persecution, people can come to experience violence as normal. In such situations, it may be difficult for an applicant to argue that she has been a personal target of political persecution or that her actions represent political protest. Political turmoil disrupts differentiations between personal and public.

Things that we in the West regard as normal (such as educating girls) may be the focus of political persecution elsewhere. Engaging in an otherwise normal act (teaching girls to read) becomes a political act, whether or not the teacher belongs to a political party or has a public profile for her activities. Because women's activities are often part of the domestic, rather than the public sphere, their personal lives are especially vulnerable to the disruption of the difference between the personal and the public. Further, women accustomed to participating in domestic life may also perform political protest through that sphere.

The categories of women, the everyday, the domestic, and the personal converge with the category of the traditional. Not all, but significant categories of violence and of resistance that do not qualify for asylum are associated with tradition. Thus domestic violence may be understood by the officials to be an unfortunate part of the traditions of a particular group, or rape similarly may be relegated to the category of the kinds of horrible things men do to women, or, even more obviously, FGM, honor killings, and violations of rules against public romance are understood as dimensions of traditional culture.

Then, not so surprisingly, women's resistance to these acts of violence also is categorized as, if not traditional, still not political. Women use handicrafts to create visibility for the disappearance of their loved ones; they escape, they resist, they talk with other women, they find covert ways to protect other women. In the immigration officials' world, these activities are not necessarily political. They might be actions of resistance, but they do not include manifestos or organized parties. Interestingly, one of the asylum officials in the film *Well-Founded Fear* notes that when he sees a case with a lot of documentation, probably it is backed by an NGO, and NGOs wouldn't be likely to take a case without merit (Robertson and Camerini, 2000). But having an NGO behind you not only signals merit, it also designates the case as political, as the political business of an NGO rather than as merely a personal claim. Often, cases of domestic violence require publicity to render them recognizable for political asylum in the eyes of immigration officials. Sometimes, as in Mende's case, it is the very public exposure itself that the officials recognize will put the person at risk should they return to their home country. In other cases, publicity alone makes the case seem more political.

The feminist slogan, "the personal is political" is useful here. When first used, the phrase meant that the oppression experienced by a person was not only a matter of personal circumstances; rather the conditions of oppression were reproduced in multiple cases, and these conditions could be identified as the political, social, cultural power relations in which individuals experienced discrimination or persecution. Later, the phrase, less usefully but still having some validity, came to mean that whatever one does personally could be taken as political action. So, for example, the choice to be a vegetarian, a personal choice, is also a political statement. Even more recently, the phrase has been used in debates about privacy, for example, discussions about whether the relationship between Monica Lewinsky and Bill Clinton was private or political. However, the personal is political precisely because women are often excluded from participation in the political process. As Robert Barsky points out:

> There is no reason why an adjudicating officer who believes that Pakistani women cannot themselves participate in political opposition should ask if the female claimant was persecuted for her political beliefs. If she makes a claim on those grounds, it is quite likely that the appropriate questions to deal with her claim will not be asked, or, if the adjudicator does ask the appropriate questions, s/he will do so within a limited structure of presumed answers.

> (2000: 290)

Restricted access to the political process is certainly the case for many women applying for asylum. Many, not all, women experience persecution as women, and they resist within the gender frameworks of their societies, not out of preference or even custom, but because of restricted access to more public fora. They have been penalized for this in the political asylum process, though things are changing, especially regarding practices identified as traditional. US asylum officials are more willing to recognize the discriminatory practices of what they regard as backward societies as political persecution. What remains undisturbed, or in Susan Gal's terms (2002), not recalibrated, is the association between the women, the everyday, and the private.

The classification of violence in the family as private and away from the reach of the state is a much broader notion in the law; it is one of the reasons that the law came so late to prosecute domestic violence and rape within marriage at all. Recent reclassifications of gender violence as qualifying for political asylum require a shift in the relationship between the state and the family. Instead of protection of the family from the interference of the state, the failure to protect women from family violence can be regarded as justification for a political asylum claim. As the Refugee Women's Resource Project argues:

"Private" issues commonly associated with women are not inherently less political than those taking place in the "public" sphere. Conflicts concerning the demarcation of privacy (for example, freedom to choose to wear the veil or not, to have an education or undertake certain work, to be sexually active or not, to choose her partner, to be free from male domination and violence, to exercise reproductive rights and to reject female genital mutilation) are conflicts of a political nature.

(2003: 102)

Rape is always both personal and political. But, for a rape to be considered political by the asylum officials, it must be an act of one group against another. For example, a woman is raped to terrify her husband or her community. The rape in this case is symbolic of a larger act of aggression. Feminists have argued that rape always has this symbolic power. It is never just a physical act on the body but is always an act against a woman's humanity.

Even to acknowledge that they have been raped places women in some societies in a vulnerable position, where they might face further violence as a consequence of categories of impurity and desecration. The extreme of this risk can be seen in Pakistan where a woman who claims she has been raped can be prosecuted for having extramarital sex unless she can produce male witnesses, a very unlikely possibility. Thus familiar men (the husband, brothers, father, or others present in the courtroom) are potentially dangerous to a woman who has been raped. Unfamiliar men, the lawyers, judge, asylum officials, are also threatening, especially to a woman who has been raped by an unfamiliar official.

Conclusion

We have argued that the general trend in asylum law and policy is one of raising the bar. The numbers of applicants are down, the rates of successful claims are down, and new laws and policies have cut off previous avenues for winning asylum. The one exception is that of gender-based asylum claims, where there has been a contrary trend. When gender-based claims were first made in the 1990s, they were viewed with skepticism. More recently, however, women both in the US and the UK have had more success in claiming asylum on gender grounds. We believe that the increasing tolerance of gender-based claims parallels the increasing willingness in our own societies to protect women from such crimes as rape, domestic violence, and other gender-based harms. In the international context, the recognition of women's rights as human rights has also had an effect on the framing of these issues for asylum. The development of "new" interpretations of the bases for asylum, which is what gender-based claims are, legally, itself comes from changes in cultural values. As, for example, domestic violence became a front-burner issue in the West during the 1970s, so, later did it become an issue in asylum.

Oxford argues that a gendered regime is not good for women as it may undermine gender justice (2005). Her view epitomizes the gap between scholars and practitioners in this field; for the immigration lawyer, anything that works is fine. Lawyers believe that a woman is better served using whatever basis she has for a claim so she does not have to return to face the persecution she fled, than by seeking "gender justice" at the expense of her chances to gain asylum.

There has been a similar history of the expansion of circumstances in which women get asylum in the UK. Bhabha points out that the earlier applications for asylum by Iranian women who would not conform to the rules for female behavior were generally denied. As time went on, the threat of the Islamic revolution increased, as did its potential spread elsewhere in the Islamic world, and its conflict with "Western" values. In response to this change in attitudes, later cases were more sensitive to the reality of dissidence over gendered norms (1996:18).

We have seen that one of the problems of asylum policy is the fear of the accepting country of interfering with the sovereignty of the homeland of the applicant. This tension is especially clear when the persecution complained of is legal in the country of origin, like honor killings and Islamic dress codes in some Middle Eastern countries. Asylum policy wrestles with the issue of whether it is appropriate to grant a woman asylum for behavior which is either required by law in her country of origin, or part of the prevailing normative culture (Bhabha, 1996: 11). This was the situation in the case of Fatima, whom we met earlier, who was at risk of being killed for her crime of getting pregnant while unmarried. In that case, the barbaric nature of the behavior trumped the concern for the sovereignty of Iran. It may also have been significant that Iran has been an enemy of the US since the revolution there. We saw elsewhere that the discourse of asylum assumes that a country which is a friend of the US by definition can't produce asylum seekers, while those countries we consider enemies can (see Macklin, 1995: 264). We also saw in Chapter 5 that the line between persecution and prosecution sometimes revolves around whether we consider a prosecution a human rights violation rather than the legitimate exercise of sovereignty.

The reframing of opposition to oppressive norms from personal to political is another development in process. The UK Refugee Women's Resource Project report says:

> The fact that women oppose repressive social norms that restrict their civil and political freedom is not interpreted as a political act by the Home Office, although as the RWLG [Gender Guidelines] makes clear these personal acts of defiance are often highly political.

> (2003: 102)

Here we have another example of the authorities not following the policy set up by another unit of government, resulting in the limitation of gender-based cases being granted asylum.

Henri Lefebvre wrote, "A revolution takes place when and only when . . . people can no longer lead their everyday lives"(cited in Langbauer, 1992: 50). This is, essentially, what makes the personal lives of asylum seekers political. But this is also where the categories collapse, where the destruction of everyday life also makes asylum seekers into economically motivated migrants. But remember, asylum law provides safe haven not for people whose lives have been destroyed, but for people who have a well-founded fear of return. It is here that the idea of "the personal as political" is insufficient. Even though the conditions that produce personal suffering are always political, not all suffering could be predicted to recur, a condition generally necessary for asylum. Feminists also observe that it is not enough to recognize that personal life has political conditions. Gayatri Spivak, for example, "redefines the everyday, not as lived experience, or 'real' underlying consensus, but as the ongoing deconstruction of that illusion of experience" (cited in Langbauer, 1992: 61). This, as Spivak herself notes, is impossible for oppressed women. Instead, it is incumbent on them to present their experience as a reality. The significant tension is not between the everyday and the political but between the everyday and its destruction. We would reframe the significant tension in asylum cases as between the everyday and catastrophe. There is more than one kind of everyday. What is "business as usual"? If the annihilation of ordinary people becomes business as usual, that is political persecution justifying a fear of return. But if women resist business as usual, that is personal. Notice the narrative here, the becoming. How does catastrophe become ordinary? Of course it does not become ordinary for the victims, but it does become ordinary for the asylum officials who hear the same story too many times, who believe that "bad things happen in Algeria" (Robertson and Camerini, 2000), or who make distinctions between public and private violence. There are two different kinds of repeated violence here, the repeated violence of everyday life, which does not warrant asylum, even though a woman might legitimately fear its recurrence, and the repeated violence against people who politically resist. When catastrophe, trauma, violence can be categorized as everyday (that is, not political), asylum can be denied.

7 Safe haven for whom?

Asylum in the late twentieth and early twenty-first centuries is a complex concept with built-in contradictions, especially the impossibility of bringing all those who are persecuted elsewhere to the West. The fundamental idea of Western nations offering safe haven is complicated by national histories and ideologies, and by current attitudes toward immigration. It is not always possible to separate the legitimate asylum seeker from the economic immigrant, so asylum seekers are vulnerable to policies driven by the economic need to open or close borders, as well as by compassion for their plight. Regardless of the rationales for separating the legitimate from the bogus applicant, the most fundamental contradiction in asylum policy is the classification of people fleeing persecution without proper documentation as criminals. Many policies in the US and the UK cause further harm to asylum seekers, from incarceration to inquisition, to deportation.

Asylum systems in the US and UK use conceptually inconsistent legal standards to determine whose claims merit asylum. After World War II, the international community developed a system of asylum because the lukewarm or negative response of so many states to those trying to flee from Nazi persecution seemed, in retrospect, to be ethically unacceptable. At that time, asylum policies were developed out of a sense of responsibility and a sense that one of the benefits of democracy was providing safety and state protection against persecution. In addition, displaced people are seen as a force for instability, a threat to be remedied by asylum policy. To some extent, a sense of moral responsibility still drives asylum policy, or, as some argue, it is the reason that asylum has not been discontinued altogether (Steiner, 2003: 193). However, contradictions between the earlier motivations and present circumstances also create confused categories and contribute to obstacles in asylum procedures.

Although the asylum policies were drafted following the failures to respond to Nazi persecution, the procedures followed today, especially in the US, were formulated in response to the post-Vietnam War era, when ongoing political conflicts created masses of people facing persecution by opposing governments, political organizations, tribes, and social groups. Today's asylum seekers are often displaced; the fear of return is complicated by the destruction of their homes, communities, and states. As Gil Loescher notes, contemporary practices are far more restrictive than during the Cold War.

> The present reality is that the Cold War interest in taking refugees from the Communist world has passed with the collapse of European Communism and has now been replaced by a growing state interest in keeping refugees out, or in sending them back home. This is a worldwide trend.
>
> (2003: 11)

The present asylum system suffers from both the inadequacies of the original design and the continuing challenges of providing safe haven and safe borders. If the measure of success is providing safe haven for those fleeing persecution, then the system continues to fail by denying worthy applicants rather than open the floodgates to possibly undeserving applicants. Our liberal ideology conflicts with other social needs, including our fear of terrorist attacks and of being confronted by the actual arrival of the huddled masses we (at least in the US) speak about in our founding myths. The asylum system uses the law in a doomed effort to implement conflicting political goals at the grassroots level.

We will first review how the system itself fails and then turn to a discussion of the conceptual contradictions, especially regarding how our categories of what counts as political persecution and political activism conflict with our policies.

How the system fails

Gaps in the production of knowledge

In other legal proceedings there is an adversary who argues an opposing point of view; in asylum proceedings, an additional adversary is lack of available knowledge. Denying people knowledge about their circumstances is a part of persecution, and asylum applicants sometimes do not know who targeted them or why, what happened to their family members and/or friends, and who helped them to escape. The system tests their knowledge and evaluates the merits of their claims based on both the knowledge about a site of violence brought to a case by the asylum officials and the knowledge brought by the applicants and expert witnesses. Some of the most deserving cases are denied because either the applicant or the official does not know enough or because the witness's knowledge is discounted (Kalin, 1986: 233).

The reliance on narrative as a primary form of evidence at several stages of the asylum application process

People seeking asylum face the double problem of, first, trying to narrate unspeakable events and, second, translating those personal stories into a different sort of narrative that conveys the information needed by the asylum officials. As Caroline Moorehead notes, "their story is their only real passport" (2005: 165). The stories people told us when we first met them, some of which are told at the beginnings of our chapters, often focused more on the trauma of loss and the struggle to survive than on the details of persecution. However, it is these details, about the persecutors, their interrogations, incarcerations, and torture, as well as the individual's role in a larger political, religious, or social conflict, that interest the asylum officials.

Credibility: are you who say you are and is your story true?

In the face of the lack of corroborating evidence, asylum officials devise methods to test the validity of the accounts presented by asylum applicants. These tests are not accurate measures of credibility; moreover they create arbitrary obstacles. To present a credible account, asylum applicants need to be able to substantiate that they are who they say they are, but the processes of persecution often destabilize identity or require individuals to reconfigure their identities. At the very least, escape often requires deceptive or concealed identities. Further, persecution can change one's sense of oneself, as well as who one can depend on. Deaths, disappearances, and incarceration sometimes lead to reconfiguration of family structure. The law requires identity to be a fixed category, but asylum applicants more often have multiple and changing identities, out of necessity.

Who protects whom against what?

Asylum law is designed to protect individuals from harm they would likely face if they returned to their native countries. But there are complex questions about the sufficiency of government protection and what kinds of violence are prosecuted. We are reluctant to charge our allies with a failure to protect their citizens, so we sometimes deny applications by Western asylum seekers. As Niklaus Steiner writes, "Granting asylum to a refugee is an explicit critique of another state's treatment of its citizens, so states are often quick to accept refugees from foes, but hesitant to accept them from friends (2003: 180). The irony is that the Westerners look like familiar political protesters and are more likely to fulfill the expected requirements of proving a need for safe haven.

Cultural difference

The horrors asylum applicants report are culturally specific in several ways. First, efforts to intimidate and humiliate political dissidents or members of a social, religious, or gender group are culturally specific, as are people's responses to those acts. How people respond to fear depends on the resources available as well as on cultural expectations, for example, for bribing officials, for intimidating one family member to frighten another. Second, border controls, citizenship documents, and modes of transport have spawned underground cultural institutions for creating false documents and trafficking people. These underground institutions are technically illegal, but the people who rely on them are not criminals. Third, to understand the conflict in a particular place, the role of a particular asylum applicant in the conflict, and the resources used by the applicant to escape, asylum officials need to understand the culturally specific circumstances of conflict and resistance. The law attempts to be culturally neutral, but, in the case of asylum, cultural difference plays a crucial role. Bonny Ibhawoh argues that political asylum procedures require a "weak cultural relativism," in which understanding cultural practices is crucial, but those differences should not undermine positions on universal human rights (2003: 63).

What counts as persecution?

Clearly, asylum law is intended to protect the persecuted rather than the persecutor. In some cases, the difference is clear, but in others, when a dissident uses weapons, there are complicated questions about who deserves protection.

The asylum process fails in part because of its reliance on an arbitrary and narrow definition of persecution (as described in Chapter 5). One view would say, after all, persecution is persecution; why should it matter what the motivation was? The suffering of the persecuted individual is the same, regardless of the basis for the persecution. However, the law is not designed to save people from just any dangerous circumstances, but rather to identify those individuals who qualify for refuge from very particular kinds of danger. Not all danger can be described as political, religious, or social persecution (Ibhawoh, 2003).

Persecution also is narrowly defined to exclude discrimination. People with disabilities in a country with no accommodations, who are impoverished because they are unable to earn a livelihood, could argue that they are persecuted, but this is not included in the definition. We saw in Chapter 5 the legal difference between persecution and discrimination. The question of what qualifies is further complicated by the fact that asylum cannot serve as a remedy for all of the persecution defined by the law.

The requirement that asylum seekers prove a "well-founded fear of persecution" places the emphasis on possible future harm, based on past harm. It is not enough for an applicant to have experienced harm in the past. In fact, theoretically, it would be possible for someone who had experienced no harm to prove the likelihood of persecution upon return to the native country. The stipulation of fear in the future makes sense, of course, because the purpose of asylum is to offer protection to people not protected by their own governments. However, conceptually, a future fear is quite different than seeking refuge from harm.

Law versus policy implementation

In some areas of the law, the practice is more liberal than the law as it is written (black letter law). In the case of asylum law, however, it is the exact opposite; the law is more liberal than the practice. Despite laws to the contrary, we have seen how asylum seekers are often held to impossible standards of proof and denied asylum. We have also seen that both the Home Office and the Department of Homeland Security are working very hard to limit the number of asylum seekers for reasons not necessarily connected to the strength of the claims.

The ambiguous categories of illegality (crossing borders without proper documentation), undocumented persecution, and false motives (economic rather than asylum) become conflated in a border regulatory practice intended to identify people in need of asylum but sometimes resulting in their criminalization. Border control regulatory practices are put in place in the absence of information/documentation that would provide credibility to both identity and persecution claims. And it is not surprising to find intensified gate-keeping in such ambiguous situations (Foucault, 1988). The asylum seeker suffers the consequences of the absence of information.

Failure through incompetence and inadequate resources

Neither the Home Office nor the Department of Homeland Security seems able to manage the complexity and scope of the problem of asylum seekers, not to mention immigration generally. They are not given the resources to do a good job. So they have to work with the problems of personnel burnout, and the resulting lack of training and experience caused by frequent staff turnover and lack of financial resources. The bureaucracies suffer from backlogs and the rapid, inadequately careful decision making caused by the need to reduce the backlogs. Sometimes it is not a matter of organized policy, but rather of inability to address a constantly changing problem with available resources. Asylum seekers, as well as the traffickers who bring in foreigners, are much more flexible and quicker to react than the government bureaucracy intended to respond to them. These inadequate resources affect asylum seekers directly, also, to the extent that they cannot find legal representation. We have no right to call asylum a legal procedure and then deprive people of legal assistance, as we do in the US and are beginning to do in the UK.

Confusing categories: addressing our ambivalence

Beyond these different sources of failure, there is a more fundamental reason the system fails. We ask the asylum process and policy to serve several conflicting purposes, which reflect our ambivalence about the whole system. So the system is implemented in such a way as to "satisfy" that ambivalence.

In asylum law and policy, there has always been a tension between the humanitarian need to let in deserving applicants, and concern about opening the floodgates through which millions would inundate countries offering safe haven. As with so many policy issues, there have been times of loosening policies and times of tightening them (Steiner, 2003). The events of September 11, 2001 and subsequent concerns about terrorism in the United States have, however, added complexity to asylum policy, as with all issues related to immigration. So, in addition to the usual concerns about only letting in those applicants who are truly fleeing persecution, we now have to add in the concern that asylum law may be being abused by terrorists. In the UK there is also a concern about terrorism, although it is only part of the overriding concern about opening the floodgates to hordes of economic migrants who are believed to use the asylum system to get a foot in the door. In both the US and the UK, concern about asylum masks other concerns about immigration more generally.

One of the best illustrations of how the conflicting goals are dealt with at a practical level is the use of special procedures for people who are in limbo. In the US, TPS (temporary permission to stay) is used for those whose countries are currently in a state of chaos or armed conflict, but who might not have a good enough individual claim for asylum. The government periodically issues rules allowing all those from a particular country currently in the US to stay for a specified period. In the UK the term is ELR (extraordinary leave to remain), which is used quite frequently on an individual basis when the case doesn't seem strong enough but the authorities are afraid there may be a valid human rights claim or some other barrier to their return home. These are the kinds of people no one wants to take responsibility for, nor do they want to make a decision that might create a precedent for others in the same situation. We don't want to send them home but nor are we willing to officially let them stay permanently.

Confusion between activism and terrorism

We have difficulty separating activism from terrorism. Clearly 9/11 has been a significant part of that, because the terrorists weren't actually asylum seekers, though the general public doesn't know that. However, they were political activists, whose views on political change were unacceptable to us, not only because they espoused violent means to bring about change. As we have seen, if an asylum seeker is involved in violence or weapons exchange or any possible collusion with groups identified as terrorist, they can't get asylum. Because of 9/11, however, all political activists are suspected of being terrorists. The line between good political activists and bad ones (i.e. terrorists) is a fine one.

Political activists working in opposition to a government or group in power sometimes face the challenge of proving that they are activists rather than criminals, and sometimes cultural categories of activism in other places do not match those of the West.

Some asylum seekers have had their former lives destroyed. They do not have the option of returning to ordinary life in their homelands. They are hoping to find ordinary life somewhere else. This scenario presents some of the contradictions. The typical asylum seeker is not necessarily someone who will carry on political activism once settled in the West. Some will, especially writers such as Huang Xiang, one of the asylum seekers in the film *Well-Founded Fear*, who describes himself as a "poet in exile," and Tun, who continues to work for democracy in Burma. But not all asylum seekers are political activists engaged in ongoing efforts to effect political change. Some are temporary activists protesting against persecution. Many of the asylum seekers are victims rather than activists. Many of them left the cause when they left the country. They don't appear as freedom fighters in terms familiar to us. They don't become activists in the countries of refuge.

It is beyond the scope of this book to discuss the wide variation in whether people continue to participate in the political struggles that required them to flee from their homelands. For some, resettlement marks the end of their struggle, either because it is over, because they have no resources, or because they are too damaged to continue. For others, the struggle becomes global. For example, E. Valentine Daniel quotes a refugee as saying, "You ask me about Tamil nationalism. There is only Tamil internationalism" (1996: 176).

Many changes predate 9/11; however, after 9/11, the balance shifted in the US with regard to a broad swathe of people who are considered possible terrorists, a category that includes many asylum seekers who have no connection with terrorist organizations. As a result, more and more asylum seekers languish in detention (i.e. prison) for months, and sometimes years. This hardening of attitudes in the US has its parallel in the UK and in Europe, where, as we have seen, the response to asylum seekers has been similar.

Part of our confusion is our expectation about what resistance and protest should look like. Asylum seekers' narratives do not necessarily meet these expectations. This is true of many forms of opposition, like standing up for one's religion or sexual orientation, but it is most true of political activism. What's necessary in the asylum process is not only correcting practices to better fit policies, but also evaluating our concepts of what counts as activism. This is much more of an issue in Britain than in the US, where there is a much deeper tradition of civil rights activism and protest, a tradition enshrined in the US First Amendment, which the British don't have. Perhaps as a result, the British have a more restrictive sense of political protest; there is frequent calling into question of the legitimacy, not to mention likelihood, of risk taking for political gain, which doesn't seem to happen in the American context. In one UK case, the newspaper headline read "Home Office Tells 'Foolhardy' Asylum Seekers: 'It's Your Own Fault You've Been Persecuted' " (Johnston and Breslin, 2004). The headline referred to what officials told an asylum seeker from Zimbabwe in their rejection letter. He had received threats against his life because he protested against Robert Mugabe's regime.

If someone is an activist, according to this (mostly UK) view, they bring persecution on themselves, and should know better. There is a sort of *caveat emptor* approach which totally negates the point of political activism. Clearly a political activist can always avoid persecution by not being an activist; it is not absence of knowledge of the risks involved that drives them, but a belief in the importance of the goals that drives them to continue political activity.

Our definition of activism in general and the definitions of the countries persecuting people are different. For example, the Chinese poet Huang Xiang, who appeared in the film *Well-Founded Fear*, had difficulty proving his case, based on censorship, cancelled publication contracts, and even writing in public spaces as a form of protest. Instead, as the film reports, his case depended on his proving that he had scars resulting from torture when he was jailed. Although both the US and the UK are familiar with historical and contemporary cases of the persecution of writers, we can't fathom persecuting a poet. At the same time, it is easier to accept persecuted writers than armed protesters.

Confusing the categories of the asylum seeker and the economic migrant

Asylum policies are inevitably influenced by immigration policies. The fear of being inundated by immigrants is mostly about being inundated by the "wrong" immigrants. This is also about race; it is no accident that the lion's share of asylum seekers (and immigrants in general) are not "white" (Roxstrom and Gibney, 2003: 45). The discourse on immigration is also about the need for cheap labor and the inability to enforce existing laws or create adequate laws to manage border crossing.

Asylum seekers, who often enter the country without documentation, are too easily categorized as illegal border crossers, and they then face the problem of proving their asylum claims at the same time as they defend themselves against illegal entry charges.

Asylum seekers are in one sense a category of immigrants. As we suggested in the introductory stories for this book, many nineteenth-century immigrants to the US and the UK could have been called asylum seekers. The displacement of people due to persecution is not new. Rather, the category of asylum seeker was created as part of restrictive immigration policies. Asylum seekers are forced migrants, people forced to leave homelands rather than people choosing to leave. Economic migrants may leave because life is unsustainable in their homelands, and that condition may be due to political oppression. The question is whether they have lost fundamental protections in their homeland. The refugee who seeks asylum is someone who must leave and who cannot return (Loescher, 2003: 12).

In the UK, the legal and policy changes we have described in earlier chapters are in response to the continuing political pressures (the flames of which are constantly fanned by the media) to limit the numbers of those who claim asylum. The media continue to encourage people to believe that most asylum seekers are bogus, that they are abusing the system to get a place to live and collect benefits. Though it is impossible to determine the "real" figures, it seems to us that there is indeed a larger proportion of economic migrants claiming to be asylum seekers in the UK than in the US, which may be connected to the differences in government largesse available in each country. Asylum seekers in the UK are perceived as being handed everything on a plate, while others have to work for it or do without, a perception that underpins much of the antagonism toward asylum seekers in Britain. By contrast, in the US, an economic migrant gains nothing by claiming asylum, and in fact loses the anonymity that is so essential to a life under the radar screen.

Underlying both media representations and public policy of asylum and of immigration generally is a widely held assumption that everyone wants to come to the West. The West is not the only, or even the primary, destination of asylum seekers. A counter-argument suggests that people prefer to stay in their home communities, as long as life is sustainable there (Canclini, 1993). Many people experiencing persecution suffer economic hardship and could be classified as economic migrants. In fact, poverty in the West may be worse than their lives before persecution; nevertheless there is some economic incentive even for asylum seekers.

Separating economic from political immigrants is difficult if not impossible. All political applicants are looking for a better life. We want them to demonstrate that their hardship is a result of persecution, but then, if their applications are accepted, we want them to join in the dream of the West. They are supposed to defer that dream, make no mention of it, never express their concern about having lost a sustainable livelihood until granted asylum. Then they are supposed to become model immigrants, assimilating and working hard to improve their economic position.

Confusing the categories of the undocumented asylum seeker and illegal entry

Political asylum provides governments with the possibility of doing something right, and the fact that offering asylum is the right thing to do is not questioned. But this rather simple right act gets muddied and complicated by conflating the asylum process with the process of defending borders. In this book, we have discussed some of the particular ways that the process gets confused, by challenging an asylum seeker's identity or the degree of persecution. But the larger issue, beyond the particular inequities of the process, is how the concept of political asylum challenges concepts of national sovereignty and citizenship.

As we have seen, some asylum seekers do rely upon illegal means of crossing borders. In the UK, media reports have implicated low-cost airlines in this process and have argued that these no-frills airlines are less apt to catch the use of false documents (Hickley and Slack, 2005). Illegal entry is viewed as threatening to national security, and it is this fact, rather than criminal or terrorist associations of other kinds, that creates the confusion of asylum seeker as security threat. This perception completely contradicts the Cold War identification of asylum seekers as "defectors" who represented a victory for democracy (Loescher, 1993: 21).

Moral ambivalence

Part of the problem with the system for granting asylum is that we're ambivalent about our moral obligations to the people who make claims. Increasingly we go to greater and greater lengths to strengthen the barriers to entry and to make sure that only a few people slip through the net. As Peter Mares argues:

> Simply put, the broad thrust of that policy is to stop people from ever crossing your frontier in the first place, in order to prevent them from invoking the protection obligations enshrined in the 1951 Convention on the Status of Refugees.
>
> (2001: 231)

We let in people whose experiences are so horrifying that we're shocked; others don't get in. Those running the system act as our agents in the process. They either become inured to the horror they confront so they can say this particular horror isn't bad enough, or they burn out and leave. Only the strongest psyche and the noblest soul can continue to confront the horrors and keep trying to alleviate the suffering of a few of the millions who are persecuted, by granting them asylum. Our policy is a recognition that the world is a mess and that we can't fix it, and we can assuage our guilt by allowing in a few people. Just as we feel good when we sponsor one child in the Third World, so too we can feel good when we allow in a few individuals fleeing persecution. Particularly in the US, we tend to look to individual solutions for social problems in general. In this case, the whole asylum process is an individualized solution to the huge problems of political unrest and other forms of persecution carried out on a social scale. As we saw in Chapter 6, we are also ambivalent about the barbarism of traditional culture versus crimes we ourselves commit (e.g. domestic violence). We don't want to be reminded that there is really no "they" ("barbaric" other) and "us" (civilized people). The asylum system tells us discomfiting things about who we are as a nation. As Niklaus Steiner says, asylum policy is always about national interests and how we regard ourselves (2003: 191). We saw in Chapters 1 and 2 the various ways we try to discourage asylum seekers from applying. We also saw that we turn away most of those who nevertheless apply for asylum. In the

UK, in 2005, about three-quarters of applicants were denied asylum, while in the US it was over 60 percent.

We want the asylum system in place in theory because it's an ideal to which we aspire. But we can't get there and we blame that on practical factors attributed mostly to the flaws in the applications. The system works to obstruct unworthy applicants rather than to identify deserving ones. We are less worried about those who are unfairly denied than we are about those who might be falsely admitted.

The ideal asylum seeker and the typical asylum seeker

Asylum policies and practices are based not only expectations of what counts as protest and persecution, but also on what asylum seekers should know about the asylum process. For example, applicants ought not only to be aware of political asylum as an option but also to know that acquiring asylum status requires declaring oneself upon entry. Further, applicants ought to be aware of the political situation and motives behind the persecution they experienced. They ought to have some means for documenting both their own identity and the facts of their case. We are not suggesting that it is not possible to identify typical conditions for applicants. To the contrary, our research has identified several common dimensions of the asylum applicants' experiences; we are suggesting that current practices are misinformed in their assessments and expectations of the applicants. As one of the interpreters in Peter Showler's book argues:

> I suppose the root of the problem is this process of pigeonholes. The members know so little about the countries of the claimants. They rely on categorizations, objective knowledge, learning the names of places and politicians . . . It is all a mass of generalizations.
>
> (2006: 169)

The discourse of asylum conflicts with other discourses about border control. The discourse of security – the fear of letting in the "wrong" people – is a subtext for something else, not a reason in itself. Another conflicting discourse is economic; that "these people just want to come here to make money," which is of course true, but we regard economic motives as suspicious and as inconsistent with claims of persecution. We recognize the poverty caused by civil war, as well as our complicity in those civil wars. But we rarely discuss our responsibility in having helped to create the situation of displaced people. We have several competing narratives, including the story of the activist working for political change who is forced to flee from persecution at the hands of an opposition group, and the narrative of the economic immigrant who unfairly uses the benevolence of the asylum system to gain entry to a country that is otherwise barred to him. The narratives of displacement, political struggle, and economic hardship coincide, of course. The bottom line is the question of what will happen to the people who are returned to their home countries because their applications are denied.

So where does that leave us?

We have seen that asylum is dying the death of a thousand cuts. Those left standing are the exceptions who can present themselves in a way that makes us feel good. This outcome stands in stark contrast to our countries' sense of obligation. As liberal states, the US and the UK believe in an obligation to take in people; to provide a safe haven. The US has its huddled masses myth to buttress this sense of obligation. The British don't have that; instead they have colonials coming home. But they do have legal obligations under European human rights laws, which they have incorporated into British law. These myths may be more confusing than helpful. Understanding the asylum seekers of the twenty-first century as different from Holocaust survivors or defectors from the Cold War may require a paradigm shift. To accurately identify legitimate asylum seekers, we need to stop seeing them as threats.

In responding to asylum seekers, the British are reacting to a sense of a loss of identity and are trying to figure out who they are if they aren't white Britain. It is not so different in the US, especially in California and the southwest. Asylum seekers are an "in your face" example of the other wanting to be us; they are indeed no different than the huddled masses we once were. Moreover, they claim all of the founding virtues of the US – of escaping religious persecution and seeking freedom – which are framed in human rights terms in the UK. This isn't a minor policy problem; in the case of the US it's the founding principle. In the case of Britain, it's the legacy of colonialism and being an honorable colonist: standing for something more than exploitation.

Political asylum is possible because so many countries collectively recognize the need to provide protection from persecution on the basis of politics, race, religion, and membership in a social group. There is profound agreement on what is intolerable for a civil society (even if countries providing safe haven sometime violate these agreements either by persecuting individuals or by encouraging or condoning others' persecution). Asylum is predicated on the premise that it is the responsibility of a state to protect its citizens and that safe haven must be offered in the absence of such protection – in situations of civil war, invasion, or political chaos, where the disruption of everyday life is such that people live in fear for their lives.

Asylum policy exists within two sometimes contradictory discourses: the discourse of border control and the discourse of human rights. When the human rights discourse prevails, asylum policy seeks to identify the conditions of displacement that warrant providing safe haven. When border control discourse prevails, asylum seekers are potential trespassers, at best, and criminal illegal aliens at worst. In Andrew Shacknove's terms, "Refugee policy has always been at least one part State interest and at most one part compassion. Appeals based solely upon compassion, solidarity or rights are only occasionally successful" (cited in Steiner, 2003: 181). Niklaus Steiner comments: "This literature then generally assumes that asylum policies are the result of a tug-of-war between international norms and morality loosening asylum on the one hand and national interests tightening it on the other" (2003: 181). Steiner goes on to explore the struggle between people arguing to tighten asylum policy, because its abuse is a threat to democracy (2003: 184), and those against tightening it. Steiner finds that the arguments are rarely if ever about moral obligation. He says that no one in Europe is arguing that asylum should be abolished (2003: 195). Instead, he says, the arguments about asylum policy are about identity. "How parliamentarians see themselves and their countries and how others see them is a function of what they want (interests), fulfilling expectations (norms), and doing good (morality)" (2003: 194). We would add to this the identities of the asylum seekers themselves, as victims of persecution, as political activists, as forced migrants and displaced peoples, and as people seeking safe haven. The interests, norms, and morality issues of the asylum seekers are not necessarily recognizable in the terms understood by the receiving countries.

The problem is that there are too many asylum seekers with too many reasons to flee. They do not fit a simple profile. The solution should not be to try to discredit as many of them as possible. The system as it currently exists harms too many people, whether by incarcerating people who have already suffered too much, by humiliating people who already despair of returning to ordinary life (not life as they knew it), or creating impossible standards of measurement based on written documentation when none exists. Even those asylum seekers who are successful in the application process are needlessly harmed by it. If countries of safe haven cannot take in the multitudes of asylum seekers, they can at least create a more humane process for rejecting them.

Our policies need to be driven by differentiation rather than discrimination. A more humane process would begin by recognizing the diversity of asylum seekers. Asylum seekers are sometimes treated as an undifferentiated category; we argue that some of the discrimination they face is a result of conflating categories, especially the categories of undocumented asylum seeker/illegal alien; asylum seeker/terrorist; and asylum seeker/economic migrant. These conflated categories are at best arbitrary and uninformed; at worst they are deliberately discriminatory.

These categories are conflated conceptually as well as legally. The first step is to understand the circumstances in which individual asylum seekers arrive without documentation. As we have observed in case after case, asylum seekers often have only their stories as documentation of their experiences. But challenging the story of someone who has suffered trauma by examining inconsistencies in minor details is not a useful practice for identifying legitimate asylum seekers. Instead, asylum officials need to rely on the now-extensive scholarship on trauma narrative as a better guide to determining the credibility of an account.

The second step is to understand how the asylum processes themselves (along with other border control bureaucracies) support a complex underground network of traffickers, false document producers, and others taking advantage of desperate people. The asylum seekers are the victims of both systems; attempts to prevent their entry only strengthen the illegal practices.

The third step is to decriminalize the asylum process. Some asylum seekers have been involved in conflict and are therefore suspected of being terrorists. Many are poor and are therefore suspected of being economic migrants. But unsubstantiated, over-generalized suspicions contaminate the process (Campbell, 2004). Instead, we need to better understand the particular and diverse experience of today's asylum seekers. We opened this book with stories about our own families, who migrated at a time when economic and political migrants were not differentiated. Our Jewish families migrated for centuries. For many groups, migration is part of the culture. Many groups have migrant myths and historical realities, just as many have myths of ownership and belonging (and some have both). The displacement and migration of people is an old story. But the policies of border control, both the morally responsible idea of non-refoulement and the restrictive policies of containment, interrogation, and deportation, are new.

The process is neither as equitable or as predictable as it might be, but we hope to provide greater self-consciousness of how the system responds to contemporary politics.

We recognize that this is a truly complex and difficult task. It may be one that is impossible to fulfill. Like any system, the asylum process is vulnerable to abuse. However, the greater abuse may be the suspicions and restrictions that result in criminalizing and deporting the people who are actually the most deserving and most in need of asylum. In our enthusiasm to protect ourselves from terrorists and hordes of economic migrants, we run the risk that we will turn away those who need our protection most.

Bibliography

Ahluwalia, Navtej (2004) Personal Interview, London, Nov. 23.

—— (2005a) Email Message, April 1.

—— (2005b) Personal Interview, London, Nov. 25.

Aliaskari, Mahsa (2000) "U.S. Asylum Law Applied to Battered Women Fleeing Islamic Countries." *American University Journal of Gender, Social Policy and the Law* 8: 231–82.

Amnesty International (2004) *Get it Right*, UK report. London: Amnesty International UK.

Anker, Deborah (1992) "Determining Asylum Claims in the United States: A Case Study on the Implementation of Legal Norms in an Unstructured Adjudicatory Environment." 19 *New York University Review of Law and Social Change* 433–528.

Asylum Aid (1999) *Still No Reason At All*. London: Asylum Aid.

Avery, Miranda (2004) Personal Interview, London, Nov. 19.

Bahl, Anjana (1997) "Home is Where the Brute Lives: Asylum Law and Gender-Based Claims of Persecution." *Cardozo Women's LJ* 4: 33–73.

Barnes, John (2004) "Expert Evidence – The Judicial Perception in Asylum and Human Rights Appeals." *International Journal of Refugee Law* 16(3): 349–57.

Barsky, Robert F. (2000) *Arguing and Justifying: Assessing the Convention Refugees' Choice of Moment, Motive, and Host Country*. Burlington, VT: Ashgate.

Barth, Frederick (1969) *Ethnic Groups and Boundaries*. London: Allen and Unwin.

Becker, Gay (1997) *Disrupted Lives: How People Create Meaning in a Chaotic World*. Berkeley: University of California Press.

Berger, Dan (2005) Personal Interview, Northampton, MA, Aug. 29.

Berk-Seligson, Susan (1989) "The Role of Register in the Bilingual Court-room: Evaluative Reactions to Interpreted Testimony." *International Journal of the Sociology of Language* 79: 79–91.

Bernstein, Nina (2004) "Out of Repression, into Jail." *New York Times* Jan. 15: A25.

—— (2006) "New York's Immigration Courts Lurch Under a Growing Burden." *New York Times* Oct. 8: 1, 29.

—— and Marc Santora (2005) "Asylum Seekers Treated Poorly, US Panel Says." *New York Times* Feb. 8: A1, A27.

Berthold, Megan (2003) Personal Interview, Los Angeles, CA, May 19.

—— (2004) Personal Interview, Los Angeles, CA, May 17.

Bhabha, Jacqueline (1996) "Embodied Rights: Gender Persecution, State Sovereignty, and Refugees." *Public Culture* 9: 3–32.

Bohmer, Carol and Amy Shuman (2007) "Producing Epistemologies of Ignorance in the Political Asylum Applications Process." *Identities: Global Studies in Culture and Power* 14(5).

Brownmiller, Susan (1975) *Against Our Will: Men, Women and Rape*. New York: Simon and Schuster.

Burstein, Bonnie (2004) Case report on Abdul M., Los Angeles Harbor College, April 20.

Campbell, Nancy D. (2004) "Technologies of Suspicion: Coercion and Compassion in Post-Disciplinary Surveillance Regimes." *Surveillance and Society* 2(1): 78–92.

Canclini, N. Garcia (1993) *Transforming Modernity: Popular Culture in Mexico*, trans. Lidia Lozano. Austin: University of Texas Press.

Caruth, Cathy (ed.) (1995) *Trauma: Explorations in Memory*. Baltimore, MD: Johns Hopkins University Press.

Castel, Jacqueline R. (1992) "Rape, Sexual Assault and the Meaning of Persecution." *International Journal of Refugee Law* 4(Jan.): 39–56.

Castles, Stephen (2000) *Citizenship and Migration: Globalization and the Politics of Belonging*. New York: Routledge.

CIRB (Canadian Immigration and Refugee Board) (1993) *Guidelines on Women Refugee Claimants Fearing Gender-Related Persecution*. Ottawa: CIRB.

Cohen, Juliet (2002) "Questions of Credibility: Omissions, Discrepancies and Errors of Recall in the Testimony of Asylum Seekers." *International Journal of Refugee Law* 13(3): 293–309.

Conley, John and William M. O'Barr (1998) *Just Words: Law, Language, and Power*. Chicago: University of Chicago Press.

Copeland, Emily (2003) "A Rare Opening in the Wall: The Growing Recognition of Gender-Based Persecution." In Niklaus Steiner, Mark

Gibney, and Gil Loescher (eds) *Problems of Protection: The UNHCR, Refugees, and Human Rights*. London: Routledge, pp. 101–15.

Cornelius, Wayne A. and Marc R. Rosenblum (2005) "Immigration and Politics." *Annual Review of Political Science* June.

Court TV (2004) *Chasing Freedom*. Film directed by Don McBrearty.

Crawley, Heaven (2001) *Refugees and Gender*. Bristol, UK: Jordan Publishing.

Crewdson, Patrick (2007) "Gay Asylum Seeker Can Stay Despite Lying." *Dominion Post* (Wellington, New Zealand) Feb. 5: A1.

Daniel, E. Valentine (1996) *Charred Lullabies: Chapters in an Anthropography of Violence*. Princeton, NJ: Princeton University Press.

Daniel, E. Valentine and John C. Knudsen (eds) (1995) *Mistrusting Refugees*. Berkeley: University of California Press.

Dow, Mark (2004) *American Gulag: Inside U.S. Immigration Prisons*. Berkeley: University of California Press.

Dunford, David (2004) Personal Interview, London, Nov. 19.

Einolf, Christopher (2001) *The Mercy Factory: Refugees and the American Asylum System*. Chicago: Ivan R. Dee.

Ekman, Paul (1985) *Telling Lies: Clues to Deceit in the Marketplace, Politics, and Marriage*. New York: W.W. Norton.

Ekman, Paul and Maureen O'Sullivan (1991) "Who Can Catch a Liar?" *American Psychologist* 46(9): 913–20.

Erikson, Kai (1976) *Everything in its Path: Destruction of Community in the Buffalo Creek Flood*. New York: Simon and Schuster.

Fletcher, Katharine (2005) "A Minimum of Charity." *London Review of Books* March 17: 30–4.

Foucault, Michel (1988) *Politics, Philosophy, Culture: Interviews and Other Writings, 1977–1984*, edited by L. Kritzman. London: Routledge.

Franklin-Houtzager, Ezinda and Gita Williams (2004) Personal Interview, London, Oct. 7.

Furlan, Simonetta (2005) Personal Interview, Florence, Italy, May 17.

Gal, Susan (2002) "A Semiotics of the Public/Private Distinction." *Differences: A Journal of Feminist Cultural Studies* 13(1): 77–95.

Gee, Maurice (2005) Personal Email Message, Dec. 13.

Gibney, Matthew J. (2004) *The Ethics and Politics of Asylum*. Cambridge: Cambridge University Press.

Gibney, Matthew J. and Randall Hansen (eds) (2004) *Migration and Asylum in the Twentieth Century*. Santa Barbara, CA: Clio.

Good, Anthony (2004) "Expert Evidence in Asylum and Human Rights Appeals: An Expert's View." *International Journal of Refugee Law* 16(3): 359–80.

272 *Bibliography*

Goodnough, Abby (2005) "Tensions Rise as More Flee Cuba for U.S." *New York Times* Dec. 18: 1, 31.

Goodwin-Gil, Guy S. (1996) *The Refugee in International Law*, 2nd edn. Oxford: Oxford University Press.

Greater London Authority (2005) *Into the Labryinth: Legal Advice for Asylum Seekers in London*. London: Greater London Authority.

Greenberger, Lea. (2002) Telephone Interview, March 2.

Grewall, Sheila (lawyer at Refugee Legal Centre) (2004) Personal interview, London, Nov. 16.

—— (2005) Personal Interview, London, Nov. 25.

Guild, Elspeth (2001) *Immigration Law in the European Community*. The Hague: Kluwer International.

Herlihy, Jane, Peter Scragg, and Stuart Turner (2002) "Discrepancies in Autobiographical Memories: Implications for the Assessment of Asylum Seekers: Repeated Interviews Study." *British Medical Journal* (9 February): 324–7.

Hetfield, Mark (2005) Email Message, Sept. 28.

Hickley, Matthew and James Slack (2005) "The Illegal Migrants Using Budget Flights as a Passport to UK." *Daily Mail* Aug. 4: 16.

Hing, Bill Ong (2004) *Defining America through Immigration Policy*. Philadelphia, PA: Temple University Press.

Hohenstein, Joe (2002) Personal Interview, Philadelphia, PA, May 1.

Holzer, Thomas, Gerald Schneider, and Thomas Widmer (2000) "Discriminating Decentralization: Federalism and the Handling of Asylum Applications in Switzerland, 1988–1996." *Journal of Conflict Resolution* 44(2): 250–76.

Home Office (2006) "Asylum Seekers Increase in Last Quarter." National Statistics Online, URL (accessed Feb. 2007): http://www.statistics.gov.uk/cci/nugget.asp?id=261

Human Rights First (2004) *In Liberty's Shadow*. New York, NY: Human Rights First.

—— (2007) "Material Support Update: Progress for Some Asylum Seekers; Process Still Unknown." *Asylum News* 49(Jan.). URL (accessed Feb. 2007): http://www.humanrightsfirst.org/asylum/torchlight/newsletter/newslet 49.htm

Hurwitz, Leah (2002) Personal Interview, San Diego, CA, Feb. 1.

Ibhawoh, Bonny (2003) "Defining Persecution and Protection: The Cultural Relativism Debate and the Rights of Refugees." In Niklaus Steiner, Mark Gibney, and Gil Loescher (eds) *Problems of Protection: The UNHCR, Refugees, and Human Rights*. London: Routledge, pp. 61–75.

ICAR (2005) "LGBT People as 'Members of a Particular Social Group'." ICAR Legal Developments and Issues in Case Law, URL (accessed June 2007): http://www.icar.org.uk/?lid=1808

International Herald Tribune (2006) "Terrorists or Victims?" (editorial). April 14: 6.

Jarvis, Catriona (2003) "The Judge as Juror Revisited." *Immigration Law Digest* winter: 7–23.

Johnston, Jenifer and John Paul Breslin (2004) "Home Office Tells 'Foolhardy' Asylum Seekers: 'It's Your Own Fault You've Been Persecuted'." *Sunday Herald* Dec. 26.

Joly, Daniele (1996) *Heaven or Hell: Asylum Policies and Refugees in Europe.* New York: St Martin's Press.

Jones, David (1989) "Re-Examining Rights." *British Journal of Political Science* 19(1): 69–96.

Joppke, Christian (1999) *Immigration and the Nation-State: The United States, Germany, and Great Britain.* Oxford: Oxford University Press.

Joyce, Robert (2003) Personal Interview, Boston, MA, Oct. 3.

Kalin, Walter (1986) "Troubled Communication: Cross-Cultural Misunderstandings in the Asylum Hearing." *International Migration Review* 20: 230–41.

Kassindja, Fauziya (1998) *Do They Hear You When You Cry?* New York, NY: Delta (published by Dell).

Khan, Noor (2006) "Militants Behead Afghan Who Taught Schoolgirls." *Valley News* Jan. 5: B1.

Kleinman, Arthur, Veena Das, and Margaret Lock (eds) (1997) *Social Suffering.* Berkeley: University of California Press.

Kot, Veronika (1988) *The Impact of Cultural Factors on Credibility in the Asylum Context.* San Francisco, CA: Immigration Legal Resource Center.

Kratz, Corinne A. (2002) "Circumcision Debates and Asylum Cases: Intersecting Arenas, Contested Values, and Tangled Webs." In Richard A. Shweder, Hazel R. Markus, and Martha Minow (eds) *Engaging in Cultural Differences: The Multicultural Challenge in Liberal Democracies*, pp. 309–43. New York: Russell Sage Foundation.

LaCapra, Dominick (2001) *Writing History, Writing Trauma.* Baltimore, MD: Johns Hopkins University Press.

Langbauer, Laurie (1992) "Cultural Studies and the Politics of the Everyday." *Diacritics* 22: 47–65.

Lawyers Committee for Human Rights (2002) *Refugee Women at Risk: Unfair U.S. Laws Hurt Asylum Seekers.* New York, NY: Lawyers Committee for Human Rights.

Leppard, David (2006) "Criminals Not Deported 'To Avoid Asylum Claims'." *Sunday Times* April 30: 2.

Lindsley, Fiona (2004) "Report of the Independent Monitor 2003." London: Home Office, June.

Liptak, Adam (2005) "Courts Criticize Judges' Handling of Asylum Cases." *New York Times* Dec. 26: A1, A22.

Loescher, Gil (1993) *Beyond Charity: International Cooperation and the Global Refugee Crisis*. New York: Oxford University Press.

—— (2003) "UNHCR at Fifty: Refugee Protection and World Politics." In Niklaus Steiner, Mark Gibney, and Gil Loescher (eds) *Problems of Protection: The UNHCR, Refugees, and Human Rights*. London: Routledge, pp. 3–18.

London, Judy (2003) Personal Interview, Los Angeles, CA, May 6.

—— (2004) Personal Interview, Los Angeles, CA, June 22.

—— (2006). Email Correspondence, Jan. 17.

Longman, Timothy (2001) "Identity Cards, Ethnic Self-Perception, and Genocide in Rwanda." In Jane Caplan and John Torpey (eds) *Documenting Individual Identity: The Development of State Practices in the Modern World*. Princeton, NJ: Princeton University Press, pp. 345–57.

Lynch, James P. and Rita J. Simon (2003) *Immigration the World Over*. Lanham, MD: Rowman and Littlefield.

McDonald, Ian A. and Frances Webber (2005) *Immigration Law and Practice*, 6th edn. London: LexisNexis Butterworths.

McHaffey, David (2005) Personal Interview, Boston, MA, Feb. 7.

McIntyre, John S. and Fergus I.M. Craik (1987) "Adult Age Differences for Item and Source Information." *Canadian Journal of Pyschology* 41: 175–92.

MacKinnon, Catharine (1987) *Feminism Unmodified: Discourses on Life and Law*. Cambridge, MA: Harvard University Press.

Macklin, Audrey (1995) "Refugee Women and the Imperative of Categories." *Human Rights Quarterly* 17(2): 213–77.

—— (1998) "Truth and Consequences: Credibility Determinations in the Refugee Context." In International Association of Refugee Law Judges, *The Realities of Refugee Determination on the Eve of a New Millennium: The Role of the Judiciary*, pp. 134–40.

—— (2005) "Disappearing Refugees: Reflections on the Canada–US Safe Third Country Agreement." *Columbia Human Rights Review* 36(2): 365–426.

Maiman, Richard J. (2005) "Asylum Law Practice in the United Kingdom after the Human Rights Act." In Austin Sarat and Stuart A. Scheingold (eds) *The*

Worlds Cause Lawyers Make: Structure and Agency in Legal Practice. Stanford, CA: Stanford University Press.

Malkki, Liisa H. (1995) *Purity and Exile: Violence, Memory and National Cosmology among Hutu Refugees in Tanzania.* Chicago: University of Chicago Press.

Mares, Peter (2001) *Borderline: Australia's Response to Refugees and Asylum Seekers in the Wake of the Tampa.* Sydney: University of New South Wales Press.

Martin, David (2000) "The 1995 Asylum Reforms: A Historic and Global Perspective." Center for Immigration Studies, URL (accessed June 2007): http://www.cis.org/articles/2000/back500.html

Migrations Wordpress (2004) "No More Shopping for Asylum." URL (accessed December 2004): http://migrations.wordpress.com/2004/12/

Moorehead, Caroline (2005) *Human Cargo.* New York, NY: Henry Holt.

MORI (2002) "Attitudes towards Refugees and Asylum Seekers." Research study for Refugee Week, London, May.

Mulrooney, Paul (2006) "From Judge to Refugee." *Dominion Post* (Wellington, New Zealand) June 24.

Musalo, Karen, Lauren Gibson, Stephen Knight, and J. Edward Taylor (2001) "The Expedited Removal Study: Report of the First Three Years of Implementation of Expedited Removal," *Notre Dame Journal of Law and Ethics, and Public Policy* 15: 1–155.

Nazer, Mende and Damien Lewis (2003) *Slave.* New York, NY: Public Affairs.

New York Times (2005) "A Pilgrim's Progess" (editorial). *New York Times* Nov. 9: A26.

Nolan, Lisa (2004) Personal Interview, London, Nov. 24.

Oxford, Connie G. (2005) "Protectors and Victims in the Gender Regimes of Asylum." *National Women's Studies Association Journal* 17(3): 18–38.

Perlez, Jane (2006) "Once Muslim, Now Christian and Caught in the Courts." *New York Times* Aug. 24: A6.

Phillips, Janet and Adrienne Milbank (2005) "The Detention and Removal of Asylum Seekers." E-Brief, Parliament of Australia, Parliamentary Library, Issued July 5.

Physicians for Human Rights (2003) *From Persecution to Prison: The Health Consequences of Detention for Asylum Seekers.* Cambridge, MA: Physicians for Human Rights.

Quinn, Patrick (2002a) Personal Interview, San Diego, CA, Feb. 1.
—— (2002b) Telephone Interview, Feb. 8.

Referral Notice (2006) Department of Homeland Security, May 4.

Refugee Women's Resource Project Asylum Aid (2003) *Women Asylum Seekers in the UK: A Gender Perspective Some Facts and Figures*. London: Refugee Women's Resource Project.

—— (2006) *"Lip Service" or Implementation? The Home Office Gender Guidance and Women's Asylum Claims in the UK*. London: Refugee Women's Resource Project.

Robertson, Shari and Michael Camerini (2000) *Well-Founded Fear*. PBS documentary, Director: Michael Camerini. New York: Epidavros Project Inc.

Roxstrom, Erik and Mark Gibney (2003) "The Legal and Ethical Obligations of UNHCR: Temporary Protection in Western Europe." In Niklaus Steiner, Mark Gibney, and Gil Loescher (eds) *Problems of Protection: The UNHCR, Refugees, and Human Rights*. London: Routledge, pp. 37–60.

Schoenholtz, Andrew (2005) "Refugee Protection in the United States Post September 11." *Columbia Human Rights Review* 36(2): 323–64.

—— and Jonathan Jacobs (2002). "The State of Asylum Representation: Ideas for Change." *Georgetown Immigration Law Journal* 16(summer): 739–72.

Schooler, Jonathan W., Delia Gerhard, and Elizabeth F. Loftus (1986) "Qualities of the Unreal." *Journal of Experimental Psychology, Learning, Memory and Cognition* 12 (2): 171–81.

Schrag, Philip G. (2000) *A Well-Founded Fear: The Congressional Battle to Save Political Asylum in America*. New York, NY: Routledge.

Schuster, Liza (2003) *The Uses and Abuses of Political Asylum in Britain and Germany*. London: Frank Cass.

Sengupta, Somini (2006) "Is Public Romance a Right? The Kama Sutra Doesn't Say." *Meerut Journal* Jan. 4.

Shah, Prakash A. (2000) *Refugees, Race and the Legal Concept of Asylum in Britain*. London: Cavendish Publishing Ltd.

Showler, Peter (2006) *Refugee Sandwich: Stories of Exile and Asylum*. Montreal: McGill-Queen's University Press.

Shuman, Amy (2005) *Other People's Stories: Entitlement Claims and the Critique of Empathy*. Urbana: University of Illinois Press.

Shuman, Amy and Carol Bohmer (2004) "Representing Trauma: Political Asylum Narrative." *Journal of American Folklore* 117: 394–414.

Siman, Farzad (2002) Personal Interview, New York, May 3.

Sinha, Anita (2001) "Note: Domestic Violence and U.S. Asylum Law: Eliminating the 'Cultural Hook' for Claims Involving Gender Persecution." *New York University Law Review* 76(Nov.): 1562–98.

Spijkerboer, Thomas (2000) *Gender and Refugee Status*. Burlington, VT: Ashgate.

Squires, Nick (2006) "MPs Revolt Over Plan to Put Asylum Seekers on an Island." *The Telegraph* (London) Aug. 11.

Steiner, Niklaus (2003) "Arguing about Asylum: The Complexity of Refugee Debates in Europe." In Niklaus Steiner, Mark Gibney, and Gil Loescher (eds) *Problems of Protection: The UNHCR, Refugees, and Human Rights.* London: Routledge, pp. 179–95.

Steyn, Johan (2006) "Authoritarian Tendencies." London: *Guardian Weekly* April 28–May 4.

Swarns, Rachel L. (2006) "Study Finds Disparities in Judges' Asylum Rulings," *New York Times* July 31: A15.

Tichenor, Daniel J. (2002) *Dividing Lines.* Princeton, NJ: Princeton University Press.

TRAC Immigration Report (2006) "The Asylum Process." URL (accessed Feb. 2007): http://trac.syr.edu/immigration/reports/159/

Troper, Harold (1995) "In Search of Safe Haven." In Elizabeth McLuhan (ed.) *Safe Haven: The Refugee Experience of Five Families.* Ontario, Canada: Multicultural History Society of Ontario.

UK Asylum Appellate Authority (2000) *Asylum Gender Guidelines.* URL (accessed June 2007): http://www.asylumsupport.info/publications/iaa/gender.pdf

UNHCR (1985) *Executive Committee Conclusion No. 39: Refugee Women and International Protection.* Geneva: UNHCR.

—— (1991) *Guidelines on the Protection of Refugee Women.* Geneva: UNHCR.

—— (1992) *Handbook on Procedures and Criteria for Determining Refugee Status.* Geneva: UNHCR.

—— (2002) *Handbook on Procedures and Criteria for Determining Refugee Status.* Geneva: UNHCR.

—— (2005a) "Asylum Levels and Trends in Industrialized Countries." Geneva: UNHCR. URL (accessed Jan. 2007) http://www.unhcr.org/statistics

—— (2005b) *2004 Global Refugee Trends.* Geneva: UNHCR.

USCIRF (United States Commission on International Religious Freedom) (2005) "Asylum Seekers in Expedited Removal Executive Summary." Washington, DC: USCIRF.

United States Department of Homeland Security (2006) *Yearbook of Immigration Statistics 2005.* Washington, DC: Office of Immigration Statistics.

US Department of Justice (1995) "USINS Distributes New Gender-Based Guidelines." News release, US Department of Justice (INS), 26 May.

Vrij, Aldert (2001) "Detecting the Liars." *The Psychologist* 14(11): 596–8.

Waters, Tony (2001) *Bureaucratizing the Good Samaritan: The Limitations of Humanitarian Relief Operations.* Boulder, CO: Westview Press.

Weber, Leanne and Loraine Gelsthorpe (n.d.) *Deciding to Detain: How Decisions to Detain Asylum Seekers Are Made at Ports of Entry*. Cambridge: Institute of Criminology, University of Cambridge.

Wechsler, Lawrence (1990) *A Miracle, A Universe: Settling Accounts with Torturers*. New York: Pantheon.

Westerman, William (1996) *Fly to Freedom: The Art of the Golden Venture Refugees*. New York, NY: Museum of Chinese in the Americas.

Whittaker, David J. (2006) *Asylum Seekers and Refugees in the Contemporary World*. London: Routledge.

Wiebe, Virgil and Serena Parker (2001–2) "Asking for a Note from your Torturer: Corroboration and Authentication Requirements in Asylum, Withholding and Torture Convention Claims." *Immigration and Naturalization Handbook*, vol. 1. Washington, DC: AILA, pp. 414–35.

Woodhurst, Erika (2004) Personal Interview, London, Nov. 19.

Wright, Shelley (1988–1989) "Economic Rights and Social Justice: A Feminist Analysis of Some Human Rights Conventions." 12 *Australian Year Book of International Law* 241–64.

Yeo, Colin (2004a) Personal Interview, London, Oct. 14.

—— (2004b) Email Message, Nov. 4.

—— (2005) Personal Interview, Nov. 24.

—— (ed.) (n.d.) *Country Guidelines Cases: Benign and Practical?* London: Immigration Advisory Service.

Zolberg, Aristide R. and Peter M. Benda (eds) (2001) *Global Migrants, Global Refugees: Problems and Solutions*. New York: Bergahn Books.

Cases cited

A v. *MIEA* (1997) 142 ALR 331.

Appellant S. v. *Minister for Immigration and Multicultural Affairs* (2003) HCA 71.

Attorney-General v. *Ahmed Zaoui, Inspector-General of Intelligence and Security, and Human Rights Commissioner as Intervenor* (SC CIV 19/2004), 2005 NZSC 38.

Chen Shi Hai v. *Minister for Immigration and Multicultural Affairs* [2000] INLR 455, Aust HC.

Country Guideline and Starred case of IG (Nepal) [2002] UKIAT 04870.

Eduard v. *Ashcroft* (2004) 379 F.3d 182.

Habtemicael v. *Ashcroft* (2004) 370 F.3d 774.

Hernandez-Montiel v. *INS* (2000) 225 F.3d, 1093.

Higuit v. *Gonzales* (2006) 433 F 3d. 417 (4th Cir.).

Huang v. *INS* (2005) 421 F 3d 125.

In re Soto Vega (2004) A-95880 (BIA January 27).

In re Toboso-Alfonso (1990) 13 Immigr. Rep. (MB). B1-29. (BIA).

In the Matter of A and Z (1994) I.J. Dec. (Dec. 20) (Arlington, VA), reported in 72 Interpreter Releases 521 (Apr. 17, 1995).

In the Matter of RA (1999) 22 I & N Dec 906 BIA.

INS v. *Elias-Zacarias* (1992) 502 U.S. 478.

Jimenez v. *U.S. Attorney General* (2005) 132 Fed Appx 811.

Khodaverdyn v. *Ashcroft* (2004) 111 Fed Appx 489.

Lazo-Majano v. *INS* (1987) 813 F2d 1432 (9th Cir.).

Matter of Chang (1989) Int. Dec. 3107, 1989 WL 247513 (BIA May 12).

Miranda Alvarado v. *Gonzales* (2006). 449 F 3d. 915 (9th Cir.).

Mohammed v. *Gonzales* (2005) 400 F 3d 785.

Neli v. *Ashcroft* (2003) 85 Fed Appx 433.

R (on the application of Virjon B) v. *SSHD* [2002] EWHC 1469 (Admin).

Rresphja v. *Gonzales* (2005) 420 F 3d 557.

Pitcherskaia v. *INS* (1997) 118 F 3d 641.

Shaikh v. *Ashcroft* (2004) 119 Fed Appx 141.

Singh v. *Ilchert* (1995) 63 F 3d 1501.

Thomas v. *Ashcroft* (2004) 359 F.3d 1169.

Younis et al. v. *Gonzales* (2005) 131 Fed Appx. 584.

Yun Jun Cao v. *Attorney General of the United States* (2005) 407 F.3d, 146.

Index

eBooks – at www.eBookstore.tandf.co.uk

A library at your fingertips!

eBooks are electronic versions of print books. You can store them onto your PC/laptop or browse them online.

They have advantages for anyone needing rapid access to a wide variety of published, copyright information.

eBooks can help your research by enabling you to bookmark chapters, annotate and use instant searches to find specific words or phrases. Several eBook files would fit on even a small laptop or PDA.

NEW: Save money by eSubscribing: cheap, online acess to any eBook for as long as you need it.

Annual subscription packages

We now offer special low cost bulk subscriptions to packages of eBooks in certain subject areas. These are available to libraries or to individuals.

For more information please contact webmaster.ebooks@tandf.co.uk

We're continually developing the eBook concept, so keep up to date by visiting the website.

www.eBookstore.tandf.co.uk